OPPORTUNITY, MONTANA

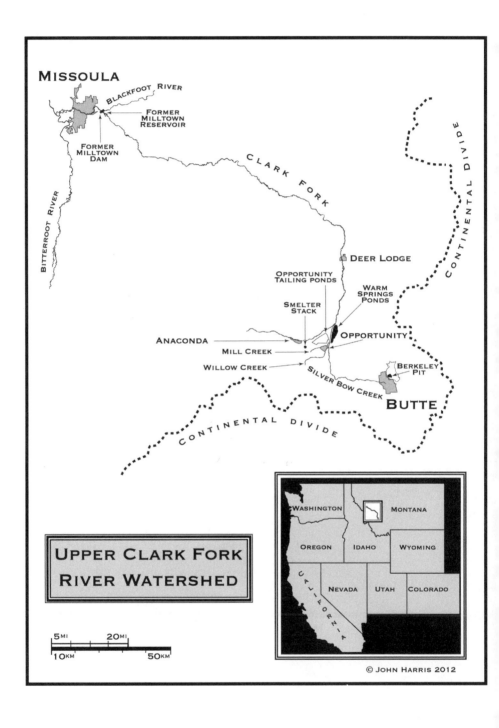

MISSOULA

BLACKFOOT RIVER

FORMER MILLTOWN RESERVOIR

FORMER MILLTOWN DAM

BITTERROOT RIVER

CLARK FORK

CONTINENTAL DIVIDE

DEER LODGE

OPPORTUNITY TAILING PONDS

WARM SPRINGS PONDS

SMELTER STACK

ANACONDA

OPPORTUNITY

MILL CREEK

WILLOW CREEK

SILVER BOW CREEK

BERKELEY PIT

BUTTE

CONTINENTAL DIVIDE

UPPER CLARK FORK
RIVER WATERSHED

5 MI    20 MI
10 KM        50 KM

WASHINGTON    MONTANA

OREGON    IDAHO    WYOMING

CALIFORNIA

NEVADA    UTAH    COLORADO

© JOHN HARRIS 2012

# OPPORTUNITY, MONTANA

## Big Copper,
## Bad Water, and
## the Burial of an
## American Landscape

Brad Tyer

BEACON PRESS ✛ BOSTON

BEACON PRESS
25 Beacon Street
Boston, Massachusetts 02108-2892
www.beacon.org

Beacon Press books
are published under the auspices of
the Unitarian Universalist Association of Congregations.

16  15  14  13      8  7  6  5  4  3  2  1

## Note about Spacebreak Ornament ☩

The spacebreak ornament, a square cross with four terminal circles,
is an alchemical symbol for the element copper.

This book is printed on acid-free paper that meets the uncoated paper
ANSI/NISO specifications for permanence as revised in 1992.

Text design and composition by Wilsted & Taylor Publishing Services

Library of Congress Cataloging-in-Publication Data
Tyer, Brad.
Opportunity, Montana : big copper, bad water, and
the burial of an American landscape / Brad Tyer.
    pages  cm
Includes bibliographical references.
ISBN 978-0-8070-0329-9 (alk. paper)
    1. Copper mines and mining—Waste disposal—Montana—
Opportunity Region. 2. Copper mines and mining—Environmental
aspects—Clark Fork Watershed (Mont. and Idaho) I. Title.
TD899.C59T94 2012
304.2'809786—dc23                                    2012041716

*For my dad, Bobby Ray Tyer*

*In rearing the great structure of empire on the Western Hemisphere we are obliged to avail ourselves of all the resources at our command. The requirements of this great utilitarian age demand it. Those who succeed us can well take care of themselves.*

—WILLIAM A. CLARK,
*U.S. senator from Montana,*
*retirement speech, 1907*

*I come from the water*
*That weren't no easy thing*
*It's more than nature*
*It's like my destiny*
*I stood upon these legs*
*And held my head up high*
*Emerged beneath the sun*
*To start a new life*

—TOADIES,
*"I Come From the Water,"*
*Rubberneck, 1994*

# CONTENTS

# PREFACE

From this distance it looks almost like a half-buried, old-style Mc-
Donald's: two pale, parallel parabolas arcing side by side in a lateral
shaft of sun. Snow clouds roll in behind the wind. The wind stings.

Maybe it's the angle, but the structure appears to be solidly on
land, and entirely surrounded by water. Maybe it's some kind of
sculpture or earthwork, something designed for looking at and
wondering why. There's rarely anybody out here to look but maintenance guys in company trucks and duck hunters. Some birders
probably. Binoculars would help.

I'd like to throw the canoe on the water and paddle over to see,
but I hadn't planned on the ponds being iced over when I drove
up here to squeeze in one last late-season paddle. The sheet ice
isn't thick yet, but it doesn't take much to freeze all the fun out of a
canoe. Still, I drove all the way up here. The light is remarkable,
with shape and volume, as if it's displacing the dark air. I'll walk.

Beavers and bobcats and coots and ducks and geese and gray
partridges and minks and mourning doves and mule deer and white-
tails and muskrats and otters and sandhill cranes and snipes all live
here, and in the proper season, with the approved equipment, you
can kill them. I don't see any hunters today, though 'tis the season.
The geese are out on Pond 3, standing on the ice, and a few ducks
cluster at the outlet pipes that connect one pond to another, where
movement keeps the water just a little too warm to freeze.

The berms cut out into the ponds at right angles to each other,
more or less square to the shores, chopping the water into cells.
The berms are flat-topped, with ruts on the flats, where company trucks drive out to open and close the pipes. There aren't any
trucks out here today either.

Half a mile out on the first berm I come to a left turn, and the ruts roll off toward an angular rise holding back a higher-elevation cell. I follow the ruts for three-quarters of a mile and they take me right alongside the arched whatever it is. The little dike I'm on dips to a low spit, and on the spit is planted a pole-mounted, quarter-fed binocular like the ones at Niagara Falls, except this one's heavy metal eyepieces are gone, like some monster magpie has pecked the sockets clean.

Who knows why it'd been put here in the first place. It wasn't to look at the bridge, which is what the arched thing turns out to be. A historical marker at the edge of its island says so. The bridge is just a few steps away, across a shallow slip of water.

It's called the Morel Rainbow Arch Bridge. It was built in 1914, in the flush of a national initiative known as the Good Roads Movement, to cross Silver Bow Creek, thus completing the dirt county road that connected a then-thriving town called Anaconda with a now-traceless substation called Morel on the long-defunct Chicago, Milwaukee, St. Paul, and Pacific line nearby. The Rainbow Arch design had been copied from a similar bridge patented by its builder, Iowa's J. B. Marsh, in 1912. It's made of poured concrete: cheap and strong and erectable with no more skill than could be rounded up by a local prison warden.

The superstructure isn't even slightly impressive, maybe twenty feet long and a horse cart and a half wide, hardly more than head-high. But it was the only one of its style ever built in Montana, and it was decommissioned just two years after the cement dried, so the state got it listed in the National Register of Historic Places and planted a silver metal marker on it: "The bridge was abandoned in 1916 when the Anaconda Mining Company—which owned the surrounding land—built Pond 2, one of a series of settling ponds that separate old Highway 10 and the interstate. Today, Atlantic Richfield, a BP affiliated company, maintains the water treatment facilities and the State of Montana manages the site for wildlife and recreational use."

Even prison labor is too precious to waste hauling away concrete bridges, so here it remains. Over the years sediment piled up like a pearl and turned water and thin air into an island. The gray-white concrete rises out of browned bunches of cocklebur and a wheat-colored carpet of scrub grass emerging from the white down of the season's first snow. Milky matte-green sagebrush sprouts at either end. A sentinel clump of red osier dogwood glows like backlit rust. A gold-fronded patch of cattails turns black from the frost.

The Rainbow Arch no longer spans water to connect land. Now, stranded, isolate, without function—it connects nothing.

The creek is long gone too, of course, drowned with water and filled with silt.

What a perfectly odd place to be. I've given up the prospect of canoeing on solid water to stand on a bridge I had to step across liquid to get to, in the middle of a wetland filled with submerged mine waste, freezing my fingers at the Warm Springs Ponds.

This bridge that isn't a bridge spans two centuries, two kinds of wealth, two ideas of what water is good for. I'm straddling the spot where a river died, looking out across the landscape of its rebirth. On a clear day, I can almost see Opportunity from here.

# PART I

# HEADWATER

*Montana seems to me to be what a small boy might
think Texas is like from listening to Texans.*

—JOHN STEINBECK, *Travels with Charley*

The first time I saw the Clark Fork I wasn't sure I'd found what I
was looking for. I'd imagined something else.

When I announced I was moving to Montana a decade ago, my
friends in Houston hummed bars of Frank Zappa: *Movin' to Montana soon / Gonna be a dental floss tycoon.* My mother dropped exploratory references to the Unabomber, trying to act casual. I had never
heard the song and I had no intention of blowing anybody up.

I packed a small green truck with two dogs and not much else.
I'd sold most of my books and all of my records. I'd kept some
clothes, a few keepsakes, a camera, some camping gear, a couple of
paddles, and a life jacket. On top of the truck were two canoes and
a kayak tied down with nylon straps that hummed in the wind
and rubbed the paint off my hood in patches.

I left Houston headed due north, going the long way through the
Great Plains, bisecting Oklahoma, Kansas, and Nebraska—because
I'd never seen Oklahoma or Kansas or Nebraska—and continuing
up through Wyoming toward Montana via Yellowstone National
Park. I'd used baling wire to mount a memento of home—a deformed steer skull, one horn curving up, the other curving down—
to the truck's grill. A Yellowstone ranger, concerned that fellow
tourists might think I'd scavenged the skull from park grounds and
follow suit, made me cover it with a plastic garbage bag.

I flirted through the window at 35 mph with a couple of 4-H queens driving an old GMC truck around some worn-out Wyoming farm town, burned my brake pads to smoke coming down out of the Bighorn Mountains, and saw a sign I'd never seen before and don't mind if I never see again, a yellow rectangle on a steel swing-gate standing ready to block the highway: "Closed for Snow—Return to Cody." It struck me at the time as the most tragicomic mandate a highway department could issue. I had just been through Cody, and nothing could make me want to go back.

Yellowstone delivered me into Montana alongside a splishy little stream running beside the road, pebble-bedded, cold, and clear, and a jagged horizon of mountains to awe any flatlander. I stopped next to a carved wooden sign reading "Welcome to Montana" to take my picture. It was a border crossing I wanted to remember.

I was on Interstate 90 northwest of Butte when I picked up the Clark Fork. I knew it was supposed to be the biggest river in the state, and one of the waters that ran through Missoula, where I was headed. The gazetteer showed it shadowing 90 for a while, but I had a hard time matching the squiggly blue line with the view out the window. That river looked not much bigger than a Texas ditch, and long stretches were lined with stone riprap to reinforce and define the channel, shaped to suit a highway surveyor's transit. Sometimes it moved from one side of the road to the other when I couldn't remember crossing it.

I'd picked Missoula off a map.

I'd gotten married and quickly divorced two years earlier, then been laid off from a longtime newspaper job. I didn't have any family left in Houston. My mother had remarried and moved to Dallas. My sister had gone to school in Tennessee and followed a career to Atlanta. My dad was living north of Houston in Humble, where I rarely saw him, and usually regretted it when I did. I loved Houston, which is a thing only a Houstonian can or will say, but I wasn't exactly in love with it anymore.

I lived off severance and unemployment for the allotted seven months, looking less for a new job than for someplace to go. I spent two months driving around the Southeast, camping at state parks, paddling Arkansas's Buffalo River, Georgia's Chattahoochee, North Carolina's New, scouting a move. I had Asheville in mind, but when

I got there the hippie egg joint downtown had no salt on the table and the local weekly paper was touting a Jimmy Buffett cover band as the best live music in town, so I kept driving. Nothing against Jimmy Buffett—I bought all his 8-tracks when the format died and they hit the discount racks—I just don't like being around too large a crowd that likes him too.

On my way back to Houston, still undecided, I stopped in Atlanta to visit my sister, Cameron. She had a little girl, my first niece, three years old, and, with an understandable affinity for boyish names, Cameron had named her Nelson. A second baby girl on the way had the name Bradley Rivers waiting for her. Bradley was for me, and Rivers was a family name from my brother-in-law's side, but I hogged pride in it whole. It's a name I wish I'd had.

We considered my options. Cameron had spent a summer between college semesters working at a dude ranch on the Smith River in central Montana, and on the way there she'd flown into Missoula and visited Flathead Lake—the largest freshwater lake west of the Mississippi—to the north. Now she offered up a coffee-table book of Montana landscape porn: snow-draped peaks, steep creeks, weathered homestead cabins, and bighorn sheep grazing alpine meadows.

Cameron found a map and we sat on the floor and drew a red circle around Missoula. There was plenty of moving water and a university there, and surely no Jimmy Buffett cover bands so far from any beach.

Six months later, when I crossed the Montana state line, I still didn't know anything about Montana except what the picture books showed, so I expected an uninterrupted trove of scenic superlatives. The rivers would all come crashing down out of real mountains, sudsy with whitewater and lined with browsing bears, grazing elk, and free-range bison. A few weeks after I arrived I found a job editing a weekly newspaper, the Missoula *Independent*, and began to see past the surface.

I wrote and assigned and edited stories about purple-state Democrats, federal land management controversies, and the local development battles endemic to those parts of the Rocky Mountain West where settlement had stuck. I acculturated to a seasonal news cycle in which every spring someone drowned during runoff, trapped in a log jam that hadn't been there the day before or crack-ing their skull on rocks ill-pillowed by big water. Every summer, a season I used to associate with hurricanes, marked the nervous start of a new wildfire watch, when hundreds or thousands of acres might spark into flame from lightning or campfire coals, pouring soot into the valleys like black fog. Every fall generated videos of a stockpiling bear wandering into town or falling tranquilized out of a tree onto a makeshift trampoline. Every winter the city's ski hounds counted the accumulating snowpack like gold coins, alert for powder days unsullied by the climatic inversions that some-times capped the valley in smog.

I played at poker tables with hippies who hung Tibetan prayer flags from their front porches and hunted elk with arrows in the fall. I poached weekend potlucks where the tables were laid with fresh salmon from someone's recent trip to Alaska and morel mushrooms someone else had picked from the charred floor of last year's burn.

I spent my weekends, evenings, and weeks off floating the Bitterroot, the Blackfoot, the Missouri, the Smith, the Ruby, the Madison, the Flathead, and the Clark Fork, in inner tubes, kayaks, canoes, and rafts. Some of these rivers did come crashing down out of real mountains, sudsy with whitewater. Others meandered quietly. They all ran muddy come spring. And I finally saw a bear, a cinnamon-colored cub wading Rattlesnake Creek just a few yards from the 1950s-era Sears kit log cabin I rented one year.

Writer Caroline Patterson describes Missoula as "drunk with rivers." The vocabulary of moving water suffuses the lingo here, and it's a rare conversation that doesn't include the abbreviation "cfs"—cubic feet per second—the rate of river flow. Montana's riv-ers freeze up in winter, surge with snowmelt in spring, and ebb in late summer when irrigators drain them to water parched crops. Fly fishers and kayakers watch the water gauges like osprey, Mis-soula's ubiquitous fish hawks.

I gradually began to gather that the Clark Fork wasn't quite what I'd thought it was. The river I had shadowed on my drive in had long been choked by the detritus of a century's worth of copper mining upstream. The "Treasure State" of Montana's license plates was sourced in metal, and it had been mined for a century in Butte and refined at an enormous smelter nearby in a town called Anaconda. Butte copper had wired America, strung across the country to deliver residential electricity and telephone connections, feeding power to unbridled industrial growth and cladding the bullets that won two world wars. That copper was in my cell phone and my laptop and my refrigerator. It wired the pickup I drove upstream to launch my canoe.

The Clark Fork I found bore little resemblance to the river that Meriwether Lewis named for his partner William Clark in 1806. Upstream at Butte, untold tons of ore-bearing rock had been crushed to liberate millions of pounds of the red metal it held, and the waste rock, leaky with poisons, still littered the watershed, moving downriver with every rain. Over the course of a century, millions of tons of it had washed up behind the Milltown Dam, an aging powerhouse built in 1908 that pinched the river just east of Missoula. Among those sediments were mine tailings laden with copper, arsenic, cadmium, and lead, toxic heavy metals and refining by-products that were eventually discovered seeping into area wells.

In 1983, the Environmental Protection Agency had defined the river's upper reaches as the largest Superfund site in the United States, a cluster of interrelated environmental catastrophes and corollary cleanups blossoming upstream to their source in Butte. Arguments over the best way to deal with the contamination lasted for two decades and generated sophisticated public relations campaigns. ARCO, the oil company that inherited the site when it bought the Anaconda Mining Company in 1977, wanted to leave the dam in place, arguing that removing it would just stir up trouble downstream. A local nonprofit called the Clark Fork Coalition advocated taking the dam out and removing the sediments—a more permanent and much more expensive solution.

Cleanup negotiations were never far from the front page. Environmentalists plastered Missoula with bumper stickers saying "Remove the Dam, Restore the River." Contrarians produced "Remove Missoula, Restore the Valley."

Come summertime, I would drag an inner tube to the river just below the dam and joined thousands of floaters spinning downstream into Missoula, partly to support the cleanup, but mostly because it was another excuse to get on the water.

Finally, in 2008, the dam came down. Governmental potentates presided, environmentalists celebrated. The Clark Fork would be rerouted into an artificial bypass channel, the artificial lake behind the dam allowed to dry up, and contractors would begin removing three million tons of contaminated sediment from the reservoir bed. Soon the river would be restored to the engineers' best guess at its natural channel, and the tributary Blackfoot River would flow freely into the Clark Fork, instead of stagnating upstream of the dam, for the first time in a hundred years. Within a decade, it is hoped, the arsenic plume contaminating Milltown's water will disperse, and without the weight of the reservoir pushing contaminants down into the aquifer, the health of Milltown's drinking water, and Missoula's aquifer, will be restored.

Thus began the multigenerational work of remanufacturing a river.

Nobody's ever rebuilt a 120-mile river before. Nobody knows what it's supposed to look like. The goal is a naturally functioning river. How do you design one of those?

That question was the current connecting the myriad topics tackled at the 2010 Clark Fork Symposium at the University of Montana in Missoula, two seminar- and workshop-packed days during which a parade of federal bureaucrats, state functionaries, nonprofit administrators, academics, environmentalists, landowners, biologists, chemists, and entrepreneurs dissected the river into its component issues: migratory riverbed corridors, streambank erosion, dissolved copper content, arsenic contamination, fish kills, phosphorous loading trends, brown trout populations, algae blooms, gradient scouring, and a dozen other esoteric fields of inquiry.

Outside the conference rooms, adjacent to a university parking lot, the Clark Fork itself flowed past perturbed, over a rubbled weir dam diverting water to an irrigation ditch, around an island dog-walking sanctuary Missoulians call the Bark Park, beneath a suspension footbridge, and past the DoubleTree Hotel's Finn & Porter restaurant, where diners are regularly treated to the graceful casts of a fully bedecked fly fisherman on the rock beach below. Local rumor holds that hotel management hires fly fishers to work that precise spot, where Rattlesnake Creek pours into the river from the north, to provide out-of-town visitors—graduation-weekend parents, trout-seeking tourists, symposium attendees—with the expected ambience. The rumor is almost certainly untrue. Fishing is a pastime in Missoula, rarely a profession.

The symposium offered a field trip to the site of the former Milltown Dam, a few miles upstream. Several dozen of us stood on a bluff and looked down at a muddy expanse of brown dirt where Milltown Reservoir used to be, complete with cottonwood stumps left behind more than a century ago when the trees had been cut before the river bottom was first submerged behind the dam. Those logs had been turned into lumber at the nearby mill in Bonner, the mill the dam was built to power, itself finally shuttered in the face of cheap Canadian competition the year before the dam came out. The timbers had been carried on trains back upstream to Butte and used to frame the ten thousand miles of mining tunnels there. The trees eventually ended up underwater anyway; the Butte mines have been flooded since 1980, when the massive pumps that kept the tunnels dry, deep beneath the water table, were turned off.

Mining is the process of turning the earth inside out. Buried rock is dragged to the surface; mountainside trees go underground.

By the time the symposium rolled around in the spring of 2010, temporary rail tracks transected the former reservoir and bright yellow front loaders fringed the site. The river ran in a stone-caged channel around its northern perimeter, awaiting release into the not-yet-recontoured bed in which it would lie, along the northerly bend beneath the cliff where we stood. A restoration specialist commented approvingly on the unexpected wealth of original seed bank unearthed by the project. The stumps had been a happy surprise.

I had canoed that poisoned reservoir several years before, slipping after the sounds of a heron rookery there, the paddle stirring shallow silts into dark clouds in the water. I'd wondered then about the tall blue cylinder rising above the northern shore like a Claes Oldenburg lipstick. I didn't learn until later that it held drinking water for the residents of Milltown whose wells had been tainted by the arsenic seeping out of those same silts into the aquifer below.

When one of our group asked if all the effort had been successful, our guide replied that it would take at least another twenty-five
years to know.

Back at the conference, guest speaker Rick Bass tried to envision a more satisfying response. Like me, Bass grew up in Houston,
and his book *Winter* had helped spark my own flight north. Thirty years ago Bass packed his bags and moved to the remote Yaak
Valley of northwestern Montana, and he's been there ever since,
tramping the mountains and forging himself into a fierce defender
of his adopted home. He delivered the conference keynote, admitting that he's not particularly a river person. He prefers the forested high ground. Bass noted the pleasing geographical irony that
the hard-used Clark Fork flows north of the town of Wisdom, and
south of Paradise. He described Milltown, site of the just-removed
dam, as "the place where the wound was," where soon "there won't
even be a scar."

"We haven't been here very long," he said, speaking of Anglos,
"and in that time we've done enormous damage."

The symposium closed on Friday, and on Saturday I went paddling
on Missoula's other river, the Bitterroot. While the Clark Fork carries the brunt of mining's burden, and the Blackfoot slowly recov-
ers from clear-cutting, the Bitterroot suffers only from too much
love, an abuse easy to forgive. Trophy homes occasionally crowd
the banks, and stretches are lined with cabled assemblages of old
cars, strung along the bends in a vain attempt to prevent erosion,
but for long stretches the Bitterroot is as pretty as any postcard.

The Bitterroot is the first river I canoed when I moved to Missoula. It had been late September, a few weeks after I'd arrived, and
something about the way the light deepened the shallow water and
framed the mountains in sheets of laundered blue made me think
this was where I was supposed to be. The scenery is spectacular
down near Stevensville where I was drifting, where the river never
wanders far from some fresh panorama of the sawtoothed Bitter-
roots looming to the west.

I knew from my guidebook that mountain man Old Bill Williams had yelped "Thar floats my stick!" when he found a stream he liked, and I've whispered that exclamation many times on the Bitterroot. It's where I take new friends who want an introduction to paddling, or first dates. The Bitterroot is where I went when Bob died, two years after I'd left Houston.

I don't know what else to call him. "Father" sounds too formal, and "Dad" is too familiar. His birth certificate says Bobby Ray Tyer, an informality he considered hickish. He did business as Robert Ray Tyer, accommodating the professional world's assumptions, just as he taught himself to talk about sports, which he disliked, to get along with businessmen who felt otherwise. He considered Bobby—any name ending in an "ee" sound—an inappropriate diminutive for an adult, and to my knowledge he let no one but his mother and his wife call him that, and it rankled him even then. Everyone else called him Bob. I'll call him Bob.

He'd been dead for days when I got the call from my aunt back in Texas. Bob and I hadn't spoken for almost five years. He'd been recently engaged again after two failed marriages, and he and his new wife-to-be were paddling a canoe on a golf course pond near the house they were about to buy in Humble, Texas, when his back seized up and he went clammy and cold. He let his fiancée paddle him back to shore and the episode passed, but it put enough fear into him to go to the local hospital for tests. They kept him overnight and didn't find anything wrong. The next day, as a nurse wheeled him out of an elevator back toward his room after another inconclusive test, his heart blew up. They couldn't revive him. I'm told he died more or less instantly.

He was just sixty. He still looked, I imagined, like he always had: two parts Glen Campbell to one part Johnny Cash. He'd tried a beard once, during a bout of considered nonconformism, but found it wanting. He'd been a sideburned, strong-jawed American striver, and when I thought of him I thought of a salesman.

I flew back to Houston to meet Cameron, who flew in from Atlanta, to deal with what could be dealt with. He didn't leave a will— "fuck 'em," one of his estranged friends told me he'd said when it had been suggested that he should get one in order—but I eventually ended up with his effects anyway, for lack of other takers.

Cameron and I inherited his one-man company, despite the fact that neither of us had been in touch with him for years, and despite our mutual lack of interest in running it. He called the company AerResearch, and what he did was design, sell, and install aeration systems for municipal wastewater treatment plants. To oversimplify: he pumped bubbles into sewage lagoons to efficiently oxygenate shit-eating bacteria. We finally sold the company and a few patents that came with it to another man who oxygenated shit-eating bacteria. He was our only suitor and claimed to be Bob's best friend. He never paid up and we didn't pursue it. It wasn't our money anyway.

I knew from his tackle boxes, shipped by his fiancée in hastily taped cardboard, that he'd taken up fly-fishing. I also got the canoe, the sixteen-foot aluminum Grumman he'd been paddling when he started to die. I abandoned that in Texas with friends. No reason to waste a perfectly good boat, but there's no way I'm paddling it. I'm not superstitious, but narrative inevitability is self-propelling.

It was weeks after his death before I got back to Montana and had a chance to take my own boat out on the Bitterroot. There's a sewage treatment plant on the bank near the takeout at a parking lot in Lolo, not far upstream of the Bitterroot's confluence with the Clark Fork. I might have scattered his ashes as I drifted past, if I'd had any, but by the time I thought to ask, they'd already been buried in Texas.

He didn't like me, and I didn't like him. He said he loved me, as a father surely feels he must, but always in the context of correcting me, as if to establish his judgmental bona fides. I can't say that I loved him, but I owe him, which may be more binding.

I let the canoe spin down the current and tried to imagine having a son, and discovering that he disappoints me. What could you do with a realization like that? Bob's solution had been to enlist me as an ally. He spent the last conversation we had explaining his disappointment in me in detail. "I want you to understand," he told me. He wanted my approval for his disapproval.

I couldn't give him that, even if I'd wanted to. There was no room in that box to shape a life of my own. I left Texas and six generations of fathers to find that room.

Leaving home always includes the prospect of return, but when Bob died the prospect vanished. There could be no rapprochement now, no forgiveness, no homecoming. Return to what?

—✝—

In the aftermath of Bob's death—there'd been no funeral, no wake—I flew back to Missoula. Nonstops to Montana are rare. You have to connect through Seattle, Denver, Salt Lake City, or Minneapolis. There's not enough market to justify the direct flight. The Montana Office of Tourism knows this, and an advertisement in the in-flight magazine tried to turn the inconvenience into a lure. The full-page come-on featured an aerial photo of one of Yellowstone National Park's boardwalk-rimmed thermal pools in vivid shades of iridescent blue, green, and orange, with a tagline selling the counterintuitive draw "There's Nothing Here"—a simultaneous acknowledgement of and corrective to flyover sensibilities. "Nothing but living color everywhere you least expect it. An otherworldly landscape filled with bears and wolves. Where abundant herds of bison and elk follow the earth's ancient rhythms. With nothing on the fringe but charming towns full of creature comforts."

Don't expect truth in advertising. Ninety-six percent of Yellowstone is in neighboring Wyoming, and wildlife in Montana is an intricately managed resource. Of the fewer than a thousand endangered grizzlies hemmed into the margins of Montana's 147,046 square miles, about a dozen are killed every year by people, poached with rifles or run down by trains. A third of those are classified as "management removals," which is to say that state wildlife personnel take the bears out any time they become too comfortable in the company of human communities, as they're increasingly forced to do. A fed bear, local public service bulletins warn, is a dead bear.

Wolves, controversially reintroduced in the 1990s and still a reliable argument starter anywhere in the state, were delisted as an endangered species in 2011, and are now closely supervised by the state with a toolkit full of hunting licenses and trapping permits. Wolves kill calves, so ranchers kill wolves. Meanwhile, binocular-bearing ecotourists watch wolf puppies frolic in distant meadows and subsidize ranchers for the calves that wolf pups grow up to kill.

Montana's most abundant herds of bison are hybridized with cattle and belong to one-time media mogul Ted Turner, the nation's second-largest private landowner and proprietor of several Montana ranches, including the 166,000-acre Flying D southwest of Bozeman. Turner serves bison burgers at his sixteen-state chain of Ted's Montana Grill restaurants. As a sideline, his Montana Hunting Company charges trophy hunters $14,000 to bag elk on state trust land bordering his 22,000-acre Bar None Ranch.

Montana's genetically pure buffalo are largely confined to one national wildlife refuge and Yellowstone National Park. At the park, the state's Department of Livestock agents routinely haze the beasts with ATVs and helicopters when they stray past the borders into cattle country. Politically powerful ranchers fear the spread of brucellosis, a stillbirth-causing disease carried by the bison, so every year the state slaughters hundreds of buffalo stubborn enough to roam, and the gun-toting Democrat in the governor's office instituted a lottery-driven buffalo hunt for sportsmen. Hook-and-bullet advocates like the Rocky Mountain Elk Foundation and Trout Unlimited never tire of reminding newcomers of the paradox, unsatisfying but true, that there's no more powerful lobby of support for wildlife and habitat conservation than hunters and fishermen, who can't kill what's been driven extinct. Value attaches to what we can use. There's a growing consensus that the only way to preserve Montana's most iconic megafauna—the Montana quarter, in an unintentional instance of truth in advertising, features a bison skull—is to eat them. Buffalo, fortunately, makes excellent jerky.

Ancient rhythms and creature comforts. Welcome to Montana.

✝

No matter where your layover, the approach to Missoula—western Montana's busiest airport, all six gates of it—is always the same: from the south up the Bitterroot River valley, or down it. Up because you're headed north toward town, but down because you're headed downstream. The Bitterroot River flows northward, draining eighty-eight miles out of forked creeks melting from the mountains near Montana's southern border with Idaho, so in local parlance to drive southward against the current is to go "up the Bitterroot." Several drainages to the east you can drive "up the Big Hole" and nobody snickers.

The Bitterroot joins the Clark Fork in Missoula's western outskirts. The Clark Fork doglegs into the Bitterroot from the east, like a tributary, and yet it's the name Clark Fork that the river bears going forward. River names, for the most part, honor volume. The combined flow sucks up Grant Creek, Petty Creek, and Fish Creek before opening wide to swallow the main stem of the broad turquoise Flathead, itself braided from three mountain forks. The river then pours across Montana's western border into the still water of Idaho's Lake Pend Oreille. From there it rolls into Woody Guthrie's mighty Columbia, acting the tributary part at last, and finally into the Pacific.

I can't see that far from the plane, at ten thousand feet and dropping fast, but I can see a lot. As the pilot starts his descent the deepwater green of the mountain forests, dusted with the confectioners' sugar of an early snow, gives way to tawny foothills the color of wheat, or a lumpy rug of deerskin. Below is the Bitterroot River, blue and braided in its valley. To the west is the craggy Bitterroot Range of the Rocky Mountains, named for a native flower and the bane of Lewis and Clark, who but for friendly Nez Perce Indians almost starved trying to navigate its passes in early winter. To the east are the Sapphires, gentler in contour and namesake of the state gemstone.

As the plane dips into its final approach over Missoula, the Clark Fork slips into view, emerging from Hellgate Canyon to spill through this mountain-bound juncture of five valleys. The bowl used to be a lake, 15,000 years ago, thousands of feet deep, plugged where the Clark Fork entered Idaho with a two-thousand-foot ice dam that periodically floated and burst under the pressure, sending towering walls of water crashing across Idaho and Washington toward the ocean and leaving telltale ripples and eddy lines in the landscape at a scale best appreciated from space.

This vantage clarifies the Clark Fork as Missoula's heart, the river, more than writer Norman Maclean's Blackfoot, that runs through it. It's not an especially scenic river, certainly not the prettiest in Montana, though it does have its moments, its right profiles. And it's hardly Montana's best fishing, being far surpassed on the Big Hole to the east, or the Bitterroot to the south, or any number of smaller streams.

I grew up fishing on Texas lakes, spin-casting for bass, bait-fishing for crappie, and bobbing dog food for carp. Fly-fishing carries too spiritual a cast for my taste, and the prospect of learning to fly-fish in Montana seems every bit as embarrassing as an atheist practicing the rosary on a stroll through St. Peter's.

Canoeing is how I relate to rivers, a paddle plying current, and the Clark Fork isn't even the best canoeing near Missoula.

What the Clark Fork is, is the most fucked-up river I've ever met.

┽

When my plane lands in Missoula, I grab my bag and walk to the curb to wait for the friend who's agreed to pick me up. Standing at the edge of the arrivals lane beside me is a tall man, maybe fifty, dressed from the casual-wear pages of a fly-fishing catalog. Like me he's breathing deeply in the sixty-degree air, drinking in the horizon of hills that makes Montana's sky look so famously large by providing point of perspective. It's an illusion. Montana's skies are actually impinged by the intrusion of so much elevated terrain. I'm the kind of Texan who doesn't enjoy saying stuff like this, but the skies are bigger in Texas.

I overhear the man talking to a loitering curb-mate. He used to live in Seattle, he says, owned a business there, but then one day he flew into Missoula to fish for trout, as out-of-state businessmen do, and found the place he really wanted to be. He went back to Seattle just long enough to sell his business, bought a house by the river, and never looked back.

It's a common story in Montana, one of those American states that exert a magnetism and inspire a loyalty far out of proportion to any sober appraisal. People move to places like Houston to make money. Once they've made it, if they have any sense, they retire to places like Montana. They are not drawn by Superfund sites.

John Steinbeck, whose late-career road trip brought him to Montana in a custom-built camper truck with his dog Charley, was equally uninterested in the state's contradictions. "For other states I have admiration, respect, recognition, even some affection, but with Montana it is love," he wrote. "And it's difficult to analyze love when you're in it." What Steinbeck saw in Montana was a blank canvas for the imagination of adventurous boys. From Lewis and Clark to Teddy Roosevelt to Ted Turner, that's how America has always seen Montana. That's how I saw it too.

"There's Nothing Here" sells the same promise: Unspoiled wilderness. Big Sky Country. The Last Best Place. A frontier refuge from frantic American modernity. That's why we come.

There's a phrase I learned from a woman in Missoula, looking at the sky one day and making plans. The cloud cover was thick and unencouraging, but there was a window of bright blue the clouds hadn't obscured, the sliver of a possibility of accommodating weather on the horizon. I had pointed to it hopefully.

That, she informed me, is a sucker hole.

Which is just another name for a good lie, and I'm an easy mark. Charley, Steinbeck's typically bright standard poodle, probably knew better.

✛

Healing had been Rick Bass's laudable symposium theme, and restoration, in his eyes, amounted to a sort of penance. To localize the point, Bass quoted "The Towns We Know and Leave Behind, the Rivers We Carry With Us," by the late Richard Hugo, Montana poetry's hardscrabble and hard-drinking favorite son:

> I forget the names of towns without rivers.
> A town needs a river to forgive the town.
> Whatever river, whatever town—
> it is much the same.
> The cruel things I did I took to the river.
> I begged the current: make me better.

But Richard Hugo's confession—poetry being poetry, and Hugo being Hugo—bears an imprecise relationship with Clark Fork facts. There is a town whose name has been forgotten in the self-congratulation of restoration—a town that's not just unforgiven by its river, but ruined by it.

By geographical rights, Opportunity, Montana, should claim

the Clark Fork, flowing just half a mile from the nearest doorstep, but too much cruelty has been taken there.

Opportunity is a rural suburb of the town of Anaconda, founded by the Anaconda Copper Company in 1912, ostensibly as a garden community for retired smelter workers. For most of the twentieth century, the adjacent Opportunity Ponds—four thousand acres of them—were used as a dump for Butte's mine tailings and Anaconda's smelter waste. Now even more waste, the tons that washed downstream from Butte, spreading across the floodplain and piling up behind the Milltown Dam, are being scooped up with front loaders, packed into rail cars, and shipped back upstream to Opportunity.

About five hundred people live in Opportunity today. The Clark Fork burbles between poisoned banks alongside Opportunity's pastures. The copper that wired America had a price, and Opportunity paid it. The restoration of the Clark Fork has a price too, and Opportunity is paying again.

For two days, the symposium's speakers had presented their talks and slideshows and, at the tail end of each, had made a point of thanking anyone and everyone with a hand in helping to restore the river. Nowhere on the schedule was Opportunity represented. No citizen from Opportunity traveled to Missoula to raise her hand to question or protest the repository role their community had been assigned. Opportunity's protests had been drowned out years before. Only three times did I hear the town's name mentioned at all.

Vicki Watson, the gray-ponytailed symposium organizer and an eminence in the University of Montana's Environmental Studies Department, drew appreciative chuckles from the crowd when, ticking off the milestones of the Milltown Dam removal, she cheered the "last train to Opportunity."

Joel Chavez, the state's man running the restoration, bragged that Opportunity's six-plus square miles of tailings ponds were managed to keep the dump site "separate from the active environment," and likened the strategy of storing the restoration wastes at Opportunity to "putting all the rats in one trap."

Dan Cain, the USGS scientist delivering the talk about how copper contamination influences "mayfly richness" (not well, it turns out), felt compelled to clarify that "the Opportunity sites are basically an outlier, so let's just forget about those."

To include the portion of the Clark Fork riffling past Opportunity, Cain said, would too badly skew his otherwise encouraging findings. Opportunity was off the charts, and so better to ignore it. There's nothing there.

It was as if a lecture on human shit had failed to acknowledge toilets.

Four months after the symposium, I pulled into Skip's Mini-Storage on Stewart Street in Opportunity. I was moving upstream. I wanted to see the disaster before it was undone, and done unto others.

Skip's wife Millie, in her sixties, was already working the sheds. A couple of the units had their steel doors rolled up and Millie was out there in the sun, moving floor lamps and end tables and cardboard boxes from inside out to the gravel drive. I had called ahead, so I introduced myself and nodded at the clutter.

"Busy day. Moving two deadbeats out and one in," she said, without any rancor that I could see. I also couldn't see anyone besides me moving in. We went into her shady breakfast room, sat at a kitchen table, and went through the rules, filled out the paperwork. She made me to understand that there was no lock I could put on her sheds that she couldn't cut. I wrote her a check for six months of storage and told her I didn't plan to make her prove it.

It took a few hours to unload a six-by-twelve U-Haul trailer of pretty much everything that hadn't been skimmed away in previous moves: bookshelves, a rolled-up rug, Rubbermaid tubs full of canoeing and camping gear, cardboard boxes filled mostly with books, and Bob's old rods and tackle. I transferred the cheap lock I'd bought for the trailer to the sliding clasp on the shed door and snugged the straps holding the canoes on top of the truck.

From Opportunity, the five-mile drive into Anaconda is a portal into America's industrial past. First you pass the highway sign marking the turnoff to Wisdom, fifty miles to the southwest. For years, out at the other end of Mill Creek Road, where it intersects

State Highway 43, there was a sign at the juncture with divergent arrows pointing the way to Wisdom and, alternately, Opportunity. The sign got replaced during a resurfacing project a decade ago, part of the slow and steady erasure of Opportunity from the map. No point in steering people toward someplace no one would choose to go.

The turnoff to Wisdom is followed closely by an unnatural-looking grassy knoll, a mile and a half long, that I would learn is the entombed remains of the Anaconda Pond, a former waste pit where toxic heavy metals settled out of suspension and dropped to the bottom before the water carrying them was released into Mill Creek, flowing through Opportunity toward the Clark Fork. The pond has since been filled in and fenced off, a minor achievement ticked off of a long list of cleanup tasks associated with the Anaconda smelters. Just next to it is an unchecked box: a low mountain of black sand half a mile long, twenty-five million tons of granulated smelter slag, like a Hawaiian beach washed up in the foothills of central Montana.

Looming over all of it is the Washoe smelter stack, the tallest brick masonry structure in the world, 585.5 feet high, taller than the Washington Monument. The Washoe was considered progressive pollution control when it was built in 1918, the idea being that the higher in the sky the smelter belched its by-products, the more arsenic and sulfur would disperse harmlessly in the atmosphere instead of scattering back to earth. The Washoe was the last of several smokestacks the Anaconda Company built at its successive Anaconda smelters, and it's the only one still standing. After it was decommissioned in 1980, when the EPA arrived to demolish the structure, Anacondans lobbied to leave it standing. The stack marked their heritage. Today it's the site of a state park that's never welcomed a visitor. The ground around it is too toxic for the public to walk on, and bricks may fall from the sky.

You can see that stack from twenty miles away on a clear day, but a clear day is the last thing Anaconda residents ever looked to the stack for. For most of the twentieth century, they'd wake up each morning and look to the stack for assurance. If it was smoking, the smelter was up and running, and there would be work that day. If not, then there was a labor strike, or copper prices—published daily on the front page of the *Anaconda Standard*—had fallen low enough to put the smelter on standby.

I drove past the Copper Bowl Lanes and Cafe, past the Happy Endings Casino, past the Volkswagen-sized iron ladles that had once poured molten copper, now salvaged from the smelter and parked around town, spilling copper-colored marigolds into the medians. Past the Montana Hotel, lop-topped to a stub of its former glory, its once-grand ground floor now occupied by a podiatrist's office and a Subway sandwich shop advertising $5 foot-longs, a shabby motel named after Anaconda founder Marcus Daly appended out back.

Unlike its older brother Butte, where the streets are named for the metals extracted from the mines—Iron, Aluminum, Platinum, Gold, Porphyry, Silver, Mercury, headed uphill toward Copper Street—Anaconda's thoroughfares are named for trees: Pine, Alder, Elm, Cherry, Maple, Tamarack, Locust, Hickory, Oak, Cedar, Chestnut, Birch, Ash. Not all are native to the valley. Those that are were stripped from the hillsides to feed the smelter's furnaces, or cut down by the arsenic pouring from its stack. The streets on the east end of town, expanding to follow the smelter in the early 1900s, are named for presidents Washington, Adams, Jefferson, and Monroe. Another president, William Howard Taft, visited his cousin's home at 105 East Seventh Street in the early 1900s, an address now featured on an architecture-appreciation walking tour. Anaconda's streets are boulevard-wide, built in Daly's anticipation of his town becoming the new state's capital. The snow-plowing costs, combined with dwindling tax base, now constitute a municipal hardship.

Anaconda proper begins to peter out at the Safeway grocery at the western edge of town. Tidy rows of modest homes on cramped lots give way to a rural procession of trailers and country places, usually outfitted with a fishing boat and ATV in the gravel drive. Warms Springs Creek, more or less invisible in Anaconda proper, becomes a pretty if largely inaccessible roadside presence. Its cool supply of fresh water, melting out of the Pintler Mountains overlooking the road's southern flank, is why the smelter, and thus Anaconda, was built here in the first place.

Then, Warm Springs Creek—it's pronounced "crick" in Montana, like something you wake up to find in your neck—was a ready source of industrial coolant, and a handy way to fill the smelter's fifteen redwood tanks, each fifty feet in diameter and fourteen feet deep, where copper was leached out of roasted ore in a bath brewed from seventy thousand gallons of fresh water, thirty-five tons of sulfuric acid, and fifteen tons of salt.

Today that creek, running clear and cold upstream of the smelter site, signals different uses, suggested by the steel silhouettes that welcome visitors approaching either end of town: an elk, a deer, a snowboarder, a downhill skier, a pair of golfers, and a fly fisherman casting into the wind. This is no longer Anaconda, Smelter City, but Anaconda, Gateway to the Pintlers, the showcase range in the 158,615-acre Anaconda-Pintler Wilderness, a quintessential Montana fantasy landscape loaded with bears, wolves, and mountain goats, crystalline alpine lakes, tumbling creeks, glacial moraines, serrated and talus-skirted peaks, and forty-five miles of the Continental Divide National Scenic Trail.

For almost a hundred years men came to Anaconda to secure their wages at the smelter. Today they come, if they come, to fish and play.

Either way, it's about water.

Water is why I've come, too. That and because friends offered to loan me a remote Montana cabin. A boy could hardly imagine a finer retreat, clinging to a mountainside, up several hundred yards of steep, rutted switchbacks, with four stair-step levels, from a basement bedroom carved into the slope to a well-windowed reading loft perched among the upper boughs of pine, larch, and fir.

From the corner windows I can look out at the peaks of the wilderness, the granite outcrop of Mount Haggin drizzled with overnight snow in August and melted bare again by late afternoon, the green sub-timberline slopes striped with the dying rust of beetle infestation. Out another window, just a few miles up the road, a sliver of Georgetown Lake, glossy blue on still days or white-capped in the wind. I look that direction for clouds, mostly, stacking up over the Sapphires behind the lake, the evening sun dropping through the curtain of them, heavy and dramatic, purple and orange. Here at 6,700 feet above sea level, hail falls pea-sized out of clear, blue skies on a seventy-degree afternoon. One night I saw a shooting star that left a trail of glowing green in the sky as thick as my thumb.

In the mornings I sip coffee on the railed porch and watch hawks circle the pasture across the road, or ride the thermals closer, right over the cabin, too close for binoculars, winging fat shadows across the ground. Hummingbirds flit among the flowering weeds beneath the porch. I see coyotes trotting in the meadows and watch the green pond at the forest's edge for the moose said to frequent it. Soon after I got here, driving back to Safeway to stock groceries, I passed the hulking carcass of a dead moose on the side of the road. It was gone by the time I returned. I choose to believe that it wasn't *my* moose, and keep an eye out. With fall coming on, the elk have begun bugling their hollow love songs in the drainages to the east.

It's Steinbeck's young boy's Montana fantasy in spades. It's also an engineered facade.

Georgetown Lake shouldn't be a lake at all. It was once Flint Creek, dammed at the edge of the designated wilderness—itself a human-drawn border—into the East Fork Reservoir, and then again, further downstream, into Georgetown Lake. Likewise Storm Lake, to the east, a mountain reservoir held back by earthen berms. Silver Lake, the least natural-looking of the three, penned in by the rubble grade propping up Scenic Highway 1, its pumping station stranded in deep water at the end of a long pier, is the only natural lake of the bunch, and even it has been tinkered into industrial service. Find the side roads and you'll cross the relict concrete aqueduct, and the even more relict wood-planked pipeline that once fed water to Butte, forty miles away. The whole system has been rigged since anyone was here to rig it, engineered and reengineered to suit whatever purpose was most immediate to hand.

The purpose was usually mining, or the watering of miners. The place is lousy with holes in the ground. Fifteen miles down the road, Philipsburg, a tourist town built on the remains of a silver mining camp, now boasts antique candy shops and proximity to Discovery, a family-friendly ski hill. Slightly closer to home, in the mountains above Georgetown, a few ghost structures hang on at Southern Cross, where a thin vein of gold was once tapped out. Just around the flank of the hill from my borrowed cabin is a black hole into the mountain, another former mine, unsecured and sagging. The quietest collapse would bury you alive and nobody would ever know.

Even this cabin, all modern convenience and weekend amenities, is a pastiche. The kitchen, bathroom, and breakfast table are contained in the heavy log shell, caulked with concrete and orange spray foam, of what used to be the pay shack for gold miners who tunneled that hole into the backside of this hill. The living room and loft are finished from the gutted remains of a frame cottage salvaged off a residential lot in Opportunity. It's got new cedar siding on the outside, new double-paned windows mounted in solid new frames, and a new green steel roof that rattles when the wind gusts, but you can still see remnants of the original dull-white paint peeking out from under the eaves. It's white lead paint, another product of the Anaconda smelters.

There are no rental listings in Opportunity, no Craigslist, not even a Wikipedia entry. Opportunity is as knotted with power lines and wired with satellite dishes as the rest of America, but in terms of mobility, economy, or sociability, it might as well be off the grid entirely. You can't get much closer than this displaced cabin, whence I spy on Opportunity from space, via Google Maps' ubiquitous satellite view: a tiny cross-hatched corner of green abutting an enormous inverse crater, bleached blotchy white with toxic mineral salts.

It's otherwise almost invisible, as if there's nothing there at all.

When the sun sinks over the lake this time of year, Orion comes out in the eastern sky, skimming the treetops, sword sheathed. I was taught to see Orion drawing an arrow on his bow, and from here it looks like he might be taking aim at some unlucky bull elk in the Flint Creek Range to the north. Bob first showed Orion to me decades ago, as a billion fathers have shown a billion sons, teaching me to look for the bright three-star asterism of the hunter's belt.

He was an engineer—of course he taught me to look for the straight line. The only other constellation I can reliably find is the Pleiades, the Seven Sisters, a cluster that's most distinct in peripheral vision, wobbling and fading under direct observation.

Orion is making copper up there right now. Rigel, one corner of the hunter's hem, and Betelgeuse, his shoulder, are massive stellar furnaces a thousand times the size of the sun, between six hundred and eight hundred light years from Opportunity, slowly churning out neutrons that collide and combine with iron and other heavy elements. When these supergiants explode into supernovas, the pulverized dust will race through the universe until it finally coalesces into new stars and new planets, and some of that dust will be copper.

Four and a half billion years ago, the earth formed out of just such clouds of stellar debris propelled from the limbs of long-dead constellations. Millions of years later the earth's tectonic plates collided outside of Butte, raising the Rocky Mountains into the sky and spewing molten rock toward the crust. Surface water from some prehistoric Clark Fork seeped deep into the fractured globe to dissolve minerals out of the magma, and then, superheated into steam, carried them back toward the surface to deposit in the thick veins threading Butte's hills.

People have been using copper for ten thousand years, but nobody knew where it came from until two Italian astronomers, Donatella Romano and Francesca Matteucci, figured it out less than a decade ago. Right from the start, water and sky were copper's conduits, transporting it from exploding supernovas into the core of a forming planet trillions of miles away, and from that core to the crust, where men shattered it with picks and dynamite, shoveled it to the surface, and shipped it to their own furnaces, creating their own dust. That dust poisoned a valley and killed a river, so now we're digging it up again, moving it upstream, against the current, to a place from which we somehow expect it never to move again.

I remember Rick Bass in Missoula, talking about this Montana, the one that most people never see. "The poison hasn't gone away," he'd said. "It's simply redistributed. We need new stories to tell this truth, new stories built with old words."

One of those stories is about Opportunity. It's also about a wastewater engineer and his son, a mineral and its mess, and the connections forged by water. It's a buried history of Americans' attachment to progress and estrangement from consequence. The only way to read it is through a lens made of metal.

# PART II

# VENUS RISING

*And every civilisation when it loses its inward
vision and its cleaner energy, falls into a new sort of
sordidness, more vast and more stupendous than the
old savage sort. An Augean stables of metallic filth.*

—D. H. LAWRENCE, *St. Mawr*

How far upstream before you're at the beginning?

The more closely you consider a river, the less discrete a reality it becomes. Follow it upstream from anywhere and sooner or later you'll be presented with a fork, and then others off that, each with their own tines rising into mountains, and you can only walk uphill so far before the thing you think of as a river ceases to be an observable entity.

Running water diminishes as it rises closer to the sky: river, bayou, anabranch, creek, stream, brook, freshet, slough, rivulet. Higher up, or in dry low country, the words are arroyo, coulee, draw, gully, and wash, all defined by intermittency. There's rarely water in them. You are now hiking, and hiking is for people who have an argument with gravity.

I could step into the Clark Fork just outside of Opportunity and start sloshing upstream, past the fuzzy demarcation where the river becomes a creek named Silver Bow. Past the new Mill Creek electrical switching station, past the Blue Lagoon, where old train-derailed tailings color a pond Caribbean blue, through cramped Durant Canyon, up along railroad tracks past the truck-stop town of Rocker, where ten-by-ten mine timbers were once soaked in recycled arsenic as preservative, and on into Butte, trudging through culverts and marsh and muck across town.

Just off Harrison Avenue, the creek winds between scaly black walls, a human-made canyon. The walls are made of compressed slag from early Butte smelters, twenty feet high, stacked along the creek bank, because creek banks were handy. Mine waste is heavy, and there's no profit in moving it farther than you have to. For decades, and largely still, Butte's tailings and slags have been left where they lie.

Legend has it that Silver Bow was named for the way sunlight lapped the ripply creek, sparking reflective bowties off the surface. Another story delegates the silver to sunlight and the bow to the way the waterway curves through Butte's flats. There's poetry to both, but not much specificity. Every creek ripples and bends, and they all reflect the sun.

At least one Butte tour guide will tell you that by the late nineteenth century, Silver Bow had entered the local lexicon as the original Shit Creek. The original part seems unlikely. The word "shit" dates to 1580, and waters have been fouled since there were humans to foul them.

Keep walking upstream and you'll cross another unmarked boundary into a 1.5-mile stretch of water with no poetry at all. In the 1960s the state designated this stretch of Silver Bow as Butte's "Municipal Storm Drain," a bureaucratic euphemism for Shit Creek if ever there was one. In 2010, a group called the Silver Bow Creek Headwaters Coalition filed suit to force the state to refer to the creek by its proper name. Calling it a storm drain, a coalition spokesman told the local paper, hampers restoration efforts. Names matter. Who wants to pony up to restore a storm drain?

If I really want to be a completist, I can splash up the storm drain, past the strip-mined Berkeley Pit, then into the tributary Blacktail Creek, and from there up Yankee Doodle Gulch all the way to the top of the Continental Divide, overlooking town from 6,350 feet above sea level. That ridgeline, part of 3,100 miles of North America's meandering mountain spine, is the defining terrain of water in the United States, and as close to an ultimate source as you're going to get. Rain that falls on the eastern slope eventually finds its way into the Missouri River, and from there into the Mississippi, which carries it to the Gulf of Mexico. Rain and snow on the western slope trickles into the gullies and gulches feeding Silver Bow Creek, the uppermost link of a watery chain feeding the Clark Fork, then the Columbia, and finally the Pacific.

But I'm being too literal. Rivers, like journalism, encourage obsession with sources, and sources aren't always what they seem. The Clark Fork's symbolic source is Butte, and Butte is mostly holes in the ground.

Approach Butte on Interstate 90 from either direction and you'll pass billboards plugging the town's prime tourist attraction: an abandoned strip mine. It's called the Berkeley Pit, and if you've heard anything about Butte, the pit is probably it. The billboards' panoramic frame serves better than most vantages to give a visual identity to a feature of the landscape that's almost too large to comprehend. The Berkeley Pit is a mile by a mile and a half across and, the billboard reads, "1700 feet deep." The sign doesn't specify that the 1,700-foot-deep pit is filled with toxic soup a thousand feet deep and rising.

A flock of 342 Canadian snow geese succumbed to the pond's lure in 1995, laying over on their migration south. The next morning, in a news curiosity that appeared in papers nationwide, their carcasses were fished out of the pit with gaffs and johnboats. The acidic mine water didn't agree with them.

The billboards' compressed aerial view peers over the lip of the water-filled gouge, rendered in abstract chemical green, orange, and blue, an enormous absence, a giant hole full of history. An American century's worth of waste has poured into that hole, and out of it, soon enough, will spring one of the West's great rivers. The sacrifices required to turn that trick will make hardly a ripple.

✝

In September 1991, a couple of married German tourists named Helmut and Erika Simon went walking in Italy's Ötztal Alps, near the Austrian border, and stumbled across a mummy emerging from the meltwater of a glacial gully. Austrian authorities extracted the corpse with jackhammers and ice-axes, and gawkers poached scraps of clothing as souvenirs before the body was trucked to Innsbruck for tests.

Ötzi the Ice Man turned out to be an archaeological sensation, the oldest mummy ever found in Europe, having died some 5,300 years ago. Ötzi stood just under five and a half feet tall and weighed 110 pounds. He may have been a high-country shepherd, or part of a raiding party. Either way, he was well equipped for mountain travel with a parka made of woven grass, leather snowshoes, and a bearskin hat. He carried a flint knife, a fire-starting kit with dried moss tinder, and pouches filled with seeds and grain. Fleas covered his corpse. His last meal was an ibex steak. Genome sequencing determined that he had brown eyes, Lyme disease, and suffered from lactose intolerance.

He had company when he died. Blood on his arrows suggests a skirmish involving several men, and a bone-deep gash on his thumb says Ötzi put up a hand-to-hand fight before an antagonist's arrow pierced his shoulder from behind. It's unknown whether the wound killed him or just disabled him sufficiently to let starvation and cold finish him off. He lay facedown on a granite slab for five millennia while the ice crept over.

Of all the iceman's accoutrements, the one least expected was an ax, yew-handled and headed with a 3.7-inch blade of solid copper, 99.7 percent pure and manufactured a thousand years before scientists had thought Europeans knew how to work copper. That discovery required a backdating of the Chalcolithic era, the interstice when stone tools began to give way to metal implements. Scientists found copper particles and arsenic in Ötzi's hair. They suspect he may have been an early smelterman.

I've never found anything remotely that interesting on a hike. A heat-glazed smelter brick, yes, a steel railroad spike, but not even an elk shed, and antlers are as common in Montana as ATVs. Every garage has at least one.

Today Ötzi is ensconced in the South Tyrol Museum of Archaeology in Bolzano, laid out in a refrigerated crypt behind a fifteen-inch-square peek-a-boo keyhole into the metallic origins of modernity.

✛

Copper had already been known for thousands of years by the time Ötzi forged his ax. Archaeologists usually locate humankind's earliest use of the element in modern-day Turkey, Iran, and Iraq, the same spots that spawned civilization. A copper pendant found in northern Iraq dates to 8,700 years before Christ, plenty old enough to engender myth. The Greek island of Cyprus took its name from copper's Latin *cuprus* and the plentiful stores of green rocks that made it the go-to source for the copper-seeking civilizations of Greece, Rome, Phoenicia, and Ionia in the three thousand years predating Jesus. Venus was copper's goddess, wearing an Egyptian ankh, emerging from the waves near her island protectorate to confirm her charms in a mirror made from the polished pink metal. The Greeks knew copper as an antiseptic and mixed glittery flakes with honey as a dressing for wounds.

The patron saint of the Sinai Peninsula, another early copper bonanza, was named Hathor, the Egyptian goddess of the sky, music, dance, and art, also known as Lady of Malachite. Malachite and azurite, copper ores colored blue and green, were ground into the makeup that painted Egyptian eyelids aqua.

The first copper, like first peoples, went by the name "native," and as with first peoples, the title points to purity. Native copper poked out of the ground unadorned, as recognizable as a mineral shop specimen, in stone crevasses from which it could be pried with sticks and bones and hammered into shape with a rock. Casting came next, melting native copper over fire and pouring it into stone molds to cool. Ötzi's ax was stone-molded, then cold-hammered to a cutting edge ideal for felling small trees.

My own first conscious use of copper was sucking on a penny in the driver's seat of my mom's Camaro to mask high school alcohol breath. I'd heard you could beat a Breathalyzer that way, though I never got to test the theory. I just wanted to get through my parents' front door without raising a stink. I remember thinking the penny tasted like blood.

Human blood does contain traces of copper, but our blood is primarily iron-based, via the hemoglobin that delivers oxygen to the cells. Iron is red. Crabs have copper-based blood. It's blue.

Native copper, the orange-pink variety scattered in plain sight, is rare, and mostly picked over. The metal is more commonly found in ore form, bound in rock. The word "ore" is derived from an Old English combo of *ora*, meaning unworked stone, and *ar*, or copper. The almost alchemical art of turning stone into metal is called smelting, from the Old English *meltan*: to melt. Copper's inaugural liquidity is unrecorded, but metallurgy was probably born by accident in the unexpected leakage of a fireplace stone.

Smelting refines metal from ore, a reduction from the many to the one, but the word "smelting" also applies to the melding of different metals, the combination of elements into alloy. Bronze, the earliest alloy, is copper combined with arsenic or tin. Brass—copper fused with nickel—came later. The Bible uses "brass" and "bronze" interchangeably. Either way, it's a biblically base metal, defined by impurity, associated with snakes and symbolic of God's judgment, humankind's technological rise and moral fall epitomized in a single candlestick.

Smelter sites in modern-day Israel, Jordan, and Syria date to 4,500 BC. Sumerians introduced copper craft to the Egyptians, who turned it into farm implements, cookware, razors, and tools. Egyptian temples built five thousand years ago featured copper plumbing that is functionally intact today.

Smelting opened the door to the age of industrial pollution. Ore samples from Greenland's ice caps track global copper contamination, like frozen tree rings, to the dawn of metallurgy, between seven thousand and eight thousand years ago, spiking during the age of the Roman Empire. Having plundered Cyprus, the Romans sourced far-flung ore all across Europe and the Mediterranean, inducing slave labor to produce as much as 17,000 tons of refined copper annually for architectural accents, pipe organs, and coins.

Millennia-old Roman smelters in Jordan, Cyprus, and Sinai are still littered with mountains of glassy black slag, a waste-metal by-product of the smelting process, and browsing livestock at southern Jordan's Wadi Faynan, home of the Middle East's largest historic copper deposits, show elevated levels of copper in their tissues even today.

After a mine's easy ore gives out, water tends to leach out of underground workings, picking up residual heavy metals as it flows. At the Rio Tinto mine on the Iberian Peninsula, Roman copper scavengers faced with diminishing returns discovered that such wastewater could be poured over iron to precipitate the suspended copper. They regraded the works to facilitate drainage and sent laborers underground with brass-rimmed leather buckets. For latter-day Roman slaves, mining copper became a matter of carrying water. Their feet developed stinging sores from walking in the acidic wet.

Producing the stuff is filthy work, but the result is paradoxically self-cleansing. For the same reason that copper is bad for riverine macroinvertebrates—i.e., fish food—it's repellent to germ life everywhere. The Chinese were probably the first to use copper for coinage, and Roman coins were called coppers. Gold and silver were too valuable for common cash, and copper was well suited as a medium of hand-to-hand exchange due to the oligodynamic effect, documented in 1893 when a Swiss scientist found that ions of certain heavy metals—silver, copper, and copper alloys foremost among them—have a deleterious effect on bacteria. If your home features brass doorknobs—and it's been estimated that a billion American entries are so adorned, accounting for more than 500 million pounds of zinc-alloyed copper—you've probably been saved innumerable sick days. A brass doorknob disinfects itself in about eight hours.

The modern American quarter and dime are 92 percent copper, and the nickel is 75 percent. Between 1793 and 1981 the U.S. penny fluctuated between 88 and 100 percent copper (excepting 1943, which any casual coin collector can tell you produced a war-shortage version of zinc-coated steel). Only in 1982 was the one-cent coin rejiggered to its current composition of 97.5 percent zinc, with just 2.5 percent copper in the plating to maintain the look. The price of the metal had surpassed the nominal value of the coin containing it. Americans were melting pennies and selling the copper, at a profit, for scrap. In 2012, Canada, faced with the fiscally suspect prospect of paying 1.5 cents to produce each one-cent coin, abandoned the penny entirely.

In 2010, Serbian scientists uncovered a seven-thousand-year-old village near Belgrade littered with copper axes, hammers, needles, and hooks, bumping the Chalcolithic back another 1,700 years before Ötzi and shifting its center westward.

History rewrites itself each spring, cutting fresh channels into the past, like a river running off.

✝

Spaniards arrived in the Americas in 1492 floating on copper-clad hulls, and found copper already here. Antonio Herrera de Tordesillas, chronicler of Columbus's fourth expedition, described trading canoes launching from the Yucatan Peninsula with "small hatchets, small bells, and plates made of copper." Bernal Diaz del Castillo, a Spanish conquistador and eyewitness to Hernan Cortez's early-1500s incursions into Mexico, reported that "each Indian, besides his ornaments of gold, had a copper ax."

The Aztecs were already advanced metallurgists with two kinds of bronze under their belts, and pre-Columbian Andeans had been forging copper tools and jewelry for almost two thousand years.

Post-Columbus explorers of North America from Florida to Canada, most of them looking for gold, arrived to find copper implements in the hands of native cultures that didn't know smelting from a hole in the ground. English explorer and Hudson Bay namesake Henry Hudson encountered tribes smoking tobacco from copper pipes and wearing copper necklaces in 1609. Some had pure copper axes and knives. The copper had come from Michigan.

When French explorer Samuel Champlain founded Quebec in 1608, friendly Algonquin tribesmen gifted him with a chunk of solid copper "a foot long, very handsome and quite pure" that Champlain shipped to his patron, King Henry IV, either as a token of New World wealth or as a shiny curiosity.

The British weren't much interested in Michigan copper at the time. They already had the world's greatest copper smelter in Swansea, Wales. The French were little more than curious as well. Copper wasn't quite a precious metal, and its uses were usually decorative or utilitarian. It doesn't take much copper to make an earring, and there was no shortage of supply sufficient to satisfy demand for cookware and hull-plating. Copper certainly didn't carry the rarity to justify freight from the region that would become Michigan, a land described in a letter from French cartographer Baron de Lahontan to the king of France as "the fag end of creation." The French had grander goals in mind for the Great Lakes. Their seventeenth-century letters describe Lake Superior's shores as studded with rare gems and veined with silver and gold.

Like all El Dorados, Lake Superior inspired more fiction than fact, and the embellishments far predated stipend-seeking French fabrications. Long before Champlain was given his hunk of copper, the Ojibwa deity Missibizi was said to reside on a canoe-shaped island in Lake Superior called Michipicoten, fifteen miles long and made of solid copper, that Missibizi liked to paddle across the waves from his helm on the island's hilly crest. Michipicoten's surf-splashed flanks were reputedly littered with copper nuggets the size of softballs, and, according to legend, when passing fishermen decided to take a few for themselves Missibizi jealously struck them dead.

The Ojibwa invested the metal with magic and handled their heirloom stashes of copper fishhooks, pebbles, needles, and knives with superstitious zeal. The Ojibwa weren't miners so much as gleaners. The art that produced their prized artifacts had been lost for centuries by the time European explorers arrived in Michigan to find the inexplicably abandoned works, filled with tools and half-extracted copper rocks.

Michipicoten may not have been solid copper, but Lake Superior's Isle Royale wasn't far from it, and the island's metallic core drew it into the sphere of the fledgling United States. A lobbying contingent of East Coast businessmen and three Ojibwa Indians so convinced Benjamin Franklin of the baby nation's interest in a seemingly limitless supply of copper that Franklin threatened to gridlock the 1773 Treaty of Paris, whereby the international boundary between the United States and Canada was hashed out, unless America got title to the island. Franklin prevailed and Isle Royale is the only island in Lake Superior specifically mentioned in the treaty. The international boundary line jogs north on its path through the lake specifically to encompass the prize.

It would be another twenty-eight years before Paul Revere

founded the nation's first manufacturing company, the Revere Copper Company in Canton, Massachusetts, and started cranking out the rolled copper sheets that cover the dome of the Massachusetts state capitol.

Visitors to North America from the earliest French explorers on had been treated to field trips to the must-see geological oddity of Michigan's Upper Peninsula: a 3,708-pound solid copper boulder that famously lay on the banks of the Ontonagon River. In 1843, an enterprising Detroiter named Julius Eldred purchased the rock from a local chieftain, bought it a second time from a disputatious miner who'd claimed it for his own, and barged it to Detroit for display at twenty-five cents an ogle. Newspaper writers called it "a supreme gesture of nature" and "a veritable nugget from the Gods." Then the U.S. War Department pulled rank and seized it for the Smithsonian. It's still there, in the National Museum of Natural History, in storage. In 1991, Keweenaw Bay Ojibwa sued for the boulder's return under the Native American Repatriation Act, but the repatriation office decided the tribe had failed to sufficiently prove the stone's sacredness.

It was hardly the first time Michigan's copper riches had been plundered. Extraction on a mass scale had begun thousands of years before at the hands of an ancient race of itinerate pre-Columbian miners.

Missibizi had ruled a landscape of haunted copper mines—shallow pits dug with stone and bone—that still stumps archeologists. Isle Royale, now a national park, is dimpled with some ten thousand holes in the ground where Missibizi's predecessors scrounged for shiny red rocks. Exactly who those excavating predecessors were remains a mystery, but a good guess is that the depressions were scooped by some arm of the Mississippian Mound Builder cultures that flourished from their eponymous delta to northern Michigan between 3400 BC and the sixteenth century.

More fanciful theories were floated over the years, including Dr. Henriette Mertz's claim, in her 1986 book *The Mystic Symbol*, that ancient Phoenician mariners raided Michigan's Upper Peninsula specifically to restock the depleting copper stores of Sinai. Other theorists and cranks have tried to peg the mysterious Mound Builders as displaced Vikings, Mayans, Eskimos, African survivors of Atlantis, and the Ten Lost Tribes of Israel.

Nobody knows. They left few artifacts and no known graves. Apparently they showed up every spring and left every fall, taking the copper with them.

Whoever they were, they scattered Michigan's riches prodigiously. Upper Peninsula copper has turned up in ceremonial mounds all over the eastern half of the continent. Five thousand years ago prehistoric miners and merchants were crisscrossing the country to trade copper earrings and fishhooks. It was as if copper were motive. It wouldn't stay put.

✝

Alto, Texas, is home to the Caddoan Indian Mounds State Historic Site, where 1,200 years ago Caddo Indians constituted the southwesternmost extent of the Mississippian mound culture. The Caddoans comprised a more recent variant, from about AD 900 to 1450. They wore copper-covered stone spools in their elongated earlobes and copper combs in their hair. The earthen lumps in Alto were burial mounds. I learned that from the roadside historical marker. The mounds were on the route to my grandparents' house in Whitehouse, near Tyler, and my family always stopped at historical markers along the way. Bob called them hysterical markers. We laughed the first time.

It was in Alto that I first stepped into a canoe. It was Thanksgiving, and the family was visiting Bob's parents at their deer lease on Lake Duran, just outside of town. Lake Duran was as spooky as any grave-packed hillock that night. We arrived after dark and what moonlight there was filtered through brittle oak leaves and tattered drapes of Spanish moss. There had been rain and the dirt road leading to the stilted plank cabin that served as a hunting camp was flooded out. Lake Duran, all cattails and marsh, had spilled its shallow banks and inundated the lowlands.

A caretaker named Cotton, white-haired and overalled, met us where the road went under and put us in an aluminum canoe with a square stern mount for a little 1.5-horsepower Johnson outboard. The boat carried us in shifts across flat black water to the cabin, Lake Duran's glassy skin reflecting the light of copper-churning stars in a sky held taut by nothing more than surface tension.

✛

The Mound Builders were industrious but they never crossed the line into industrialism. By the time refined coal started fueling England's industrial revolution and reactionary Romantic poetry in the late nineteenth century, they had died out—felled by exploratory germs or repatriated to Atlantis, who knows. The East Coast emigrants who in 1843 began flooding into Michigan didn't care. They'd heard the legends of solid copper shorelines and read reports of the astounding Ontonagon Boulder.

Prospectors arrived in droves, and those who couldn't wait for the next overbooked schooner hired French Canadian voyageurs to paddle them to the peninsula in baggage-laden canoes. They "salivated" the prospects, spitting on rocks to bring out the green that indicated copper in the composition. In 1843 Congress ratified a treaty with the Ojibwa by which the United States acquired thirty thousand square miles of the Upper Peninsula and three hundred miles of Lake Superior shoreline. The deal turned out to be worth billions in copper, timber, and iron, the core of a mining district that eventually produced hundreds of millions of dollars in dividends.

You'd think the government could give back the boulder.

By 1849, Michigan's copper country was providing 85 percent of the U.S. supply. In the early twentieth century, the Keweenaw Peninsula claims produced more copper than anyplace else in the world, and the dominant Calumet and Hecla Consolidated Copper Company employed 66,000 people. In the increasingly machined wake of the Civil War, demand for copper doubled every five years and the price spiked to almost fifty cents a pound.

The Michigan range eventually had some 8.5 billion pounds of copper pried out of it. The remote, lush Upper Peninsula emerged just a bit worse for the wear. Angus Murdoch, writing *Boom Copper* in the early 1940s, noted the happy accident of geology that made the majority of Michigan's copper pure. It didn't require stamp mills to pulverize ore into heavy metal and airborne dust, or smelters to burn off noxious fumes. "The copper country foliage is still green," Murdoch wrote, "and its trees and forests as verdant as in the days of the pre-Columbian miners."

America's first copper country, unlike the one that succeeded it, "never became an industrial wasteland."

Some states have all the luck.

England's phlegmatically named Humphry Davy invented the first incandescent lightbulb in 1802, using a platinum filament and powering his weak light with what was then the world's most powerful electrical battery, at the Royal Institution of Great Britain. Davy was the first of dozens of lightbulb inventors leading up to Thomas Edison, who usually gets all the credit.

Science in the early nineteenth century had not yet reached its age of specialization, and Davy was a man of wide-ranging interests who indulged them all. His first love was poetry, and in 1875 he published his debut book of verse, *The Sons of Genius*. His second love was chemistry, and Davy maintained a lifelong regimen of experimentation with nitrous oxide, aka laughing gas, which he indulgently advocated as both a substitute for alcohol and a hangover cure. He introduced the gas to his poet friends, including Samuel Taylor Coleridge, who, perhaps in gratitude, perhaps under the influence, declared that had Davy "not been the first chemist, he would have been the first poet of his age." (Another versifying contemporary and fellow nitrous enthusiast, Robert Southey, opined less effusively that Davy "had all the elements of a poet; he only wanted the art.")

Davy's poetic reputation may not have survived his century—though his chemical treatises are still available via Amazon .com—but he deserves a nod for his almost forgotten transoceanic contributions to the world of copper, including experiments with copper ship sheathing and his invention, in 1815, of the Davy lamp, a safety lantern designed for use in underground mines.

Bob, my engineer-inventor father, wanted me to be an engineer as well, which is a standard-issue paternal wish. For my elementary school science fair he built a cardboard triptych explaining basic electrical theory, with a battery-operated lightbulb and a tray of iron shavings you could move with a magnet. When my seventh-grade class had an Earth Day poster-making contest, Bob helped

me Magic Marker a three-tiered birthday cake with candles celebrating the tenth anniversary of the 1970 establishment of the
Environmental Protection Agency. I didn't know what the Environmental Protection Agency was, but he did. The EPA establishes
and enforces water standards. It costs money to clean water. Some
of that money went to wastewater engineers like Bob.

His steerage didn't take. I spent high school reading Kurt Von-
negut and Allen Ginsberg. Later, when I was in college, Bob cut off
his financial support after I flunked first-year calculus and stopped
signing up for the science prerequisites. I was young. I wanted to be
an artist. I took a series of odd jobs to make up the difference and
went on to collect an English degree with a minor in photography,
but he'd set a tone that said his way or the highway. He said if I
wanted to be independent, then he would make me independent.
I thought I was being punished for pursuing my own path. I didn't
know that he'd taken my preferences personally. He'd read my rejection of his profession as a rejection of him, and he would never
forgive me for that.

✛

Twenty-one post-Davy inventors laid claim to advancements of
the incandescent lightbulb before Thomas Edison struck gold
with a refined carbon filament in 1879, but the bulb itself wasn't
Edison's money moment. The invention that would make Edison's
glass globe more than a glowing curiosity was the electrical system
into which he plugged it: a coal-fired steam engine driving a high-
voltage dynamo generator packed with heavy copper and brass
bars. In 1892 Edison expanded on his Menlo Park demonstration
system with his first electrical power station and distribution hub,
built around a twenty-seven-ton dynamo named Jumbo, after an
elephant then in the employ of P. T. Barnum. Jumbo fed 100-volt
direct current through twenty miles of underground copper wiring and set the stage for the nationwide electrification that would
follow, rendering gas lighting obsolete and creating overnight demand for the system's core metal.

Edison's first customer, recipient of the world's first electricity
bill, was the Connecticut-based Ansonia Brass and Copper Com-

pany, with offices a few blocks from Edison's Pearl Street Station. The bill came to $50.44 and marked the early codependence of commercial electricity and copper.

In 1911, at a luncheon feting guest of honor Edison at a New York City "Electrical Exposition," copper producers gave the inventor a gift: a cubic foot of solid Cu, a 486-pound squared-off Ontonagon boulder of appreciation inscribed with statistical gratitude. In 1868, the year Edison's first patent had been approved, annual copper production in the United States had amounted to 378 million pounds. By 1910, it was 1.9 billion pounds and rising.

It was 1886 when the French military inaugurated full metal jacket bullets encased in a copper alloy called cupronickel, and by 1924, in the interim between two world wars, *The Story of Copper* author Wade Davis could write, "A man cannot be killed in a modern manner without copper."

Neither can a person live in a modern manner without copper. Electricity flipped the switch. While the premodern world's use of copper depended on hardened alloys with other metals, the industrialized world's dependence relies on unalloyed copper, purged of impurities, to conduct electricity. Today an average American home is laced with 439 pounds of copper wiring and plumbing, with another hundred pounds embedded in household appliances like water heaters, air conditioners, and refrigerators. The average American car contains almost a mile of copper wiring, and a typical commercial jet is strung with more than 600,000 feet of the stuff. In the United States alone, 130 million cell phones are retired every year, containing 2,100 metric tons of copper—enough to build twenty-six new copper-sheathed Statues of Liberty. Craft beers and liquors are brewed in shiny copper stills. Fly fishers ply Copper John trout flies, wound with copper-wire abdomens, in running waters everywhere. The shiny raw copper color attracts trout—just one form in which the metal slays unsuspecting fish.

⚲

The Clark Fork wouldn't have been destroyed without the millions of tons of copper gouged out of the ground at its headwaters. Opportunity's ponds wouldn't be buried without the smelter that sent Butte's treasure out into the world. Missoula couldn't have its historic confluence of rivers restored without Opportunity's ponds to absorb the waste. What once polluted the Clark Fork by accident and neglect is now being visited on Opportunity by design. In another decade, the river's banks and bottom will be spread out atop Opportunity's dusty plateaus, miles from where they are today. This landscape is disappearing. I want to remember it.

I launch my canoe onto Silver Bow Creek from a patch of bare dirt in the easement of the Scenic Highway 1 crossing, twenty-six miles downstream from Lake Berkeley. There's no formal access to the river, no boat ramp, just a rubble-reinforced bridge abutment and a mucky slope to the water. There are no "No Trespassing" signs in sight, no fencing to cross, but I still feel like I'm somewhere I'm not supposed to be.

I will cross and thus encompass the Clark Fork's nominal starting line somewhere between here and the next bridge, maybe a twenty-minute float. I won't notice it because there's nothing there to notice. It's just a name. The water, whatever it's called today, may have been bound in a cloud last night, or part of four-month-old snowpack melted in the morning's sunshine. It may be ocean tomorrow, or sky. It may circle back on itself behind an eddy line, reluctant to leave this shaded trickle under two concrete lanes connecting Opportunity to the world.

The water is low and slow here in July. Spring's rain is well on its way to the Pacific, or diverted downstream for summer irrigation, or bottled up behind dams in far western Montana and Idaho, and the upper Clark Fork, a big river only at flood stage, looks more like what most people would call a stream. Not that most people would call the Clark Fork at this point anything at all. Most people don't see this stretch.

I load the canoe with a camera, a bottle of water, a nylon dry bag with a rain jacket and an extra set of clothes, two paddles, and a waterproof box containing a digital recorder. The spare paddle and the clothes are ridiculous contingencies for a sunny summer day on eighteen inches of slow-moving water, but I've wrecked boats in nicer weather than this and driven home in borrowed clothes, so I tend toward caution.

The recorder is for taking notes with my hands busy paddling. It doesn't strike me that there might be anything weird about floating down a Superfund site under blue skies in a broad Montana valley, talking to myself.

The water is translucent brown tinted algal green, shallow and riffled and warm under the sun, and the little boat twitches from side to side under my knees. In deep water you can brace a paddle in the current and lean on it for stability, but there's hardly enough water here for a paddle blade to find purchase. The streambed is about twenty feet wide and twisty, and not all of it is deep enough to float a boat. I have to hug the shore in the deeper water, swinging around the bends, and stay off the shallow sandbars sweeping out from the insides of turns. Where the bed drops slightly—and it can be hard to remember, paddling through prairie, that water is always running downhill—small ripples pile up over stony miniature spillways and I have to watch close for the telltale tongues of smooth green water that mark the marginally deeper channels. They are the difference between weightless transit downstream and scraping the canoe's ass across rough rock or, worse, hanging it up entirely and having to get out and drag. There's nothing so objectively terrible about stepping out of a canoe in ankle-deep water to nudge it off an obstruction, it's just embarrassing, whether anyone's watching or not. Choosing a course on moving water is called picking your line, and to pick a viable line you have to correctly read the river. Ass-dragging through shallows and head-butting banks means you missed your line. It means you weren't paying attention. It means you don't know how to read.

The banks require translation too, layered and crumpled like a cake that's been left out in the sun. Rising out of the water they're soil-brown, as you'd expect them to be, but without vegetation to hold them in place. They crumble and slump toward the water, and into it when it rises. On top of the soil you can see why: another three-foot layer of sediment, sickly orange fading to gray. This is mine waste, pulverized rock washed down from the tailings piles of Butte in high water and deposited on the floodplain when the waters receded. In addition to nutrients and organic matter, the normal freight of floodwater, Silver Bow carries copper, cadmium, arsenic, and lead, thus the dearth of plant life—and fish-ers. Every time it rains the water erodes the poisoned banks and what fish have braved these extremities die.

You can see where the sediments have settled down around cop-pices of riverside ghost willows, choking the roots and killing them where they stand. Their spindly stalks are brittle and bleached, two heads high and shining matte silver on shores punctuated with ane-mic green shrubs. Where especially high metal concentrations have congregated, plant life is absent entirely. Acreage-sized swaths, es-pecially at the bends where water slows and sediment drops, are entirely lifeless, just sunburned scabs.

About a mile down I pass under Opportunity's Stewart Street bridge. Even in the low flow I have to duck. I pass a beached tube of rusty culvert, then a USGS gauging station, a pale blue outhouse-sized shack dangling a flow meter into the channel. Farther down, a profusion of wild pink roses has managed to blossom on top of a dead-dirt bluff.

Then I'm at the triple-bridged takeout. There's one bridge for the access road that feeds Interstate 90, which has followed my me-ander downstream in a straight line, another for the railroad track that follows I-90, and finally the bridge carrying I-90 itself.

I've paddled just three or four miles. I've seen a few ducks, some swallows, and a deer browsing on a sandbar. I had wanted, improb-ably enough, to find some huge hunk of copper half-buried in the bed, but no such luck. The only things glinting are tiny flakes of fool's gold swirled into the cocoa-colored sand.

Within the year, everything I've just seen will be gone but the water, scooped up and trucked to Opportunity's ponds and re-placed. The birds and deer will return, and trout as well. The next paddler will have a different river to read.

# PART III

# RED HARVEST

*Wealth falls on some men as a copper down a drain.*

—SENECA

In May of 1864, prospectors Budd Parker, P. Allison, and Jim Esler stumbled across a hole in a slope above Montana's Silver Bow Creek, not far upstream from a fledgling placer camp where they'd been washing gravel for glitter. They weren't Butte's first fortune-seekers—the pit already held elk antlers that looked like they'd been used for digging—but they were the first that history recorded. The three men put shovels to the task and took their spoil down the hill to wash in the creek, harvesting a few small grains of gold. It was just tobacco money at first, but the bedrock of at least two great American fortunes, and the glimmer of a thwarted third—none of them accruing to Parker, Allison, or Esler—found their geneses in that shallow pit.

Unlike the overnight exploitation of Nevada's Comstock or Montana's Virginia City, Butte's boom was years in the making. There was plenty of ore in the ground, but extracting it was laborious and inefficient in the days before steam-driven jackhammers and the widespread availability of dynamite, which wouldn't be patented until 1867. There was no railway to Butte yet, and no smelter to process ore closer than New Jersey, requiring a two-hundred-mile oxcart journey to the nearest shipping depot on the Missouri River at Fort Benton. There just wasn't much profit in minerals on so distant a frontier. The timing was wrong. By 1868, copper historian Ira Joralemon wrote in his 1934 book *Romantic Copper: Its*

*Lure and Its Lore,* "Butte was about ready to join the dismal ranks of abandoned mining camps. The only miners left were those who did not have money enough to leave and a few enthusiasts . . . who did not have sense enough to go."

Butte's first census, in 1870, counted 241 lingering souls, but fortune soon reversed itself. Ten years later the population had jumped to more than 3,000. That number would triple by 1890 and more than triple again, to 30,000, by 1900.

You wonder if whoever left those antlers behind hung around to watch the riches emerge. It was just a hole in the ground, an unpromising king high in Texas hold 'em that you fold, saving your limited ante to play another day, only to watch two more kings come on the flop.

Arthurian legend dates from the sixth century AD, but it was introduced to me in T. H. White's *The Sword in the Stone.* A young king-to-be, schooled by the magician Merlyn, ascends to the British throne after extracting a metal sword from recalcitrant stone—as good a metaphor for mining as I've heard. He who can wrest metal from mountains is king.

*The Sword in the Stone* was one of the first books Bob ever gave me. I was probably twelve. When I got to the end he sat me down to talk about it. He wanted to know which of the book's characters I most identified with. I remember the furrowed brow on his face when I named Merlyn. He'd wanted to instill a sense of quest and aspiration in his only son. He thought he was molding a boy king in waiting, not some would-be wizard.

Butte mythology minted three copper kings: William Andrews Clark, Marcus Daly, and Augustus Heinze. Any one of them, I suspect, would have earned Bob's approval.

⊹

As an adult, I want to love Bob, fix him in my mind as a stable entity who won't bite, but as a child I mostly wanted to please him. I wanted what all sons want: a father's pride. The way to get it, I thought, was to achieve.

Bob was not a sports fan—he neither cared for nor encouraged activities that involved joining teams—so I never got put through the Little League wringer or pressured to suit up for high school football. Academics is where the pressure was applied, and where I more or less excelled, collecting A's and winning spelling bees and bringing home awards for my essays. I don't recall Bob ever expressing pride in these accomplishments; they were just the outcomes he expected.

Not everyone was so stingy with praise, and when eight of my high school friends and I were named semifinalists for a competitive national scholarship in our junior year, the school saw fit to parade us on a stage at an evening assembly. I wasn't used to being singled out for such laudatory attention, and I liked it. It felt good to hear the parents clapping, and up on stage we grinned at each other and tried to figure out what to do with our hands.

My pride, or any illusion that Bob might share it, was short-lived. The drive home was silent, and when he parked the car in the driveway and stepped out, tension tightened his steps. I didn't know why, but inside the privacy of the house I found out. It was my hair, which was slightly long, and about which he'd already expressed displeasure. He thought I looked like an idiot on that stage, and he'd been embarrassed. The recognition was not for me to enjoy, apparently, but to affirm his parenting. He told me to cut the damn hair. I was seventeen, and hair seemed important. I told him the hell I would. We stared, we yelled, and when that failed to produce a desired result, he took a swing and hit me. Surprised, I swung back.

It was an ineffective fight, fueled more by adrenaline and fear than aggression or skill, and conducted with shoves and open palms, but it was fight nonetheless, and at the end of it my face was bruised, Bob's eyes were wild, and a pane of glass had been busted out of the back door against which I'd tried to pin him. My mother screamed at us to stop, and when we finally did, panting and scared, she retreated to her room in shock, already formulating, I see in retrospect, her exit plan.

It was just one fight, never repeated, but if things between us had never been quite right before, they were wrong after that. I learned not to bother trying to make Bob proud. What I didn't understand is that he wanted me to be proud of him.

✝

William Andrews Clark appears to have been an ass. Photos show a tightly wound little man with a densely thicketed van dyke and, in certain lights, a psychotic glare in his eyes. He had red hair and blue irises, stood five foot seven, and possessed a personality, in the words of a contemporary, "as magnetic as last year's bird's nest." He is not the William Clark of the 1804 Lewis and Clark expedition, who had followed the Missouri River west, crossed the Continental Divide, and traversed the same Hellgate Canyon in which William A. would install his Milltown Dam little more than a hundred years later. The Clark Fork is named not for Clark the exploiter, but for Clark the explorer.

William A. was a second-generation Scots-Irish immigrant, born in a log cabin in Connellsville, Pennsylvania, in 1839. He spent his late teens teaching school and studying law in Iowa, and enlisted on the Confederate side in the Civil War in 1862. Somehow—some sources suggest he deserted—that same year Clark extricated himself to Central City, Colorado, where he went to work in the quartz mines. It was in Central City that he caught wind of new strikes in the Montana Territory.

Tapped-out veterans of the California gold rush and at-a-loss Southerners at the end of the Civil War had begun trickling into Montana looking for a fresh frontier, and the influx makes a hash of Montana's iconic westernness. Manifest Destiny wasn't a steady march across the continent from east to west. The Far West, California, was populated first. Only later did settlers and fortune-seekers turn back inland toward the interior West of Idaho, Montana, and Wyoming. Many of the first pioneers to populate Montana, which wasn't made a U.S. territory until 1864, traveled east to get here.

Clark's path to Montana took him north from Colorado, but before he left he trekked to Denver to gear up on mining-camp supplies. He bought a wagon and four oxen to haul his goods to Bannack, near the present-day Idaho border in southwestern Montana, in 1863. Clark also brought three books with him on that trip: Edward Hitchcock's *Elementary Geology*, Theophilus Parsons's *The Law of Contracts*, and a collection of poems by proto-Romantic Scotsman Robert Burns.

Bannack was booming on a gold strike in 1863, but just days after Clark arrived he heard word of yet another strike, not yet overcrowded with claims, just a day's walk away at Colorado Creek. He arranged to haul a Bannack merchant's tobacco and liquor down the road to pay his way.

Hauling was no easy employment around Bannack in the 1860s. The sixty-five miles between Bannack and Virginia City, Bannack's gold-boom successor, was one of the most dangerous roads in history. The arrival of thousands of miners in a span of months to a nugget-rich territory beyond all legal jurisdiction created a vibrant trade in highway robbery. The highway robbery inspired ad hoc retribution by Montana's infamous vigilantes. Road agents murdered hundreds of men plying the roads in Bannack's early days, and the vigilantes lynched and hung at least twenty-seven, including sheriff Henry Plummer, a handsome man said to have been in surreptitious league with the marauders.

The first book published in Montana was Thomas Dimsdale's *The Vigilantes of Montana*, which paints the self-appointed arbiters of law and order as founding heroes. Their calling card was a chalk-scrawled 3–7–77, a warning to targets that it was time to leave town. What those numbers stand for is one of the state's lasting mysteries. A lot of people have decided that they represent the dimensions of a grave: three feet wide, seven feet deep, and seventy-seven inches long. The modern-day Montana Highway Patrol has worn those numbers on its uniform's shoulder patch since 1956 and claims official ignorance of the numbers' definitive source. It's rather an homage, they say, to the state's first organized law enforcement. You wouldn't want a Montana highway patrolman to catch you sucking a penny behind the wheel.

Clark was prospecting near Bannack, he later wrote, when he "found a very fine pair of elk antlers, which I brought into Bannack, and for which Cy Skinner, who kept a saloon and who was afterwards hung by the Vigilantes near Hell Gate, offered to give me $10, and this I readily accepted."

Clark finished his season on Colorado Creek a couple of thousand dollars in the black and determined to keep earning through the winter, when frozen ground made pickaxing impossible. First he signed on to cut and haul firewood for a local hotel at $2 a day, but he abandoned that job three days later after he got trapped in a blizzard. Clark would do anything for a buck but die. He invested his placer profits in a new wagon and team and drove them four hundred miles to Salt Lake City on another supply run, hoping to "make expenses and possibly something more."

It was the wrong time of the year to be traveling primitive roads in the Rockies. On the return trip Clark watched his oxen freeze to death in the yoke. When he finally arrived back in Bannack, he saw a train robber and would-be horse thief named "Dutch John" Wagner hanging frozen from a rafter, the first victim of the same vigilantes who later got Cy Skinner.

Freezing was a theme for Clark that season. Among the supplies he'd brought back from Salt Lake City and flipped at a hefty profit, he'd had the foresight to include several crates of eggs that he "well knew would freeze" on the trip. But eggs were rare in camp, and Clark knew that frozen eggs worked just fine in a brandy-and-eggnog cocktail called Tom and Jerry that was popular in Bannack's saloons that year. He sold them for three bucks a dozen at a time when hard-rock miners of Nevada's Comstock Lode, the best-paid laborers in America, were making $4 a day.

Clark wasn't cut out to be a laborer. He was built to be rich—a later historian described him as "an aloof little man with a penetrating gaze and a knack for making money"—and he figured out fast that the way to get there wasn't gambling on holes in the ground, but providing what desperate miners lacked. If they were running low on tobacco, he'd hitch up a wagon, make a smoke run to Salt Lake, and pocket a 500 percent markup on his return.

Bannack's miners were paid in gold dust, creating a market for currency. Clark started showing up every Sunday-morning payday and buying the miners' wages for $18 on the ounce. Then he turned around and sold the gold to the Philadelphia mint. He quickly began making $1.5 million a year that way. The money trade suited him, and by 1870 Clark was living in Deer Lodge. He was thirty-one years old, married to the twenty-four-year-old Pennsylvania-bred sweetheart named Katherine he'd imported after him, with an infant daughter named Mary. He opened a bank and a grocery store. He secured a contract to move the U.S. mail from Missoula to Walla Walla, Washington, and let his brother run it.

Two years later Clark moved his family and his capital to Butte

and expanded, loaning money to mining concerns hoping to improve their claims at 12 percent interest. When they succeeded,
Clark earned loyalty and interest. When they defaulted, he repossessed the properties and backed into mining again as an owner. By
1872, Butte's low-hanging gold was pretty thoroughly picked over,
and what was left was bundled in stone. Early Butte tried but failed
to build working refineries, so raw ore was dragged in wagons to a
new smelter at Corinne, Utah. A few early miners shipped their ore
all the way to Swansea, Wales. The freight expense consumed any
prospect of profit, and Butte's ranks started to thin again. As fast as
miners abandoned their claims, Clark snapped them up at fire-sale
discounts. A ruthlessly methodical calculator, he could afford to sit
and wait. His less fastidious brethren, one historian wrote, "hated
him cordially."

An ambitious Butte entrepreneur named Bill Farlin finally built
a mill to treat Butte's ores and Clark invested $30,000 in the en-
deavor, with Farlin's Travona mine as security. When the Travona
began to unearth unprofitably low-grade ore, Clark foreclosed on
it. Once Clark's ownership was established, the Travona began producing suspiciously high-grade ores again. Clark soon controlled
mines (the Colusa, the Original, Mountain Chief, Travona, and
Gambetta), a mill to crush gold out of the dust (at a monopoly
charge of $30 a ton), banks to provide financing, and mercantiles
to supply miners. He started making money at a sprint. He took
a year off to study metallurgy at the Columbia School of Mines
in New York City, where he cultivated the backing of the Boston
and Colorado Smelting Company, and in 1880 he made the first of
many self-improving trips to Europe, collecting art and admiring
architecture with the enthusiasm of an arriviste.

In 1884 Clark commenced construction of an elaborate mansion at 219 West Granite Street in Butte. His daughter Mary was
fourteen, and she'd been joined by siblings Charles W., William
A., Jr., and Katherine Louis, all born in Montana, and Paul Francis,
born in France. The thirty-four-room redbrick Victorian featured
hand-painted ceilings, and a live-in French craftsman carved paneling and filigree in imported oak, ash, walnut, bird's-eye maple,
cherry, and mahogany. Nine fireplaces were imported from Europe. The windows glowed with stained glass inlaid with gems.

One such installed over the front door is centered with the magnate's entwined initials: WAC.

Today the structure does business as the Copper King Mansion bed-and-breakfast. A sign out front says the mansion's contemporary quarter-million dollar price tag represented half a day of Clark's income. You can take a tour for $7.50. For $75 you can spend the night in the butler's room. For $125 you can sleep where Clark laid his little head.

Clark, though, doesn't seem to have spent much time at rest. His industriousness across the turn to the twentieth century is almost unimaginable. He bought the *Butte Miner* newspaper and established the city's first waterworks and trolley car. He expanded into timber and ranching. In 1888 he bought the United Verde copper claims in Arizona for $80,000—an investment that paid off in the billions over the next twenty years—and later founded the master-planned community of Clarkdale there to house his new smelter's workers. He established the Los Alamitos Sugar Corporation in Los Angeles and built the San Pedro, Los Angeles, and Salt Lake railroad to ship his ores to port. Along the way he bought and then auctioned the land around a pit-stop train-service town that became Las Vegas, in eponymous Clark County, Nevada.

Clark's core business strategy was to never invest in anything he couldn't own outright, and the theory extended to statesmen. It was 1889 when Clark first ran for the office of U.S. senator from Montana, and his campaign strategy was straightforward. U.S. senators were elected by state legislatures at the time, and Clark purchased their votes for $10,000 a pop—a strategically defensible expense, considering at least one historian's judgment that "[h]is personality gave him no hope of winning popular votes." When the scandal reached Washington, the Senate voted unanimously to unseat him. Clark waited until Montana governor Robert Burns Smith was out of town and then sent his letter of resignation to Lieutenant Governor A. E. Spriggs, a Clark crony. Spriggs accepted Clark's resignation and then turned around and appointed none other than the very same William A. Clark to fill the seat created by his own resignation.

That trick proved too much to swallow, and Governor Smith finally nullified Clark's appointment and sent a replacement to D.C., but Clark was unrepentant. "I never bought a man who wasn't for sale," he said, resigning under pressure and blaming his competitors for the bribery allegations. The Senate couldn't keep him out when he ran again in 1901 and won, more or less legitimately. He spent his sole six-year term bolstering his business interests, casting his vehement nay on some of the nation's inaugural conservation measures, and inspiring the enmity of the century's greatest critic, Mark Twain, who had given the Gilded Age its name in the title of his 1873 novel. In a 1907 hit piece titled "Senator Clark of Montana," Twain wrote: "He is as rotten a human being as can be found anywhere under the flag; he is a shame to the American nation, and no one has helped to send him to the Senate who did not know that his proper place was the penitentiary, with a ball and chain on his legs. To my mind he is the most disgusting creature that the republic has produced since Tweed's time."

Clark hadn't come to Montana for the scenery, and his interest in rivers was purely mechanical. He was a builder of industry, infrastructure, and wealth—he was a greedy bastard—and he draped his pursuits in the cloth of dominion with one of the great self-serving declarations of the twentieth century: "In rearing the great structure of empire on the Western Hemisphere," Clark told his Senate colleagues on the occasion of his retirement in 1907, "we are obliged to avail ourselves of all the resources at our command. The requirements of this great utilitarian age demand it. Those who succeed us can well take care of themselves."

That dismissive confidence would come back to haunt the state from which Clark lifted so much of his lucre. Clark knew exactly how unbridled wealth extraction was laying waste to Montana, or he wouldn't have bothered defending his "obligation" to extract it, and he was probably sincere in his judgment that the wholesale destruction of landscapes was worth it. There are still state legislators all over the West who will tell you that a river that reaches the sea is a waste of good water.

Two years before his retirement from office, Clark had commissioned Milltown Dam on the Clark Fork, a caged stone-and-timber stopper rigged to feed electricity to his nearby timber mill upstream of Missoula—the mill that produced the beams that staved Butte's mines. That was about the last Montana saw of him.

His wife, Kate, had died in 1882—the year a French sculptor's copper draping reached the Statue of Liberty's waist—and Clark had taken up with his teenage ward, a Michigan girl named Anna Eugenia La Chapelle. They had a child, Louise Amelia Andrée Clark, in 1902, when Clark was sixty-three and Anna twenty-four, and took the occasion to announce to a curious public and a confounded family that they'd quietly married in Paris a year earlier.

Rich westerners marked their cultural arrival on the coasts, and Clark spent the next decade and well north of $10 million erecting one of the gaudiest temples to ego and aspiration the young American century had seen. The address was 952 Fifth Avenue, overlooking New York City's Central Park, and the May 31, 1908, edition of the *New York Times* took an exclusive first look at what the headline called "New York's Most Expensive Private Residence."

Up to two hundred laborers a week were toiling on Clark's palace, and in preparation Senator Clark had purchased a granite quarry in Maine and a marble quarry in Maryland, and established a woodworking shop, stonecutting factory, and metalwork foundry on Long Island. The house featured 4,200 electric lights, a passenger elevator accommodating twenty, and a ventilation system that funneled air from New York's city streets through filters of cheesecloth. Servants shoveled five tons of coal daily to fire the home's boilers. Fifteen bathrooms tiled in opaque Italian glass and twenty-five guest rooms augmented Clark's own ground-floor suite of offices and anterooms. Separate day and night nurseries housed Clark's two daughters with Anna—the last, Huguette, had been born in France in 1906—with a quarantine tower in case one fell ill. Thirty-five servants were quartered in gender-segregated wings on the fifth and sixth floors, beneath the laundry. For relaxation there were Turkish baths and an indoor swimming pool. For entertaining, there were four dining rooms plus a banquet hall with a seventeen-foot ceiling and the country's largest chamber organ. For reflection, there was a library exhumed whole from a Normandy castle. Tapestried hallways ninety feet long converged on a vault-ceilinged rotunda ringed with columns of violet Breche marble three stories high, and life-size statues of Diana and Neptune flanked the fireplaces. The doors were enameled white and the cornices leafed with gold. Clark had his private rooms lined with satin. He'd scoured Europe to amass a trove of Constables, Rousseaus,

Delacroixs, and Millets. The main picture gallery rose two stories, with an addendum designed to house his collection of Faience pottery. The Grand Salon featured a ceiling inlaid with a sprawling canvas by Fragonard, the cost of which, the *Times* panted, "would startle the imagination of even this money-mad town."

Clark already had the castle in Butte, plus homes in D.C. and Los Angeles, and the lavish Manhattan apartments where he lived while his ultimate ode to self was compacting the earth at the corner of Fifth Avenue and Seventy-Seventh Street, but this one, the *Times* reporter wrote, was the magnate's purest expression of taste and, in the bargain, "the highest expression of American artisanship" extant in the annals of architecture.

If the *Times* approved, other reviewers made a show of holding their nose. Volume 19 of the American Association of Architects' *Architectural Record* lists the senator's house for posterity as "Architectural Aberration No. 21." When it was finally completed, a prominent humorist named Wallace Irwin wagged at Clark's pretension with a ditty that began:

> Senator Copper of Tonopah Ditch
> Made a clean billion in minin' and sich,
> Hiked for New York, where his money he blew
> Buildin' a palace on Fift' Avenoo.
> "How," says the Senator, "can I look proudest?
> Build me a house that'll holler the loudest—
> None o' your slab-sided, plain mausoleums—
> Give me the treasures of art and museums;
> > Build it new fangled,
> > scalloped and angled,
> Fine like a weddin' cake garnished with pills.
> > Gents, do your duty,
> > trot out your beauty.
> Give my money's worth—I'll pay the bills."

Butte's second copper king, and Clark's eventual nemesis, was an Irish immigrant named Marcus Daly. In the morality myth that's fogged their posthumous reputations, Daly has emerged as the people's choice, the billionaire with whom you'd rather share beers. Public personalities aside, there seems to be little basis for the distinction. They were equally self-made men, the only differences being that Clark, with his penchant for the sure thing, held his properties close, while Daly was a speculator. And where Clark preferred cultured ostentatiousness, Daly indulged his wealth in the early-twentieth-century version of NASCAR: horse racing.

Daly was born in County Cavan, Ireland, about sixty miles northwest of Dublin, in 1841. The potato famine of 1845–1852 mostly spared Daly and his six older siblings, but the environment of want left an impression, and Daly was not the kind of man to be satisfied with a merely sufficient supply of starch. He was nine when the famine ended and he went to work on a pig farm, and he was fifteen in 1856 when he abandoned Ireland in search of more fruitful labor, booking passage from Liverpool to New York harbor on a sailing schooner.

After worming his way through immigration as the "cousin" of a family he'd met on board, Daly found work in New York as a telegraph boy, leather tanner, dockworker, and street-corner hawker of newspapers. For five years he sent half his earnings home to Ireland and saved for passage to California, finally taking a freighter from New York to Panama, a stagecoach to the Pacific, and another ship to San Francisco. An inland boomtown called Placerville beckoned and Daly went to work as a mucker in the California gold mines, shoveling ore instead of pig shit. In 1865 he moved farther inland on horseback, to Virginia City, Nevada, where silver was pouring out of the ground like a geyser, and met the man whose fortune would spill over into his own.

George Hearst was already an established mining man, and his interest in the Comstock Lode in Virginia City, Nevada, was overflowing his coffers when he struck up a friendship with Daly, then in his early twenties, who was making a name for himself as a man with a sixth sense for buried metal. The two were "practical" mining men with experience born of observation underground in an age when mining "engineers" were emerging as a suspect new academic breed, and when Hearst decamped to examine an Alaska gold strike in 1866, he asked Daly to bird-dog his Nevada holdings.

Enter the Walker brothers, Samuel, Joseph, David, and Matthew, English-born merchant-bankers and Mormon converts later excommunicated from the church over their refusal to tithe, mammon proving more compelling than Mormon. In 1868 the Walkers hired Daly to supervise the Emma mine in Alta, Utah, in which they owned a profitable quarter interest. Three years later they installed him as foreman of their Ophir silver mine, where Daly met Margaret, daughter of a mining engineer, on an underground tour. He married her in 1873 in one of the Walker brothers' homes. He was thirty and she was eighteen. By the time the Walkers sent Daly to Montana, Marcus and Margaret had produced two daughters, Madge and Molly.

The call to Butte came in 1876. The Walkers wanted a look at a mine called the Alice and sent Daly to scope it out. The owners weren't encouraging tourists, so Daly hired on as a mucker and spent three weeks on the payroll surreptitiously spying the vein from the inside. He liked what he saw. The Alice's gold was almost played out, but silver was still plentiful, even if it was cluttered with copper, which most Butte miners of the day considered a nuisance metal, even waste, since the marginal profits to be made on it were eaten up by the cost of transporting it to distant smelters. The Walkers bought the Alice on Daly's recommendation and gave him a 5 percent interest to manage it. Daly moved his young family to Butte, where Clark was already consolidating power, and set up house.

Daly had his eyes on bigger prizes than 5 percent, and he thought he found one on the Butte hill's southeastern slope. The hole was owned by claim staker Michael Hickey, who'd named his prospect the Anaconda after a phrase he'd read in a Civil War–era newspaper column. New York editor Horace Greeley had declared that General George McClellan's Union army would surround Robert E. Lee's forces "like a giant anaconda." Hickey had fought as a Union soldier and the image resonated.

Daly saw money in Hickey's Anaconda. His explorations there and in the Alice told him that Butte's riches were not only barely tapped, but fundamentally misunderstood. Gold and silver were one thing, and the one thing on most miners' minds, but Daly was becoming convinced that beneath the superficial veins of precious metal lay a vast mother lode of copper, an underground Michipi-coten of red metal.

Daly relayed the opportunity to the Walker brothers, asking them to back his purchase of the Anaconda, and the Salt Lake siblings sent another expert to provide a second opinion. The expert's verdict came back negative and the Walkers passed. They were already rich; they could afford to minimize their risk. Daly didn't have that luxury yet. He sold his 5 percent interest in the Alice and used the proceeds—$30,000—to buy a controlling interest in the Anaconda.

Now he needed capital. The proper working of a hard-rock mine requires enormous infusions of cash to dig tunnels, hire miners, and pay freight, and Daly didn't have it. George Hearst did. Hearst had gone into business with fellow Californians James Haggin and Lloyd Tevis to form what would become the largest mining conglomerate in the country. Daly had turned the partners on to the Ontario silver mine in Utah that netted them $6 million in dividends on a $30,000 investment, and they were favorably inclined toward the Irishman's nose for ore.

Daly approached the consortium not long after Hearst had purchased the Homestake mine in Deadwood, South Dakota, the richest gold mine in history and later a key plot point in the HBO series *Deadwood*. The Homestake would generate $80 million over twenty years, and Hearst was already flush with cash from investments in Nevada and Utah. Daly promised that the Anaconda would produce $100 million, and despite an attempt by Clark to undermine Hearst's confidence in Daly—whom Clark slurred as an "ignorant Mick miner"—in 1881 the Hearst partnership bought in, forming the Anaconda Silver Mining Company.

If Daly was a trusted partner, he was also a sneaky bastard. Just a year into the partnership, when the Anaconda's silver started thinning at a depth of three hundred feet, Daly shuttered the mine and watched as the hill's neighboring properties dropped in value by association. With the market bottoming out, Daly tapped Hearst, Tevis, and Haggin for more money and used it to buy up the neighboring claims. At four hundred feet he'd found, but not trumpeted, a copper vein running an unprecedented fifty feet wide. Once he had his consolidated holdings in a row, Daly reopened the Anaconda and announced that he was sitting on top of the richest hill on earth and the future source of the world's copper supply. Butte's first railroad, the Utah and Northern line to the smelters at Corinne, Utah, arrived in 1881, making copper refinement on a mass scale economically feasible. After Thomas Edison perfected the lightbulb in 1889, it became necessary.

Daly had a talent for sniffing out earthbound metal, but his true genius was integration. Rather than pay commercial rail freight to ship his raw ore, he would build his own railroad, and rather than sell ore to distant refiners, Daly would open his own smelter. The site he chose was a mountain valley twenty-six miles down Silver Bow Creek and seven miles up a tributary stream called Warm Springs—the nearest industrial-scale water supply he could find. Daly platted a town to support the smelter site in 1883 and tried to give it the tongue-tying name Copperopolis, but it turned out that was already taken by another Montana mining town to the east. The company town took the company's name instead, and Anaconda, Montana began its development into one of the engine rooms of American industry.

The year after George Hearst died, in 1891, Europe's iconic Rothschild bankers, the richest family on the planet, purchased a quarter interest in Daly's Anaconda Copper Mining Company from Phoebe Hearst for $7.5 million. Phoebe invested the proceeds in her son William Randolph's newspaper business. Daly leveraged the Rothschild's confidence into a state-of-the-art copper smelter on the north-flanking hills overlooking the town site downstream. That facility almost immediately became the "Old Works" when it caught fire and burned to the ground. A new Lower Works expansion spilled down the hills. It soon caught fire and was replaced as well.

Today there's a walking trail with interpretive signs where Anaconda's early smelters once stood, overlooking the Jack Nicklaus–designed Old Works Golf Course that caps the site's legacy of contamination. The greens cover tailings dumps, and the sand traps are filled with black smelter slag. It's a stunning view, especially in fall when the slopes are painted with saffron-yellow outbursts of stunted aspen and streaked rusty red with fallen brick. Down the valley you can see what locals call the Red Sands, a fin of rust-colored tailings emerging from a vast buried pile beneath.

In their first years of operation, the smelters processed five hundred tons of ore daily. A ditch carried creek water to the smelters, and mule teams and wooden flumes funneled logs off the hillsides to feed the furnaces at the rate of 75,000 cords a year. Daly bought up stone quarries and silica mines and timber tracts for hundreds of miles around. He partnered with railroad-rich robber baron Jay Gould to build his own line connecting the Butte mines to the Anaconda smelter. He imported furnace tenders from Wales and millwrights from Michigan. Anaconda's steel and iron foundry, its electric plant, and its waterworks were all Daly productions, as were the Daly banks in Butte and Anaconda and the *Anaconda Standard* newspaper, for which Daly imported a New York–seasoned editor and state-of-the-art presses to print some of the first color comics in the country. Anaconda's Daly-built Margaret Theater was the biggest in Montana, and Anaconda's Montana Hotel, one of two Daly-purveyed accommodations, enjoyed a brief reputation as the finest in the Northwest. The other, Butte's Florence, held 627 miners at a time, two single beds per room, and offered a library, billiards, and a gymnasium.

Daly built a house for himself in Anaconda, but by this time, workingman's friend or no, he was already spending most of his time in New York and commuting to Butte by private railcar while Margaret oversaw their kids' education in France. In 1886 he bought 28,000 acres in the Bitterroot Valley, a hundred miles west, and founded the lumber town of Hamilton. On its outskirts he refurbished a mansion and established the Bitterroot Stock Farm, an agricultural enterprise that supplied his company stores in Hamilton, Butte, and Anaconda.

He built racetracks in Anaconda and Butte with grandstands for ten thousand and twenty thousand, respectively. Down the Bitterroot, Daly compiled a stable of thoroughbreds and raced them nationwide under copper-and-green silks. When Tammany, his favorite, beat East Coast phenom Lamplighter by four lengths in an 1893 match race—earning his owner a quarter of a million dollars in the process—Daly built him Tammany Castle, a turreted stable with velvet-lined stalls. Back in Anaconda, Daly had artisans inlay a wooden mosaic portrait of Tammany on the Montana Hotel's barroom floor. It was not to be stepped on.

Daly had a pet theory that Montana's thin, high-elevation air provided an edge in training horses, who could only breathe more fully in the thicker air below. The same concept, he figured, might work for human athletes too, and he was planning to train an elite team of Irish-American Olympians in Montana when he died, in 1900, at fifty-eight, of diabetes and a bum heart.

A Butte newspaper marked the occasion with an elaborate bank of headlines:

> *THE MIGHTY OAK HAS FALLEN*
> *The Architect of Montana's Greatness Is Gone.*
> *Marcus Daly Is Dead;*
> *His Name and Works Held Sacred in Montana.*
> *Love That Was His Due in Life Now Made Manifest.*
> *Marcus Daly Was a Gift of Nature.*
> *Greater than Napoleon,*
> *A Leader of Men,*
> *Died amid the Monuments of His Glory.*
> *All Montana Mourns His Death.*

Daly's thoroughbreds brought more than $400,000 in a posthumous auction at New York's Madison Square Garden. Today, a nonprofit historical society gives tours at Riverside, Daly's Bitterroot mansion, which spent most of the twentieth century boarded up. Most of the land has been sold off. A 2,600-acre chunk of it is now the Stock Farm Club, a private "golf-based" community of resort-home owners founded by investment guru Charles Schwab in 1999. Tammany Castle's acreage has been whittled down to about eleven, and the barn was converted to a 5,400-square-foot private home in 2008. In 2011 it went on the market for $2,950,000.

Daly doesn't have a proper biography, and though he named much in Montana, little is named for him. Memorial-wise, there's just a bronze statue at the entrance to the Montana College of Mineral Science and Technology campus on the hill above Butte. Here Daly's short sturdiness is topped by a round head tightly capped with thinning hair. He wears a walrus mustache and carries his hat in his hand, his pate exposed to the sky. The statue was moved to Montana Tech in 1941 after playing an unyielding role in a traffic accident in its original location at the intersection of North Main and Gagnon streets.

There are still people in Butte who will tell you that this is not the real reason the statue was moved. The real reason is that it had been poorly located in the first place. At the intersection, Daly's back faced the bulk of Butte's miners' homes. Marcus Daly, they still say today, would never have turned his back on his miners.

✝

On the heels of Daly's bonanza, tens of thousands of immigrants arrived to a town that must have seemed to have no sky. Hundreds of small smelters had followed Clark's early monopoly, and the air turned so thick with sulfur smog that streetlamps—Butte was the third municipality in the country to be fully wired for electric light—burned day and night.

What trees weren't chopped for fuel and tunnel staves withered and died for miles in every direction. Burned-off arsenic gave the air a metallic tang.

Below ground was worse. The mines were steadily deepening into the thousands of feet, aided by giant motorized hoists that lowered men in cages stacked four deep at the rate of 2,400 feet per minute and new jackhammers driven by compressed air. Miners drilled cylindrical holes in solid stone and filled them with sticks of dynamite to shatter their solidity. The dynamite-dispensing DuPont family grew wealthy from the endless explosion of Butte, and "tap 'er light" continues to be a widely understood colloquialism for "good-bye," even among a contemporary population that has never lost a family member to tamping dynamite into a hole too hard.

Miners worked fourteen hours at a time in the sweltering dark shafts, and winter shifts dragged them back into the night at thirty degrees below zero. Years later the company agreed to build walled-in "dries" with lockers, where a miner could towel off and change into clean clothes for the walk home.

Home was frequently a shanty or a crib in a boardinghouse, each room rented to two miners working staggered shifts. One would wake up and walk to his mine as another returned to collapse on a thin mattress.

Across town, Chinese prostitutes inhabited their own cramped cribs, and come payday saw the same steady rotation of workingmen.

There were few cities in America as international in flavor as Butte in the late nineteenth century. Daly imported thousands of experienced miners from Ireland's County Cork. Clark had a preference for Cornishmen. Finns, Moldavians, Italians, Poles, Germans, and Swedes each carved their own distinctive neighborhoods into Butte's foothills and flats and worked in concert beneath them. Company-posted "No Smoking" signs in the tunnels were printed in sixteen languages.

Butte worked around the clock to feed the exploding demand for copper, spiked first by the unspooling of thousands of miles of electric and telegraph wire, again by the massive factories and industrial concerns that widespread electricity enabled, yet again by World Wars I and II, and later still by the postwar boom in appliances of convenience: refrigerators, water heaters, and air conditioners.

The price of copper soared and dove, and with it the wages of Butte's workingmen, many of them immigrant Europeans with dangerous ideas about the proper relationship between management and labor. Butte's miners were unionized, and subject to far-flung rhetoric from mining companies, neighbors, and traveling union organizers. Though World War I made Butte's copper a matter of pressing military interest, plenty of miners originally from Germanic states weren't completely sold on the morality of the war effort. Strikes became common, and reached a pitch on June 9, 1917, when a frayed electrical cable sparked the paraffin paper wrapping a carbide lamp and set off the Granite Mountain Fire, killing 164 miners underground. It took two weeks to remove all the bodies, and Granite Mountain became the most vivid example of a death toll that's made Butte the most fatal hard-rock mining center on record.

Butte elected a Socialist Party of America candidate, Louis P. Duncan, as mayor in 1911, but his politics didn't keep him from being stabbed by a miner in 1914. During labor unrest in 1917, the city was placed under martial law by President Woodrow Wilson. As late as 1920, company detectives opened fire on striking miners on the road to Anaconda, wounding sixteen and killing two.

While companies advertised Butte as "the richest hill on Earth," organizers worldwide came to know it as the Gibraltar of American labor.

That's the reputation that led Frank Little, an itinerant organizer with the Industrial Workers of the World—the Wobblies—to Butte in July 1917. Little drew crowds and company suspicion in equal measure. In the early morning of August 1, he was accosted in his boardinghouse room by a gang of five masked men, beaten, tied to the bumper of a car, and dragged through the dark streets. His body was found the next morning hung from a railroad trestle, with a sign pinned to his chest: "Others take notice. 3–7–77."

No one was ever convicted for the murder.

Twelve years later, Dashiell Hammett published his first novel, a convoluted bang-'em-up of crime bosses and cop corruption titled *Red Harvest*. The action was set in Butte, where Hammett had spent a brief career in the employ of the Pinkerton Detective Agency, hired by the copper kings to keep a leash on union activity. Years later Hammett claimed the Anaconda Company had offered him $5,000 to make Little disappear, and that he had declined. Hammett disguised Walkerville, one of the city's earliest mining centers, named for Utah's Daly-backing Walker brothers, as "Poisonville."

Little is buried in the Mountain View Cemetery in Butte's flats, alongside an international cast of thousands of miners. The inscription on the cross at his grave reads, "Slain for Organizing and Inspiring His Fellow Men."

†

In 1889 William A. Clark launched his first ill-fated campaign for U.S. Senate and paid $10,000 for what he claimed was the largest nugget of gold ever found, from the short-lived Atlantic Cable Quartz Lode just a few miles from Anaconda. Daly was busily transforming Anaconda and the rural Deer Lodge Valley into the eighth wonder of the metallurgical world. That year, Fritz Augustus Heinze arrived in Butte to crown himself the city's third copper king.

Heinze was just nineteen, the Brooklyn-born fifth child of a Connecticut-born mother and a wealthy German immigrant father preceded by eight generations of Christian clergy. He took

his early education in Germany and attended the Brooklyn Poly-
technic Institute and the Columbia School of Mines, where he was
a C student who spoke fluent German, French, and English. A
fellow student gathered that "he thought a great deal of himself."
For summer vacations he traveled to Michigan to study the Calumet and Hecla mines, Pennsylvania to study coal, and Colorado to
scout silver and gold operations.

His father offered to pay his way to university in Freiburg, Germany, after Columbia, but Fritz was itchy to head west, and decamped for Colorado instead. Within months he'd made his way
to Butte and signed on with the Boston and Montana Company as
a mining engineer at a salary of $250 a month. Heinze's cosmo-
politan pedigree gave him dash in Butte, and he became something
of a socialite, known for his poker skills and vain about his sing-
ing voice. He was a tall, sturdy, brown-eyed man with a talent for
making conversational companions feel like the only person in the
room, and Butte's females responded in kind.

Clark and Daly were already well established and battling for
control of Butte's most valuable properties, but Heinze found a way
in. By 1890 he'd become convinced that an independent smelter
could make a killing by undercutting the monopoly prices miners were forced to pay the big boys. A $50,000 inheritance from
his dead grandmother allowed him to resign from the Boston and
Montana, whereupon he decamped to Germany to celebrate the
windfall. Then he returned to New York and took a job as an assistant editor at the *Mining and Engineering Journal*, which he used—
as unclear-on-the-concept journalists have done since time imme-
morial—to cultivate powerful friends. Two years later, in league
with his two brothers and backed by his new New York cronies and
his father's European connections, he launched the Montana Ore
Purchasing Company.

The MOPC leased mines and concentrated ore in Butte, shipping six million pounds of copper in its first year. Heinze bought
the Liquidator ore concentrator and bumped its capacity from one
hundred to six hundred daily tons. In 1895 he purchased an un-
derperforming mine named Rarus for $400,000 and transformed it
into the copper-spewing keystone of his burgeoning empire. Four
years later he was producing twenty-four million pounds of copper
annually.

Smelting and mining, however, weren't Heinze's truest talents. Charm, law, and subterfuge were. When Heinze leased the rights to mine a rich claim called the Estrella, he made a deal with the owners: profits from any ore assaying more than 10 percent copper would be split between Heinze and the mine's owner. Profits from any ore assaying less than 10 percent would go to Heinze exclusively. Heinze simply mixed waste rock with the Estrella's ore until it was diluted to less than 10 percent copper, taking all the profits for himself.

Even that runaround was small beans for Heinze's ambitions. His stroke of genius was his manipulation of the law of the apex, 1860s-era legislation ostensibly designed to protect and encourage small prospectors. The law of the apex said that a mine owner could follow and mine any mineral vein that broke the surface—"apexed"—within the bounds of his claim, no matter how far beyond the surface bounds of that claim the vein might wander underground.

Socked away in a back corner of Butte's World Museum of Mining today are a couple of Plexiglas-covered three-dimensional models of Butte's underground veins once used by some of the dozens of lawyers who found permanent employment arguing the hundreds of apex cases that clogged Butte's courts in the latter part of the nineteenth century. They look like tinker-toy monstrosities built by meth heads. The only way to make definitive sense of them, Heinze decided early, was to purchase the comprehension of judges.

⊹

The fortunes flowing out of Butte's ground had not escaped East Coast attention. Boston had been ground zero for the country's copper investors going back to the early days of the Michigan boom, with moneymen quietly heeding the conservative wisdom that a man could spend a fortune on a gold mine, lose one mining silver, or safely construct an empire of copper. The capital behind Michigan's mines had come from some of Boston's best families, their blood running crab-blue, and Boston's investment in Michigan's mammoth Calumet and Hecla Mining Company delivered returns of one hundred to one.

The Boston and Montana Consolidated Copper and Silver Mining Company began doing business in Butte in 1887, and a merger with the Butte and Boston Company created the second-largest operator in the city, next to Daly's Anaconda combine.

It was a Bostonian, Thomas W. Lawson, a flamboyant stock speculator turned muckraker, who helped broker the financial time bomb that in 1889 began the consolidation that would define Montana's next century as a resource colony of American industrialization.

Lawson's account of the deal, *Frenzied Finance: The Crime of Amalgamated*, fills more than five hundred histrionic pages with details of insider machinations, but the monopolistic gist is pretty simple. Standard Oil, the Rockefeller dynamo that had already cornered the petroleum market, turned its corporate eye west toward copper and decided to own it all.

According to his own account, Lawson was the scheme's mastermind, but the deal makers were John D.'s brother William Rockefeller and Standard Oil steersman Henry H. Rogers. The conspirators first formed a trust through which they could speculate with money parked there by institutional investors. The trust, with blandly admirable accuracy, was called Amalgamated.

The trust acquired New York's National City Bank—essentially an arm of Standard Oil—and used it to finance a $39 million loan to fund acquisition of the biggest Butte mines. The conspirators then published newspaper ads that now read like circus flyers, plumping Amalgamated's supposedly sure-thing prospects. Amalgamated opened the nation's then-largest public offering and immediately secured a capitalization of $75 million. Rogers and company paid their own bank back the $39 million they'd nominally borrowed and, for nothing but the price of persuasion, found themselves the owners of $39 million in producing property and $36 million in instant profit.

Later, when the manipulated stock crashed from $100 to $33, Amalgamated snapped the company back into private holdership at pennies on the dollar. The *Boston Financial News* named the finagle "[t]he greatest event in finance since the world began."

"So good does it look to us," Rogers said at the time, "that I feel it will really beat out Standard Oil as a money maker."

Lawson, whose own profit on the deal reached into the tens of millions, used his book to rail against "The System" that allowed Standard Oil—"a machine the details of which are diagrammed in the asbestos blueprints which paper the walls of hell"—to fleece investors. If that system were allowed to expand unchecked, he wrote with flourish, "the people will surely be enslaved and the public destroyed."

The scheme that Lawson called "The Coppers" was originally supposed to feature the Boston and Montana properties as its core asset, but F. A. Heinze had other plans. Heinze had filed suit against the B&M's Michael Davitt mine, alleging that the company was infringing on his own highly profitable Rarus mine veins, and the long-running litigation so tied the B&M's hands that Rogers and Standard Oil had to turn instead to Daly's Anaconda property to anchor Amalgamated's initial public offering. Daly was shrewd enough to see that Amalgamated was over a barrel, and he leveraged the situation to extract an extortionate price for his properties, plus the presidency of the resulting company.

Clark's feud with Daly ensured that Clark's properties would elude Amalgamated's grasp until his death in 1925, when the juggernaut purchased his Montana holdings—then just a fringe of Clark's multistate empire—for $8.25 million. Heinze was Butte's other holdout, and the zenith of his strategy was the Copper Trust claim, an overlooked wedge of land, just seventy-five feet by ten feet, that Heinze snapped up for a pittance. The Copper Trust's value lay not in any ore it might have contained, but in its adjacency to the neighboring Anaconda, St. Lawrence, and Neversweat mines, the Anaconda company's prime producers. Heinze crafted a legal claim that the rich veins of the three neighboring mines all apexed in his tiny (and mockingly named) Copper Trust plot.

A judge named Clancy, one of Heinze's bought allies, agreed and slapped a stop-work injunction on these biggest of Butte's mines to give lawyers time to sort out the facts. For a populist hero—it was Heinze who first purchased favor by instituting an eight-hour workday in Butte—Heinze had badly miscalculated the effects of the shutdown. Three thousand miners emerged from underground on the afternoon of the injunction to find themselves out of work, and promptly marched downhill to the judge's office, shouting

"Hang Clancy!" The injunction was dissolved by midnight. Higher courts later dismissed Heinze's apex claim as baseless.

Needling Anaconda would be Heinze's unerring modus operandi until the end of his career, and violence wasn't always averted. In 1900, Heinze started tunneling out of his Rarus mine into Anaconda's Michael Davitt, waving his apex flag. When Anaconda got an injunction stopping Heinze's work—Anaconda had learned the lawyer game by then—Heinze transferred his ownership claim to a shell company free from injunction and kept digging. Heinze sealed the corridors with concrete, but his competitors could hear his miners blasting behind them. When a court order gave Anaconda engineers access to inspect the works, Heinze refused, and the battle moved underground. Miners turned ventilation tubes filled with powdered lime on each other, and got hoses of hot water and steam in return. Two miners fighting over the inspection were killed when a dynamite blast caved their tunnel. At Heinze's Minnie Healy mine, workers tried to flood the Anaconda's adjoining Leonard. Leonard miners improvised an underground dam and turned the flood back on the Minnie Healy. Unidentified saboteurs set Heinze's smelter on fire and turned the water mains off. Only early warnings and evacuations kept the tunnels from filling with corpses.

✝

In 1906, Amalgamated finally wore down Heinze's resistance, paying him $12 million to hand over his properties and dismiss his suits. Heinze took his payout and decamped to New York, where he launched a status-seeking foray into high finance and pursued an ill-fated corner of the copper market with his own United Copper Trust. The resulting debacle not only ruined Heinze but sparked a run on New York's banks that caused the Panic of 1907, a 50 percent stock market nosedive that necessitated a bailout from J. P. Morgan and led to the formation, in 1913, of the Federal Reserve.

Heinze died in New York in 1914, pear-shaped and haggard, from complications of cirrhosis. He wasn't quite broke, but what properties he had left went to heirs unknown. There was brief talk in Butte of erecting a statue, but the talk came to nothing.

Amalgamated would become one of the defining corporate colossi of the twentieth century, based on a metal that few people would ever hold in their hand. Critics called it "the Octopus," and newspaper caricaturists depicted entire legislatures herded into the company's copper collar. The caricaturists tended to work for out-of-state newspapers, since Amalgamated owned 90 percent of the Montana press—a corporate muzzle that wouldn't be removed until the 1960s. Critics, in any case, were badly outnumbered. The company and its sprawling affiliates signed the paychecks of three-quarters of Montana's wage-earning working class.

Copper kingdoms had given way to a corporate fiefdom that turned raw dirt into a ransom in mineral wealth. The cash draining out of Montana's valleys left a ring made of poison.

╬

In 1961, Richard Brautigan wrote *Trout Fishing in America*, a surrealistic pillow of a book that wasn't published until 1967, the year I was born. Brautigan had traveled briefly in Montana as a child, and would spend several years living near Livingston in the Paradise Valley in the late 1970s, but his fantastical first novel carries Clark Fork prescience when he writes of discovering a dismantled trout stream for sale, stacked on pallets in the back of a hardware store, priced by length and accompanied by à la carte accessories: pebbles, riffles, fish.

That fictional fancy is hardly stranger than current Clark Fork truth. The thing's been chopped and shunted and hemmed within an inch of its life.

Silver Bow Creek, strictly speaking, no longer flows into the Clark Fork. The creek is impounded into a series of settling ponds, the Warm Springs Ponds, just downstream of my inaugural float's end, and the site of the Morel Rainbow Arch Bridge. If I'd continued beneath the highway, I would have been pinned against steel grates beneath stream-spanning silos just a few hundred yards across the interstate. If I'd been sucked through those grates, I would have had a load of powdered lime dumped on my head before I got flushed into the ponds.

The lime is added to reduce the water's acidity after its flow through the toxic dustbowl of Butte and twenty-six miles of Silver Bow below that. The ponds are there to catch and settle mine tailings. The first earthen dams were built by the Anaconda Company in 1911—three years before Opportunity's founding—to trap flood-borne tailings from Butte. They've been added to and modified ever since, including a major overhaul in the early 1990s after a 1989 flood topped the berms and spat banks and bottoms downstream, killing fish for miles. Today the ponds amount to 2,400 acres of placid water, shallow with toxic silt. Planted at the river's headwaters, they contain nineteen million cubic yards of toxic mine tailings—three times the poison sediment that Milltown Reservoir harbored downstream at Missoula, seeping toward the aquifer below. But there won't be any restoration of the Warm Springs Ponds. There's no nearby municipal water to threaten, and no concentrated population to complain. The ponds are too big to move. They comprise a designated wildlife area now, a haven for ducks, trout, and recreationists unbothered by the metals sequestered in their muddy bottoms, jointly managed, in a disconcerting nod to the site's bifurcated essence, by Montana Fish, Wildlife & Parks and the Atlantic Richfield Company.

The Warm Springs Ponds are a clot in the Clark Fork artery, and an engineered channel there is called Mill-Willow Bypass. The bypass is part of the encompassing Superfund site's Warm Spring Ponds "operable unit." The language is a giveaway. What happened here was heart failure. What happened next was surgery.

This is where the river's engineered disjuncture is most manifest. Not visible, necessarily, but obvious if you know what to look for. From the interstate all you'll notice are the weirdly cell-like expanses of pretty water, some studded with tiny dozer-built islands, bunched tight to the westbound feeder. Now and then you'll see a small boat. The poisons are tied up in the muck beneath the water, and the water itself is considered clean. By reputation the ponds house lunker trout that thrive in the deep, cold corners. There are no posted fish consumption advisories, but catch and release is encouraged for sporting reasons.

I drive my canoe to an overpass on the interstate feeder road and park the truck in a gravel turnout just a couple hundred yards downstream of the bend where Silver Bow Creek veers into the ponds. There's no path to the water, just a weedy embankment.

Before the ponds were dammed, Mill Creek and then Willow

Creek, pouring through Opportunity, entered Silver Bow near here. They've been reengineered since then. The new conjoined channel, the Mill-Willow Bypass, shepherds them around the reservoir and into the Clark Fork below. At its head is a rock dike separating the bypass from the pond-bound water of Silver Bow Creek. In case of extreme flooding, the rock dike is designed to give way before the ponds are topped, spilling the overflow down the winding bypass rather than flushing it straight into the river below. The bypass looks like a spring creek, but it's really a manufactured flood-control feature. It's a storm drain.

The water is shallow in July, and wet river rocks shine beneath the surface, just beginning to dull with the green strings of algae that sprout after a few weeks of warmth. I duck my head to slip under the little bridge, and then again under a highway humming with semis, and enter the snaky bypass.

An archetypical river turns in S-shaped swerves, just as trees have black holes in the trunks where squirrels live and houses have peaked roofs and smoke coming out of chimneys. The Mill-Willow Bypass, viewed from the air, looks like a child's drawing of a snake. From the water it winds so consistently back and forth as to create an illusion of purely lateral movement. For every linear mile you travel downstream, you probably paddle three miles of meander.

Mill-Willow's engineers had set out to design a "natural" watercourse. As with Silver Bow Creek and Milltown Reservoir, tailings were dug up and trucked to the Opportunity Ponds. A new streambed was shaped and steered and planted with native flora.

Paddling the result you might almost be fooled, if not for the too-geometric pond embankments looming to the east and the whine of Interstate 90 just yards beyond the brush to the west. A natural stream would never tolerate a floodplain so tightly constrained. Mill-Willow looks natural, but it has very little room in which to act that way.

The critters don't mind. Just ten years after being rebuilt, a BP/ARCO documentary claims, the bypass had achieved "100 percent biointegrity" and become one of the top trout-spawning tributaries of the entire upper Clark Fork watershed. Unlike the unreconstructed river upstream, the banks here are crowded with mature willows and grass. Fish dart through the riffles and ducks feed beneath the surface. In a little more than six miles of slow floating, I saw four beavers slap their tails in passing and I portaged two beaver dams, wading waist-deep in woody muck to drag the boat over and down. At the second dam, I could see two men standing beside a truck on top of one of the tall Warm Springs berms several hundred yards away. They were watching and wondering, I imagine, what the hell I was doing.

An hour later I was at my takeout, where I'd left a bike locked to a fencepost at the edge of a dirt parking lot for the Warm Springs Recreation Area—public staging point for the Warm Springs Wildlife Management Area. The lot is positioned to provide easy access to the outflow of the concrete spillway that dumps the lime-treated and metals-settled water out of the Warm Springs Ponds into the tail end of the Mill-Willow Bypass. The fishing here, counterintuitively, is so popular that signs suggest etiquette, asking anglers to space themselves to avoid overcrowding. The water here is pH balanced from the lime and aerated by the spillway. The toxic muck from the ponds' feeder streams has been trapped in the pond's bottom, and the toxic muck downstream hasn't entered the river yet.

As I step out of the canoe midstream and drag it onto shore there's a fly fisher plying an eddy line just downstream, in clean water at the ass end of one of the most polluted creeks in the country. The plates on the only car in the parking lot say he's from Indiana. He has no idea.

In the project-speak of the Clark Fork Superfund cleanup, "Stretch A" begins at the outflow spillway of the Warm Springs Ponds and follows the river for forty miles into the town of Deer Lodge. Aside from Silver Bow Creek upstream, Stretch A is where the worst contamination of the Clark Fork proper is concentrated. Stretch A will have some four hundred acres dug up and trucked away to the dumps at Opportunity Ponds. There is dispute over whether four hundred acres is enough, and there is suspicion among the riverfront ranchers who own the land along Stretch A about the necessity of cutting roads across their land and taking fields out of production and dealing with the heavy-machine traffic that will haul their riverbanks away. Not just their riverbanks, but parts of their pastures too. The floods that saturated the valley left metals-infused dead zones called slickens as far as a mile from the current river. If the Mill-Willow Bypass is the "After" photo in the river restoration pamphlet, Stretch A is "Before."

I drag my canoe to the water at the same Warm Springs Ponds fishing access where I took off the bypass. The flow from the ponds broadens the water and just around the bend I scratch over the first of several short rock gardens. There's no apparent reason for rocks to be down here in this dirt valley floor, and these are suspiciously concentrated. They've almost certainly been put here to help aerate the flow. These rocks do a primitive version of what Bob did for a living. By breaking river water into smaller pieces, the rock garden multiplies its surface area, increasing the opportunity for oxygen to transfer in. Fish, and the bugs they eat, need oxygen.

Bob worked on municipal wastewater treatment plants. There the job was to grow bacteria that consume sewage, leaving clean water behind. Bacteria need oxygen to grow, and oxygen was pumped into the airless sludge through a diffuser. How to turn a flow of air into a maximally efficient transfer of oxygen was the trick, and the answer is surface area. For any given volume, a spherical shape provides the largest surface area, so Bob determined that an efficient diffuser would produce the maximum possible number of the tiniest possible bubbles. He did the calculations, drew up designs, ordered custom parts, and for years our suburban garage was full of varying lengths of steel pipe and shallow, machined, stainless steel bowls rigged to be covered with a thick rubber membrane perforated with thousands of tiny slits. The invention process yielded Bob three patents.

Once Warm Springs Creek pours in, almost unnoticed, the Clark Fork comes fully into being. This is no tributary, bypass, pond, or culvert. This is officially the Clark Fork. At first the banks are crowded with grasses and willows and mature thirty-foot trees, and when they part I can see the artificial wetlands of the Warm Springs Ponds complex trailing downstream between the river and the interstate. There are four fishermen out there on little flipper-driven pontoons, circling the small islands built of fill generated by the dike restoration work in the early 1990s.

The engineered lushness ends quickly. The rich chlorophyll green dulls and soon standing-dead ghost willows are competing with live plants. Cutbanks begin to show a couple of feet of normal-looking soil capped by another couple of feet of sediment, either rusty red or pallid gray. As the banks thin I begin to see pink and orange ribbons tied to shrubs or wooden stakes in the ground, apparently marking a contamination survey. Many of them are hidden from the channel, and steep banks keep me from climbing out to explore, but when there's finally a decent landing I get out to take a look and find a huge slicken area, the size of a good neighborhood's playground, crusted with mineral salts and a sickly blue sheen of copper sulfate.

Farther downstream I find another slicken, this one grossly green and spilling directly down the bank into the river. A two-foot ledge of copper-stuffed sand abuts the small beach, washing away with every rain and rise. Depressions in the soil look like Egyptian eyes, gradients of aqua increasing toward dark jade irises. Rivulets cut the grainy surface on their way to the river.

That's where I find the first green bone. It's probably a cattle bone, almost as big as my forearm, and it was likely scattered here by scavengers. It has lain on the slickened soil as rain turned it to a puddle, and as the puddle evaporated the bone porously leached copper salts out of the soil until it was coated with copper sulfate. It is vividly pale green, an artifact from some alternate taxonomy. I pick it up and put it in a bag in my boat and wash my hands in the river. In a few years there won't be any more of these to find.

The river itself seems clean enough, flowing over a gloss of late-summer algae, and clear enough to spot the white and pink golf balls that stud the sandy bed. They're sliced into Mill Creek where it runs through the Anaconda Country Club in Opportunity, and then blow downstream. Who knows how many golf balls got dug up with the Milltown sediments and carried back to Opportunity.

Wandering east of the interstate, the Clark Fork turns into the relentlessly twisty migrating channel that characterizes the river from here to Deer Lodge. Cattle accoutrements become common: half a dozen off-cut irrigation channels, a few small diversionary weirs, one shore-to-shore steel cable designed to keep cattle from wandering across fence lines. Off to river right, the Clark Fork

Coalition in 2005 bought the 2,360-acre Dry Cottonwood Creek Ranch, where it tries to model water-wise agriculture for entrenched neighbors, and whence it can keep an eye on the restoration of Stretch A. The ranch was purchased with a donation from a CFC board member from Georgia with a second home in Missoula.

At the two-lane Galen Road crossing I meet a young woman in a Montana Fish, Wildlife & Parks uniform. She's standing on the bridge holding what looks like an old television antenna, radio-tracking tagged fish. The water is still up after several days of rain, and fish are dying again. They usually do after rain. Rains raise the water, and the water laps the poisoned banks and sloughs them into the river where the sudden pulse of copper kills the fish by provoking a mucous response that coats their gills and suffocates them.

Before I get to my takeout at Racetrack Road, I run into my first real dam. It's river-wide and generates about a three-foot drop. The water pouring over the lip is too thin to think about scraping the boat across, and even small, run-of-the-river dams are deceptively dangerous, creating recirculating hydraulics that are hard to swim out of. I climb out of the canoe in waist-deep water and lower it over the spillway with a strap. My legs sink knee-deep in muck so fine-grained it feels like liquid silk. Every dam on this river holds back poison. The copper isn't going to hurt me; copper hurts fish. The arsenic won't hurt me either, as long as I don't make a habit of soaking in it, or eating the muck.

I tie the canoe to a willow, climb around the thickety bank-end of the dam, and wade back, belly-deep, into the recirculating water, untie the boat, and walk downstream to a spot shallow enough to climb back in without jumping. You don't ever want to jump into a canoe.

✛

The second book Bob gave me to read was Ayn Rand's *Atlas Shrugged*. What he hoped it would teach me was obvious even to a teenager: self-interested men are the engines that make the world turn, and everyone else is just a drain on the system. To live a meaningful life, one has to produce. Writing, I would find out later, didn't count, which was kind of ironic, given the medium by which Bob chose to deliver his message.

I didn't give a damn who John Galt was, but his remote mountain hideaway apparently made an impression. It wasn't until years later, researching the Anaconda Company, that I stumbled across the unremembered fact that *Atlas Shrugged*, published in 1957, contains the phrase "copper king."

"At the age of twenty-three, when he inherited his fortune, Francisco d'Anconia had been famous as the copper king of the world," Rand wrote. The Anaconda Company, a near-perfect anagram for the novel's d'Anconia company, had become the globe's fourth-largest corporation of any sort by the late 1920s, and had been doing booming business at its Chuquicamata copper mine in Chile since purchasing the property, then the world's largest single copper deposit, in 1923. Anaconda bought the mine from Harry F. Guggenheim for $77 million. Harry—like Daly, a horseman, newspaper publisher, and copper magnate—was a rising scion of the über-wealthy Guggenheim clan, which amassed its fortune in mining and smelting with the American Smelting and Refining Company, itself the parent of at least twenty contemporary Superfund sites in the United States.

ASARCO had been founded in 1889 by the same Henry H. Rogers and William Rockefeller who engineered the takeover of the original Anaconda Copper Company by the Amalgamated Copper trust. The Guggenheims took over management in 1901. Even Ayn Rand must have found it remarkable, in her more reflective moments, just how few genuinely worthy producers the wide world had bred. They must have been supermen indeed.

There was, of course, a different view. Che Guevara, visiting Chuquicamata on his famous motorcycle tour of the early 1950s, encountered a stranded Chilean couple who would help catalyze Che's anti-imperialist leanings. The husband, a copper miner and Communist Party member who had been recently imprisoned for striking, was walking toward a sulfur mine in the mountains, where he hoped to find anonymous work below the blacklist radar. His wife had left the couple's children with a neighbor. "A live representation of the proletariat in any part of the world," Che wrote in his diary, they didn't even have a blanket, so the future revolutionary gave them one of his.

The next day Che hitched a ride on a passing truck to the nearby Chuquicamata mine, where he insisted on a tour over the objections of its "blond, efficient, and impertinent" American masters. Look and then leave, the administrators told him. Chuquicamata was not a "tourist attraction."

If the migrating miners of the previous night were living representations of the world proletariat, Che wasn't shy about extending that role to the landscape as well. The mountains too were "exploited proletariat." "The hills show their gray backs prematurely aged in the struggle against the elements, with elderly wrinkles that don't correspond to their geological age." How many of Chile's mountains, Che wondered, "enclose in their heavy wombs similar riches . . . as they await the arid arms of the mechanical shovels that devour their entrails, with the obligatory condiment of human lives?"

As prose goes, this is as overheated as Rand is sterile. Radicalism at either end tends to make for crappy writing. I tend not to trust extremists and ideologues. It's not about preferring the middle of the road, it's that "road" is too rigid a metaphor. On a river, you can't afford to hug strictly the right or left bank and still hope to arrive downstream. You have to follow the current where it leads, left, right, or center. Sometimes you have to get out and walk.

At least Che's florid heart is in the right place. Che and Rand saw the same future in Chile, though from vastly different perspectives. Che's dear-diary recommendation that Chile "shake the uncomfortable Yankee friends from its back" presaged Rand's plot point about Chile's nationalization of the d'Anconia mines. Both proved prescient: Chile's freshly elected socialist president Salvador Allende nationalized Chuquicamata in 1971, stripping the Anaconda Company of two-thirds of its global production. The interruption lasted only two years, though, until the Chilean military, backed by the American CIA, overthrew Allende in 1973, leading to either his suicide or assassination, depending on whom you believe. The succeeding Chilean government of Augusto Pinochet reimbursed the Anaconda Company to the tune of $250 million.

Che was executed on October 9, 1967, five days after the day I was born, and went on to fame and martyrdom as a posthumous ubiquity on the T-shirts of quasi-revolutionary college students. Rand died of heart failure in 1982, the same year Bob asked me to read her wooden book. It's hard not to wonder how much earlier her heart had actually failed her.

Bob considered himself a self-interested producer. When he and I were still talking, I'd written an article about a nationally renowned Houston poet, an elderly and lifelong sufferer of cerebral palsy, who had fallen on hard times, had or had not been exploited by her caretakers, and had been left destitute and alone in a nursing home. The night I was awarded a statewide award for the profile in a Houston hotel ballroom, I'd accepted a dinner invitation from Bob instead of attending the ceremony. I told him the article had been nominated. He'd read it, which surprised me. He didn't think much of it, which didn't. It read, he said, like an extended advertisement for the National Endowment for the Arts. That didn't make much sense, since the NEA had nothing to do with it, but it gave me a glimpse of his resentments, and his implication, skewed as it was, was clear enough: Poets require caretaking. A truly productive member of society could take care of herself. He capped the conversation by asking if I'd considered what I planned to do when I grew up. I was thirty-two, fully employed as a journalist, and winning awards for my work. I stood up from the table and walked out.

The next time I saw him, six years later, he was ashes in a box. His patented aerators for municipal sewage treatment plants had run afoul of a probably specious patent infringement suit brought by an industry leader in sewage treatment aeration systems. Legal fees had crippled him, and he'd lost his nice house in Houston's Memorial Park neighborhood and his twelve-acre weekend place on Lake Conroe. He'd gone deeply into debt and moved into a rented duplex apartment in the Houston suburb of Humble. He complained constantly, my grandmother relayed to me, about the unfairness of the legal system, how it was rigged to protect the wealthy. This seemed like a commonplace to me, and I could hardly believe how naively he'd trusted the world to reward honest hard work. I wondered what he thought of Ayn Rand now, wondered if he still thought wealth and power were the inevitable consequences of productive virtue. I wondered if he'd ever realized that the objectivist worldview only works if the game isn't rigged, and that the game is always rigged. I'll never know if he connected the dots.

His mother, my grandmother, still thinks it was the stress of those years that killed him, that he might be alive today if he'd never hired a lawyer to defend himself and gotten sucked down the rabbit hole of wealth's advantages. Could be.

⊹

I paid $12 on top of the admission fee to take one of the hourly tours at Butte's World Museum of Mining. That's the only way to get underground. Admission just gives you roaming rights through the backlit mineral museum and outside, through the replica mining camp filled with glassed-in apothecaries and Chinese laundries, under the gallows-shaped head frame of the Orphan Girl mine, so named because of its standoffish remove from the hill's more concentrated cluster of shafts, into the massive engine rooms that powered the hoists that lowered cages full of men and straitjacketed mules into the mines. It's all empty now and sparsely enough attended that the few vacationing mine aficionados you do pass on the dirt paths give off an air of fellow ghosts wandering an abandoned theme park where all the rides are out of service.

In the gift shop I found a poster reproduction of one of the Anaconda Company safety signs once posted all over the works. It's a cartoony drawing of two men in a canoe shooting a rock-strewn rapid. The man in back is oblivious, eyes to the sky and paddle in the air where it can't do any good. The man in the bow is panicked, eyes bulging, helpless from that position to steer. A tandem boat takes cooperation, and that's the message: "Safety is a two-man job." The shop was out of stock and wouldn't sell me the display. The clerk said she'd call me when she reordered. It's been well over a year.

Underground is where you can still get a sliver of a feel for what went on here. The school of mining up the hill maintains a training tunnel on the museum grounds, a cave carved at a slight decline into the side of the rise. Students practice blasting here, and drill eight-foot holes into the cavern walls to accommodate steel reinforcing rods capped with steel plates to hold the rattled stone in place. The plates anchor the chain link that cages the walls and ceiling to catch falling rocks. After an orientation in the equipment shed, where you don a battery-operated, head-lamped hard hat and an insulated jacket—the temperature in the shallow shaft drops precipitously—a student guide will walk you into the mountain.

The shaft is a couple of hundred feet long and burrows just sixty-five feet beneath the surface, but that's far enough to take you solidly into a different universe. The tunnel is scattered with historical mining equipment on slapdash display: one of the battery-operated ore-hauling cars that began to replace the primitive mule-drawn carts in the early twentieth century, sitting on an abbreviated section of small-gauge track, its yellow paint peeling; a "honey pot" car with a steel plug capping the ass-shaped hole where miners, thousands of feet from sunlight, squatted to crap; an unwieldy, jackleg pneumatic hammer of the sort that eventually replaced sledges and picks.

The tunnel terminates at a shaft—the vertical aspect of an underground mine employed primarily for transport. This is the Orphan Girl shaft I'd just explored from the surface, beneath the gallows, where the square opening that had once admitted cages holding twelve miners at a time is now roughly sealed off with heavy steel plates.

From beneath, leaning over a railing and looking up the shaft, I can see narrow slits of sunlight between the plates. Looking down, it's only forty feet to a square of water the color of motor oil, placid beneath a skin of fallen dust.

The Orphan Girl had reached more than three thousand feet beneath the surface, more than half a mile. The hill's deepest tunnels double that depth. The tunnels and stopes and crosscuts and raises that honeycomb Butte's basement are all interconnected; you could walk across town in any direction without ever coming up for sun. There's three thousand feet of vertical water beneath that scummy surface visible down the Orphan Girl shaft, and another ten thousand miles of subterranean passageways sprawling off of that, all drowned. Laid out in a radial line, they could take you through the center of the earth's core and out again on the other side of the planet. The turn-of-the-century mule corrals are still down there, preserved in acid amber. There must be hundreds of honey pots, long bubbled to the bottom; why would anyone bother to haul the last ones out? Spacious caverns thousands of feet down preserve the giant pumps that once drained the mines dry enough to work in, sucking the seeping water out and spitting it down the hill into Silver Bow Creek.

ARCO turned the expensive pumps off in 1980 when the company closed up shop in Butte. The water has been percolating up ever since, leaching toxins out of the rock and pouring over into the connected Berkeley Pit, raising the lake's level at the rate of six to eight inches every month. The pit water is projected to top 5,410 feet above sea level in 2022, and when that happens, the water will have to be treated. Once it's treated, it will be discharged downhill into Silver Bow Creek. The Berkeley Pit—an entirely human-made landscape, an anthrosystem—will spill the banks of figurative speech and become the Clark Fork's literal source.

To see the pit, you drive uptown and pay two bucks to walk through a concrete tunnel laid into an earthen berm and emerge onto a wooden viewing platform overlooking the declivity. It might as well be the Grand Canyon. The walls rising from the chemical-brown water are scalloped with terraces, and on the far shore you can just make out the little white canister towers where an experimental treatment station fails to make a dent in the inflow. Heavy silver binoculars are bolted to the railing, but at a detail level there's not much to look at. The enormity is the thing. Celtic music plays through the outdoor speakers mounted in the rafters, and if you're lucky you might hear the whistle and see the tracer of a bottle rocket fired out over the lake. The screamer is aimed in the general direction of a duck that looks like it might be thinking, like 342 Canadian snow geese, about landing. It's meant to dissuade.

If you think shooting fireworks at birds is an odd environmental protection strategy, you misunderstand Montana.

# PART IV

# CLARK FORK

*The mind that is not baffled is not employed.*
*The impeded stream is the one that sings.*

—WENDELL BERRY, *Standing by Words*

The Clark Fork leaves the state as the largest-volume waterway in Montana, draining a watershed encompassing 22,000 square miles and running a gauntlet of U.S. history. From most vantages—from a plane, or the deck of the Finn & Porter restaurant at Missoula's DoubleTree Hotel—it is remarkable only in its picturesqueness. There's little to be seen from the interstate, or from its scattered fishing access sites, to show it for what it is. Its water ripples and glints like most water, and it floats a boat as well as any water in the world, but if you peel back its surface, or peer intently enough beneath it, the river reveals layers. It has been a habitat and a pathway. It has been a storm drain for the dumping, purposeful and unintended, of that which we no longer need, and in all those facets it reflects American ideals of what we want nature to look and act like. It has been and continues to be what we've made of it. People have engineered the Clark Fork to do their bidding through evolving economic ideas of a river's highest and best use, from naturally occurring sewer to unspoiled respite. We didn't create the river, but we've made and remade it in our image, and the river, in turn, tells us ripple by eddy who we think we are.

In 1984, Montana's Department of Natural Resources and Conservation published *River Mile Index of the Columbia River Basin*, starting at the top, near the Continental Divide. The watercourses that eventually funnel their contents into the Clark Fork read like a geographical yearbook of inspiration, aspiration, and homage. Yankee Doodle Gulch, Little Blacktail Creek, Janny Gulch, Wendell Canyon, Lucky Strike Gulch, Mode-S Canyon, China Gulch, Two Bit Creek, Grove Gulch, two consecutive Whiskey Gulches, Gimlet Gulch, Seven Springs Creek, Rose Gulch, Muddy Creek, Sawmill Gulch, Alaska Gulch, Strozzy Gulch, Flume Gulch, Telegraph Gulch, Butcher Gulch, Beef Straight Gulch, and Oro Fino Gulch.

Beef Straight Gulch was named for a flour-shortage season during which miners ate nothing for three months straight but beef raised in Deer Lodge Valley. "Orofino" is Spanish for "fine gold," and not far from the state motto of "Oro y Plata" (gold and silver). Copper, *cobre*, wasn't yet on anyone's mind when the state's Spanish-naming craze ("Montana" is Spanish for "mountain," minus a tilde) was labeling the land.

There's an entity called the Board on Geographic Names ("board of" probably cuts too close to the bureaucratic quick) in Reston, Virginia, that oversees the naming of geographical features. If you find an unnamed creek on your property and want to name it after your mother, your dog, the town you left behind, or your diet, you can petition the BGN. Likewise, if you want to know how many riverine depressions in Montana are named Sheep Gulch (thirteen, with four in Silver Bow County alone, not counting Sheep Corral Gulch), you can search the BGN's online database. There is no officially registered Shit Creek anywhere in the United States.

The Clark Fork has been penned onto maps under many names over the years: Bitterroot River, Deer Lodge River, Hell Gate River, Missoula River, St. Ignatius River, and Pend Oreille River.

Salish, Pend Oreille, and Nez Perce Indians tracked the river's path through Hellgate Canyon toward buffalo hunting grounds to the east. The Salish named the confluence of the Clark Fork and Blackfoot Rivers, where Clark's dam would rise, "the place of the mature bull trout," and fished for the now-threatened species just upstream.

Lewis and Clark, for whom the river is named, had close to nothing to do with it. Returning from the Pacific in 1806, the explorers camped at a site near the Bitterroot River and then parted ways, with Clark heading south back up the Bitterroot to retrieve their boats before canoeing the Beaverhead and Jefferson rivers back to the Missouri. Lewis headed north, toward the Missouri's Great Falls. On the way he camped near the juncture of what his journal identified as the "East fork of Clark's river" (the Clark Fork) and what his Nez Perce guides called Cokahlarishkit, or River of the Road to the Buffalo, now better known as the Blackfoot. If Milltown Dam had been there at the time, Lewis would have seen it from camp.

"The junction of these streams," he wrote of the Blackfoot's confluence with the Clark Fork, "spread into a handsome level plain of no great extent; the hills were covered with long leafed pine and fir."

In 1964, an official decision by the Board on Geographic Names finally answered the nomenclature question with "Clark Fork," period, stripping the "River" from the river. They may have been on to something. What I thought was a river turns out, in many ways, to be a utensil, not so much an entity unto itself as a tool unto its handlers' purpose.

The first time I remember feeling like a semi-genuine Missoulian was years after I'd arrived, canoeing the whitewater of the Clark Fork's Alberton Gorge, west of town.

My friend Quinlan had invited me to a party at a friend's house, and the patio conversation, true to native form, ended up on the river. We met a guy who paddled the gorge frequently. Neither Quinlan nor I had yet tried. We were both relative novices when it came to whitewater canoeing. Quinlan at least owned a boat that could handle that kind of water. The guy invited us out to paddle the gorge with him the next morning, and since whitewater canoeing is the sort of thing best learned in experienced company, we said yes. If we got into any real trouble he'd be there to help out.

We arrived at the put-in the next morning, about forty-five

minutes downstream of Missoula, filled with butterflies. Quinlan likes to ask "Are you sure you want to do this?" at the launch of any even vaguely hairy river run. There's never any real doubt about his answer. "No," I always answer, half-truthfully, and then we launch anyway.

We had his seventeen-foot tandem canoe, rigged for kneeling (which anchors a paddler's center of gravity lower in the boat, aiding balance), thigh straps to allow for leaning, and inflated air bags in the boat's bow and stern. Modern rafts are self-bailing, and kayaks have sealed spray skirts to keep water from getting in. The special challenge of running rapids in a canoe is keeping the canoe from doing what neither raft nor kayak really can: fill up and sink. The airbags displace some incoming water, and canoeists more expert than I can exploit that added buoyancy to roll a canoe back upright after flipping, still strapped into their seats, but they're mostly there to give the canoe a reasonable amount of float when you have to swim it to shore after swamping.

Alberton Gorge's whitewater is Class III, maybe IV in certain flows, a pool-and-drop river packed with rock ledges and wave trains, every rapid a brief thrill ride followed immediately by water calm enough for recovery. It can be dangerous, though. Quinlan has had to help evacuate a rafter who had half his face pulverized by a rock falling off the cliff his boat was shading under. I've boated with a kayaker who once broke his back in the sucking hole at the bottom of Tumbleweed, the Clark Fork rapid I fear most. It's said the river-bottom chasm beneath that hole goes eighty feet down. I can't imagine how you'd measure it.

Quinlan drove from the stern. In a tandem canoe, the bowman in the front provides power and precision course adjustments. The canoeist in back steers the line and, when necessary, tells the one in front what to do. You want your best paddler in back.

We swamped and swam in six of the gorge's seven major rapids that morning. Every time the boat filled with water and tipped. Several times we just got blown over by wrong-hit waves. We twisted out of the thigh braces upside down under water, spluttered to the surface, started kicking the weighted tub toward the bank, dumped it, and got back in. I think Quinlan was mad by the third time, though his Wisconsin gentlemanliness didn't let it show.

It was the next week, when we came back and ran the same stretch without once falling out of the boat, that I knew I had arrived. I was no longer just drifting downstream on a bladder of hot air. I was reading the river.

✝

The Clark Fork is a different river at different flows, and it's been many different rivers over the course of geologic time. The broad contours of the Clark Fork's valley were first formed in Eocene time, between fifty-six and thirty-four million years ago. Flowing waters gouged the drainage into layers of sedimentary rock built of billion-year-old sand and mud, twice as ancient as the earliest fossils.

Between thirty-eight and seventeen million years ago, the climate and the river dried up, and with no water to carry it away, sediments filled the valley to depths of almost four thousand feet. Another wet period recharged the river roughly fifteen million years ago, eroding through the sediment, then the river dried up again, leaving a prehistoric dust bowl that lasted until about two million years ago, the dawn of Pleistocene time and the starting line for the periodic ice ages that followed. That's when the more or less modern Clark Fork began to flow.

The flow has not been uninterrupted. Fifteen thousand years ago, during the last great extent of the most recent recorded ice age, tongues of glacial ice crept down the valleys of British Columbia and plugged the Clark Fork's valley with a thirty-mile-long frozen dam at the present-day site of Idaho's Lake Pend Oreille.

For the next two thousand years, at roughly fifty-year intervals, the watersheds behind that ice dam flooded a vast pool known as Glacial Lake Missoula, an inland sea that at its fullest covered almost three thousand square miles and held five hundred cubic miles of water—half the volume of Lake Michigan. The lake was almost a thousand feet deep where Missoula sits today, as deep as the water in the Berkeley Pit.

The Clark Fork's waters stacked upstream of the lake for almost a hundred miles, lapping at the edges of Opportunity's Deer Lodge Valley. The tendriled bowl of Glacial Lake Missoula periodically rose high enough to float the ice blocking its path to the sea, flushing the lake across Idaho, Washington, and Oregon in a biblical-scale deluge, six hundred miles to the Pacific.

At constrictions like Alberton Gorge, the water would have flowed almost sixty miles an hour. At a stricture called Eddy Narrows, farther downstream, flows would have topped out at almost 4 million cfs—ten times the combined flow of every single river on the contemporary planet. By the time it got to Portland, the muddy wall of water would have been five hundred feet high.

Deep water moving that fast forms kolks, liquid tornadoes capable of sucking chunks of bedrock out of the earth and spitting them miles downstream. It was probably a kolk that hollowed the hole under Tumbleweed.

Glacial Lake Missoula filled and emptied at least thirty-six times over the course of two thousand years as glacial creep replaced the busted dam and busted again, until finally the ice retreated too far north to block the exit. You can count those thirty-six lakes in the successive shorelines that ring Missoula's Mount Jumbo—named for the same circus elephant that inspired Edison's dynamo—like a living topo map.

At the eastern end of those landscape-scale fire-hosings, where the piled-up Clark Fork poured through Hellgate Canyon into Missoula's bottoms, floods gouged the cliffs that would later anchor William A. Clark's Milltown Dam. Along the way, they blew vast volumes of sand and gravel from the valleys east of Missoula through Hellgate Canyon and dropped them in broad fans in the slacker water of the Missoula Valley. That sand and gravel, buried in the thirteen thousand years since Glacial Lake Missoula's last purge, is now the Missoula aquifer, the same one recovering from the Butte arsenic puddled behind Clark's now-dismantled dam.

If prehistoric torrents and ice ages and glacial floods defined the Clark Fork for millions of years, the digging of copper has defined it for the last two centuries and continues to define it. Of the many rivers the Clark Fork has been, the one that William A. Clark dammed in 1908 was the first fully bent to human intention. The one that's being restored now is the first to be truly human-built.

On May 13, 1908, just five months after Milltown Dam was completed, President Teddy Roosevelt convened the inaugural

Governor's Conference on the Conservation of Natural Resources. His address was titled "Conservation as a National Duty," and he used it to warn the assembled governors that "the natural resources of our country are in danger of exhaustion if we permit the old wasteful methods of exploiting them . . . to continue." The speech is often credited as the starting gun of the American conservation movement.

Three weeks later another big flood came to Missoula.

Daniel Bandmann was partial to tragedies. Born in Germany in 1840 to a wealthy manufacturing family, Bandmann launched his stage career in the Court Theatre of Neustrelitz at the age of eighteen and quickly built a reputation as a Shakespearian specialist. He arrived in America in 1858, touring with a German troupe, and polished his English at New York's Cooper Institute under the tutelage of Alexander Graham Bell, whose 1876 telephone patent, along with Edison's lightbulb, would later drive Butte's desperate dig for copper.

Bandmann made his Broadway debut as Shylock in *The Merchant of Venice* and went on to tour the world several times over, becoming one of stagecraft's most renowned practitioners of the 1870s and 1880s. When it came time to settle down, Bandmann chose Missoula. He'd made his first appearance there in 1884, opening Maguire's Opera House on West Main Street, and four years later he purchased 320 acres in what is now East Missoula. It was a spectacular spread, nestled onto a fertile bench in a broad bend of what was then called the Missoula River, surrounded by low grassy mountains and with a looming view of stone cliffs carved by prehistoric floods crashing through the constriction.

A 1943 article in the *Great Falls Tribune* excavated Bandmann's Montana career under the headline "Hamlet at Hell Gate."

Bandmann spent his final fifteen years retired to his Montana ranch, indulging the gentleman-farmer impulse common to certain artistic temperaments, establishing the University of Montana's theater program, and cultivating an air of eccentricity born of extensive travel and frequent marriage. He imported and planted the state's first McIntosh Red apple trees, and established the state's first herd of blooded Holsteins, selling thirteen of the beefs to help seed Marcus Daly's Bitter Root Stock Farm.

Bandmann's most consequential sale closed in 1905 with the transfer of twenty acres at the juncture of the Clark Fork and the Blackfoot River to William A. Clark's Missoula Light and Water Company. A few months later Bandmann dropped dead on his ranch, age sixty-five, of a heart attack brought on, the *New York Times* obituary reported, by "acute indigestion."

Clark, a senator by then, had been plucking up land and water rights near the rivers' confluence for several years. Apparently lacking an actor's instinct for auspice, he began building his dam on Friday, the thirteenth day of September 1905.

Two million board feet of timber, five thousand barrels of cement, and unrecorded tons of granite and structural steel went into the dam, a timber structure filled with stone and gravel and faced with concrete twenty-eight feet high. Clark's dam went online on Thursday, January 9, 1908. Six turbines generated five thousand horsepower, making it one of the largest hydropower plants of its era. Two eleven-thousand-volt transmission lines carried power downriver to Missoula, and another fed the Bonner sawmill.

Clark's superintendent in charge of building the dam, George Slack, expounding on his almost-finished masterpiece to the *Missoulian* newspaper, bragged that "when the last piece of timber is added to the dam it will be in such condition that the biggest waters ever known in this vicinity will not affect it in the least."

Slack must not have been counting Glacial Lake Missoula. Nor was he much of a weather forecaster. Five months later his dam was in shambles.

The rains started in May and lasted thirty-three straight days, piling down in a warm spring deluge on top of a hard winter's heavy snowpack and saturating the watershed from Butte to Missoula. On June 6 the cold snapped back and nine inches of new snow carpeted the headwaters. As it melted on top of the already soaked ground, there was nowhere for it to go but downstream.

The resultant flood, on the Texas scale of toad stranglers and gully washers, was a full-blown goose drowner, and the Clark Fork's most tumultuous flood in recorded history.

On a typical midsummer's day in Missoula, the Clark Fork

might be running about five thousand cfs, or about five feet deep at the gauges. The 1908 flood, predating official measurements, sent an estimated forty-eight thousand cfs—seventeen and a half feet—barreling through Hellgate Canyon. Fifty million board feet of felled and floated timber piled into a logjam stretching miles up the Blackfoot River behind the little mill dam at Bonner. Boardinghouses and outhouses and chicken coops rafted down the Clark Fork whole, splintering on Missoula's bridges before the bridges too crumbled and washed out. Witnesses reported seeing an island like an earthen ship, "sailing majestically down the river . . . with four great pine trees standing upright on it." Rail lines flooded out, postponing the state's Democratic convention. Governor Edwin Norris, returning from Roosevelt's Governors' Conference on the Conservation of Natural Resources, got stranded by synchronous flooding on the Missouri River near Livingston and had to walk fifteen miles across Bozeman to catch a train back to the capitol at Helena.

In Missoula, water poured over Clark's dam in waves. The powerhouse flooded ten feet deep. Company spokesmen swore to reporters that there was no threat the dam might fail, as industrial interests always do when faced with disaster, but Clark's men dynamited the dam's southern end to let the waters drain anyway, just to make sure. Repairs took more than a year.

The flood temporarily shuttered Butte's mines for lack of functioning railroads to ship their ore, but it proved an unexpected boon for waste dispersal. The early Butte mines had largely processed their copper sulfide in place. The process was called heap roasting, and it was as simple as piling crushed stone ore in a crosshatch of heavy timbers, setting the structure on fire, and letting it burn. Sulfur and arsenic smoldered off into the yellow haze that hung over Butte for years and inspired William A. Clark to authoritatively declare Butte's ladies "very fond of this smoky city . . . because there is just enough arsenic there to give them a beautiful complexion."

As airborne cosmetics wafted from Butte's heaps, copper melted out, leaving middens of brimstone ash. What ore was properly smelted left mountains of slag and dust piled behind the furnaces, or simply sloughed into Silver Bow Creek. As a result, U.S. Fish Commission biologists conducting a netting study downstream near Deer Lodge as early as 1891 "did not find any fish whatever."

When the floodwaters rose, they carried the slag, dust, and ash downstream. Archival photos show Silver Bow Creek, normally a thin ribbon, sprawling wide across Deer Lodge Valley. One hundred twenty miles later the slurry hit Clark's dam and began settling to the bottom of the six-hundred-acre reservoir behind it, clogging the pond with some six million cubic yards of sediment, shallowing its pools and silting its wetlands.

Almost as soon as the floodwaters receded, Milltown's residents could tell that something had gone wrong. A 1976 bicentennial history published by the Bonner School Bicentennial Committee contains resident Mildred Dufresne's reminiscence: "In early Milltown there was said to be only one good well. There were a few other wells that did not have very good water. It was thought they were contaminated by the copper mine residue-laden waters of the Clark Fork River."

Official confirmation that the flood of 1908 had fouled Milltown's waters with Butte's waste would take seventy-three years, with another twenty tacked on before anyone started doing anything about it.

✛

In 2003 I bought the first boat I loved. I'd been hanging around a Missoula canoe shop and it was dangling from a rafter in a corner. You could spin it and watch it sparkle. It was worse than a puppy in a window.

It was built by a Minnesota company called Bell, and the model was called Wildfire, which reminds me of the Michael Martin Murphy song and makes me cringe. I've got nothing against horses, but I indulge a strong suspicion of people who love them too much. The boat was a solo, fourteen feet long and lithe, and it glittered with interwoven threads of Kevlar and carbon fiber. The gunnels and thwarts were made of cherry and walnut, and the whole thing weighed a feathery thirty-five pounds.

It cost $1,800. When it went on spring sale at $1,350 I showed up when the doors opened at nine the next morning to take possession. I couldn't wait to get it on the water.

When you're in a canoe, it's said, you're part of the scenery.

Floating down the Smith River several years later, a friend told me it looked like I was drifting downstream in a folded leaf. I liked the hell out of that.

The first place I floated the Bell was Milltown Reservoir, behind the dam. I parked at the far end of a truck-stop lot and carried my new canoe over a weedy patch and across a riprap border to a muddy bank of the Blackfoot River, slack-mouthed at its merger with the lake, and launched there.

A natural lake is one thing, wild in its way, but a dam-plugged reservoir is a liquid scab. I don't much like paddling on stilled water, where all motion is self-propelled and aimless, momentum-free. I prefer the swell of movement, becoming over being. I didn't come to Montana to stay the same. I didn't abandon the bayous of Houston to stir a Montana mud puddle.

The water was placid enough to paddle upstream, up braided sloughs through scrubby marsh islands, before the current turned insistent, but it was hard to get far enough upstream to lose sight of the dam and its buoyed perimeter of caution signs, and it was impossible to escape the hum of Interstate 90 passing by. As living rivers go, Milltown's Clark Fork was comatose.

Congress passed the Comprehensive Environmental Response, Compensation, and Liability Act (CERCLA), in 1980. Jimmy Carter signed it into law just as he was getting run out of office by Ronald Reagan. The legislation immediately came to be better known by one of its provisions—a "Superfund" composed of a tax on the petroleum and chemical industries and used to pay for environmental cleanups when legally responsible and financially viable polluters can't be found. One student to whom I spoke about Opportunity listened politely for several minutes before interjecting: "I don't understand. That doesn't sound super fun at all." The Treasury stopped collecting the tax in 1995, and the Superfund dried up in 2003. Where Superfund work continues, it continues on the dime of legally enjoined polluters. When the polluters are out of business, the Superfund site is out of luck.

In much of Montana, "Superfund" rolls off the tongue as easily as "cfs." There are seventeen active Superfund sites in the state as of 2012 (and one proposed), each with its own collection of inter-related subunits. In Jefferson County, mining ruined two creeks and contaminated the town of Basin with heavy metals. The Barker Hughesville Mining District in Cascade and Judith Basin counties likewise spoiled groundwater, surface water, and soils with toxic metals. Same deal in Cascade County's Carpenter–Snow Creek Mining District, Mineral County's Flat Creek, and Lewis and Clark County's Upper Tenmile Creek.

Note the preponderance of waterways. Creeks are natural drains. Overburdened, they clog.

In Stillwater County, a company called Mouat Industries poisoned groundwater and the ground around it with carcinogenic hexavalent chromium. In Silver Bow County, a wood treatment company called Montana Pole left a footprint full of toxic pentachlorophenol and dioxins. In Gallatin County, Idaho Pole made a similar mess. In Yellowstone County, Lockwood Solvents left a legacy of volatile organic compounds. In East Helena, an ASARCO lead smelter saturated soil and water with lead and arsenic.

In Lincoln County, in the northwestern part of the state, vermiculite asbestos mined for decades by the W. R. Grace Company has permeated the town of Libby so thoroughly that it's been found not only in the high school track, where it was deliberately used as construction material, but nestled in the bark of the town's trees. If you've heard of a Superfund site in Montana, it's probably Libby. Some three hundred people have died as a direct result of mesothelioma, the irreversible lung disease caused by asbestos exposure.

But if W. R. Grace wins the body count, the Anaconda Company takes the prize for sheer Superfund fecundity. It's responsible for the Silver Bow Creek/Butte complex of sites near the Continental Divide, the Anaconda Smelter and Refinery complex of sites downstream in Anaconda, and the Milltown Reservoir Sediments site farther downstream still in Missoula.

As recently as 2011, EPA listed another defunct Anaconda smelter, in Great Falls, where from 1892 to 1915 the Boston and Montana Company dumped some thirty million cubic yards of antimony, arsenic, chromium, cobalt, copper, iron, lead, manganese, mercury, nickel, silver, and zinc into the Missouri River. Thirty million cubic yards, for point of reference, is 140 times the volume of concrete being used to rebuild One World Trade Center.

Those kinds of numbers are numbing, so people tend to nod and walk away. They're the price we continue to pay for a world in which metal is cheap and plentiful. As facts go, that one is not super fun.

None of Montana's Superfund sites has been completely cleaned up, and many never will be. Operations and maintenance are ongoing at most. At many, as in Opportunity, the work will continue in perpetuity.

⊹

CERCLA would probably have never been passed if it weren't for the neighborhood of Love Canal, in Niagara Falls, New York, where 21,000 tons of toxic waste buried by the Hooker Chemical Company and, subsequently, birth defects, started bubbling into the newly built bedrooms of an expanding residential area in the late 1970s. Regarding blame, it was complicated. The local school district had purchased the land over Hooker's strenuous objections—the company wouldn't take more than a dollar and included an elaborate disclaimer and warning about the property's toxic contents, which the district seemed intent on ignoring. The portion of the land used for housing had been offloaded to a developer, who sold homes to families uninformed of the chemical sump beneath their yards. Construction punctured a clay cap meant to seal the chemical soup beneath the sod, and created a dam of sorts that kept a literal underground canal of benzene, dioxin, and nine other carcinogens backed up into residential basements. Rain conspired to make it worse.

As usual, moneyed machines were set in motion to disclaim any connection between the community's wading pool of chemical waste and its 33 percent rate of chromosome damage. One percent is more typical.

A reporter named Michael H. Brown and a citizen named Lois Gibbs turned the suburban nightmare into a national cause. Around the same time, another chemical dumpsite, called the Valley of the Drums, near Louisville, Kentucky, provided a compelling visual: twenty-three acres of exposed, rusting drums leaking chemical waste into the ground. The age of polluter accountability was dawning.

Faced with the consequences, Congress had to do something. It created CERCLA, and Reagan tried to pretend the law didn't exist. In its first eight years, only 16 of 799 identified Superfund sites were cleaned up. Today there are 1,280 Superfund sites on the National Priority List. Three hundred forty-seven have been delisted post-cleanup. Sixty-two new sites have been proposed.

The year Superfund came into law, 1980, is the year that John Lennon was murdered, Mount St. Helens erupted, and Ted Turner founded CNN. It was just three years after the Atlantic Richfield Company, ARCO, flush with embargo-buttressed oil profits, decided to merge with the Anaconda Company in 1977. The timing couldn't have been worse. Almost as soon as the deal was done, the bottom dropped out of oil and copper prices at the same time.

In 1981, the Missoula City-County Health Department, having received a grant through new Clean Water Act amendments, conducted routine tests of the well water in Milltown, just across Interstate 90 from Milltown Reservoir, and was surprised to find arsenic levels far exceeding federal drinking water standards in wells supplying the taps in thirty-five homes. Arsenic can cause cancer, and Milltown's aquifer is also Missoula's aquifer: the deep layer of river rock rubble deposited by the floods of Glacial Lake Missoula. Missoula's wells lie downstream and downslope.

It was not immediately obvious where the arsenic was coming from. The Bonner lumber mill, then owned by Champion International, fell under first suspicion. The idea that the contaminants could have originated upstream in Butte had been lost in the intervening decades.

In February of 1982, two newly installed University of Montana professors, Bill Woessner and Johnny Moore, used a $20 grant to rent a chainsaw, strapped on skis, and slid out on the frozen Milltown Reservoir to carve holes in the ice and sample the sediments beneath. The sediments were tainted with arsenic all right, and enough metal to sheath an armada. The sediment averaged ten to fifteen feet deep on the reservoir floor, twice that just behind the dam, and contained an estimated 143,900 tons of iron,

19,000 tons of zinc, 13,100 tons of copper, 9,200 tons of manganese, 2,100 tons of arsenic, 1,700 tons of lead, and 70 tons of cadmium. Early-twentieth-century smelting technologies were not wildly efficient. They didn't have to be. Brass rings hung low in the trees.

The science was poorly understood at first, and debated until it was no longer debatable, but what was happening was that a) the reservoir's bottom was silted in with poison mine tailings, and b) the weight of the lake water on top of them was squeezing the heavier metals down into the aquifer below, from which they were being sucked up into Milltown's wells.

Lettuce grown in Milltown's backyards and irrigated with well water drawn from the aquifer was found to contain 1.41 parts per million (ppm) of arsenic. Spinach carried 2.66 ppm. A normal background level for arsenic in vegetables is .0001 ppm.

EPA prioritizes Superfund sites based on health risk to humans, and that much arsenic is considered a clear and present danger. By 1985, courtesy of EPA, Milltown had a new water system, tapping the cleaner Blackfoot upstream, and the contaminated wells were capped with concrete. Water heaters and plumbing pipes were replaced; arsenic had built up in lines and begun leaching out of them. Even then, not everyone—least of all locals—was convinced there was a problem. Longtime Milltowner Uno Hill told a door-to-door county sample taker, "I've been drinking this water for fifty years. I don't see any reason to change now."

EPA disagreed. In September 1983, one hundred years to the month after Marcus Daly filed the plats for the town of Anaconda, the Milltown Reservoir Sediments Unit near Missoula was listed as a Superfund site. That same day EPA listed the Anaconda Company Smelter Site upstream, and the Silver Bow Creek/Butte complex farther upstream still. Strung out along the Clark Fork, the Anaconda Company's Superfund footprint is the largest in the nation, a landscape-scale degradation requiring landscape-scale restoration.

How to do that would be a topic of debate for the better part of two decades following Milltown's Superfund designation. After the dam's owner, the Montana Power Company—itself a corporate entity spun off the old Anaconda Company—won a congressional exemption letting it off the Superfund hook, ARCO found itself saddled with cleanup costs, and ARCO was in no hurry to pour money into a toxic pond. It fell to a bunch of Missoula environmentalists to force their hand.

⁜

I met Tracy Stone-Manning at a downtown coffee shop called Catalyst, purveyor of one of Missoula's best breakfasts, and I was a little nervous. Missoula, like all towns, hosts its own emblematic breed of celebrity. Being a small town proud of its liberal conscience—you'll still occasionally hear proud reference to Missoula's sixties-era identity as the Berkeley of the Rockies, or, from less flattering sources, the People's Republic of Missoula—it tends to breed low-key celebrities from a gene pool that rewards engagement over glamour. Tracy Stone-Manning is near the top of Missoula's peculiar A-list. At the time of writing she is the field director of U.S. Senator Jon Tester's Missoula office. She's married to Missoula writer Richard Manning, author of eight books of environmental reportage and philosophy and himself a top-tier Missoula personage. Though Tracy would never say this, or even agree to it without extensive conditions, she took Milltown Dam down.

We sat at a small table in the little mezzanine overlooking Catalyst's high-ceilinged main room to talk. In person, Tracy Stone-Manning isn't intimidating at all. She's a lanky woman with a cascade of tightly curled red hair, and a stately, watchful, almost heronesque presence that suits her central role in restoring Missoula's stretch of the Clark Fork. Stone-Manning is well aware that that role alone is enough to put some people on edge in a state where it's not uncommon to see pickup windows festooned with Hippie Hater decals (an organization of Missoula motocrossers who are "tired of our local riding areas getting shut down from [sic] liberal hippies who know nothing of the sport, thinking we're tearing the land up"—which they do) and bumper stickers asking "Have You Bitch-Slapped an Environmentalist Lately?"

The Clark Fork Coalition, a nonprofit watershed protection group, had been formed in 1985 by University of Montana environmental studies professor Vicki Watson (who'd celebrated the "last train to Opportunity" at the twenty-fifth anniversary Clark

Fork Symposium the year before), Bruce Farling (who went on to found and currently heads Montana Trout Unlimited), and Peter Nielsen (now a Missoula County environmental health administrator). The group's founding purpose was to fight an effort by Champion International, the company that owned the plywood mill in Milltown, to increase its nutrient discharge into the Clark Fork from another of its facilities, a pulp mill near the village of Frenchtown, west of Missoula. Downstream communities from as far away as Sandpoint, Idaho, took buses to public hearings in Montana, and from that organizing effort the coalition was born. It quickly took on the additional goal of preventing a proposed mine in the Cabinet Mountain Wilderness, near the headwaters of Clark Fork tributary and trout-tourism destination Rock Creek—an issue that raises its head again every time gold prices spike.

Stone-Manning had joined the coalition's board in 1994, and was president when its director stepped down in 1999. Tracy sent out the call for résumés but finally got talked into taking on the job herself. The coalition was riding the wave of a high-profile victory: in November of 1998, a citizen initiative banning a form of gold mining by which large volumes of cyanide simmer through open-air heaps of ore, dissolving out the precious metal, had blocked a controversial gold mine from setting up shop at the headwaters of the Blackfoot River. Richard Manning had written a book, *One Round River*, to support the campaign.

"The obvious question," Tracy told me at Catalyst, "was where do we put the organization's resources next? We were looking for the next big thing to put people's focus on."

Milltown wasn't necessarily an obvious choice. It had begun its Superfund life as a groundwater issue, and EPA, with its primary focus on human health, was in the process of solving it the most economical way possible, by capping the wells and replacing the water supply.

In the early spring of 1996, Milltown had became a surface water issue. That's the year a ten-mile ice jam on the Blackfoot broke loose and went barreling toward the dam. Panicked at the prospect of a collision, the dam's operators opened the floodgates to spill the reservoir downstream in hopes of stranding the ice floe on the reservoir floor before it could crash into the dam. It worked, but the combination of grinding ice and untempered release sent clouds of reservoir sediment blowing over the dam. The next spring, more than half the fish in Missoula's Clark Fork were dead.

"So that's when people began to realize, 'Oh, wait, we've got a bigger problem than just groundwater.' The reservoir itself is a problem. Rivers move sediments. It's what rivers do. And it's going to kill fish. Every ten, fifteen years there's going to be an event like this that kills a bunch of fish."

Two years later, in 1998, bull trout, native to the Clark Fork, were federally listed as a threatened species. Milltown Dam, with no fish ladder or passage to let the spawning bulls upstream, became part of that problem too.

The dam was becoming a holistic issue in a world of compartmentalized bureaucracies. EPA dealt with the human health angle. Fish, Wildlife & Parks had the mandate to protect fish. The Federal Energy Regulatory Commission (FERC) held purview over dam safety. None had the overarching authority to deal with everything at once, and that's where Stone-Manning saw an opportunity. "With all due respect to those agencies, we don't care that the EPA says 'we only look at human health' and the FERC says 'we only look at dam safety' and that the Fish and Wildlife service says 'we only look at threatened species.' The public doesn't care. The public wants someone to lead on the big picture."

Stone-Manning knew that across the country, in Maine, a dam called Edwards had recently been demolished, one of the nation's first dam removals after a century of rampant dam building.

"I was looking through a bunch of files, trying to get my arms around what the coalition could do, and I just said, if there are all these problems, why don't we advocate for cleaning it up and pulling out the dam?" It was an audacious proposal—too audacious perhaps even for the Clark Fork Coalition.

"It was a very soft sell to the board," Stone-Manning says. "In our 2000 annual work plan, we put removal of Milltown Dam as goal number two, to try to bury its importance." She laughs at the absurdity of it. "Maybe they won't notice if we make it goal number two. The timing was just luck. I came into that job when the stars were aligned to have that idea work."

Stone-Manning took the helm of the Clark Fork Coalition in

August 1999. In February 2000 the coalition officially launched its campaign to tear down the dam. One of its first actions was to rent a plane and fly media over the site to provide a visual for Missoulians who, for the most part, didn't know where the dam was since it was almost invisible from the interstate and accessible only by little-used back roads. Then the coalition manufactured a news hook by asking FERC not to relicense the dam, which was up for review. At a press conference kicking off the dam-removal campaign, the city-county health commissioner, Peter Nielson, himself a former director of the Clark Fork Coalition, showed up to lend his support, and eventually convinced veteran Republican county commissioner Barbara Evans and her fellow commissioners to back removing the dam, which was beginning to be seen as a public-safety issue.

"So it immediately became not a partisan issue," Stone-Manning remembers, "which was huge. It was not about politics per se. This wasn't 'those weird environmentalists.' It was the county."

Finally, knowing that nothing comprehensive could be done without EPA support, the coalition sicced public opinion on the agency.

"The public participates in EPA processes late," Stone-Manning explains. "The EPA does a bunch of studies, it puts out a document where it has a proposed plan of action, and then the public gets to comment. We thought if [Montana EPA chief] John Wardell is going to call for dam removal, he needs to know that he's got overwhelming public support to do that, and he needs to know that *before* a public comment period. So we created our own. We started flooding them. We used all the same mechanisms—postcards . . . letters—so that they understood 'okay, if we go this far, we are going to have the public behind us.' CERCLA has eight or nine things they have to check off—one of them is local acceptance, one of them is state acceptance—and so we thought, 'Let's let them know they're going to have local and state acceptance before they even plant that flag.'" The campaign generated ten thousand comments, more feedback than any EPA issue in Montana history.

Then it threatened to become about politics. What had looked in February 2000 like an environmentally friendly Al Gore victory in the upcoming presidential elections became, in November, a George W. Bush coronation. Bush, who had regularly stymied the EPA in Texas over clean air and water regulations, and who deferred to states' rights, at least rhetorically, as aggressively as he appears to have deferred his military service, said that no dams would be coming out under his watch.

*Missoulian* editor Sherry Devlin, formerly an environmental beat reporter at the newspaper, called Stone-Manning to ask what she planned to do.

"By then I had talked to Sherry so often on this story that I was sloppy," Stone-Manning recalls, "and I didn't say, 'This is off the record.' I said, 'We're going to do a big media campaign: TV, billboards, radio ads, print ads, the whole bit,' and then I read that quote in the next day's paper."

The quote was a strategic flub, publicly tipping ARCO to the coalition's plan, but it also delivered a positive unintended consequence. A local ad agency called Partners Creative phoned to pitch its services. Partners arrived for a forty-five-minute meeting, left for two weeks, and returned with concepts and budgets in tow.

"I'm looking at these budgets," Stone-Manning remembers, "and I'm like, 'Are your creative costs embedded in these media buys? Because I don't see any line item for you.' And they said, 'Oh, yeah, no. We'd be doing it pro bono.' To which I said, 'You're hired.' I still get teary-eyed. A huge part of our fund-raising—creative costs—gone. We just had the media buys, and Missoula's a cheap market."

Over the course of a two-year campaign, the Clark Fork Coalition, with an annual operating budget of $180,000, spent about $80,000 advocating dam removal. They printed and gave away bumper stickers reading "Remove the Dam, Restore the River," which started appearing on cars and bicycles across town. They plastered billboards with the message "Not All Time Bombs Tick," and vintage images of smiling water-skiers over the logo "Ski Milltown—It's Toxic!"

ARCO, with billions at its disposal, was slow to respond. The company eventually funded a local dam-keeper organization called the Bonner Development Group, but the counter turned out to be too little too late.

"They put up a fight," Stone-Manning says, "but I don't understand why the fight wasn't bigger. Everywhere else in the basin that they worked, Butte, Anaconda, even to some extent Deer Lodge, they're company towns, and they were the company. Missoula wasn't a company town. They didn't have those inroads to the business community, or even to the city or the county, that they had in Butte–Silver Bow and Anaconda–Deer Lodge County, and so I think they didn't quite know how to get their arms around it."

The standoff followed a script familiar to any environmental reporter, or any exhausted neighborhood activist unexpectedly drawn into the maw of a corporate polluter. First ARCO questioned the science and denied that there was a problem. Studies flew back and forth. Losing that battle, ARCO tried to make the dam someone else's problem, offering to donate it to the University of Montana for "research," trying to gift it to the Bonner Development Group, and threatening to enjoin its owner, the Montana Power Company, in cleanup costs. When none of that worked, ARCO attacked the coalition's solution as both too expensive and worse than the problem. Taking the dam out, ARCO argued in a sudden fit of environmental conscience, would just slough the problem downstream and kill more fish. Sandy Stash, an ARCO VP and spokesperson throughout the Milltown brouhaha, did her best tree-hugger impression when she righteously reminded reporters, "Spawning gravels do not have the religious significance in other parts of the country that they have in Montana."

Then there was the question, familiar to cosmetics expert William A. Clark, of whether arsenic was really all that bad. President Bill Clinton, on EPA's recommendation, had enacted tougher arsenic standards for drinking water, knocking the threshold standard of 18 parts per billion down to 10 parts per billion in 2006. President Bush rescinded the new standard and then reinstated it under public pressure. A 2007 *Wall Street Journal* investigation found that ARCO had solicited scientists to prove that arsenic, at low levels, doesn't cause cancer in humans.

Here's what scientists say arsenic does in high doses: it causes cancer of the bladder, lungs, skin, kidneys, nasal passages, liver, and prostate. It causes noncancerous illnesses of the heart, lungs, and skin. It causes neurological damage. Arsenic counts in Milltown ranged as high as 1,000 parts per billion—a hundred times the federal standard.

In 1992, a University of California study had found that water contaminated with 50 parts per billion arsenic increased cancer risk by 1 percent—more than a hundred times the EPA guideline for increased cancer risk in drinking water.

One percent isn't a sexy number. The average Facebook user has 245 friends. Only 2.45 of those would die. Only 8.45 million of the site's 845 million users would die. How many do you expect to save, and how much are you willing to pay to save them? What's one life in a hundred worth?

"It really is a kind of cost-benefit," ARCO apologist Stash said at the time. "Do the chances of one less cancer death weigh against the cost a local community will have to bear putting in a water-treatment system?"

It's a logical if coldhearted question, but Stash left two important elements of her equation unstated. First was that ARCO, not the residents of Milltown, would be footing the bill for the water treatment. The second was that the question was entirely rhetorical, since ARCO had already answered it in the negative.

Arsenic is more or less harmless if it happens to be dry and stable, but Milltown's arsenic was neither. In anoxic (i.e., oxygen-free) scenarios like Milltown's, arsenic starts moving around its environment. In this specific case, researchers estimated, 7,300 pounds of arsenic were seeping annually out of the reservoir floor and into the groundwater, ballooning an underground arsenic plume beneath 253 acres of mostly residential land. Left alone, EPA estimated, the plume would continue to contaminate wells for another two thousand years.

ARCO wanted to leave the dam where it was, prohibit development in the contaminated area, and make structural dam upgrades to prevent a repeat of the 1996 ice-jam scare—a relatively painless $20 million solution. Missoulians wanted the dam out and the sediments removed—a $319 million job that EPA estimated would heal the aquifer in just three to four years.

ARCO had already spent some $75 million on maintenance and cleanup over the course of its unfortunate Montana residency, and it wasn't eager to add to the tab.

"Is it worth ten times more money?" Stash asked, again seemingly rhetorically. "Is it worth spending ten more years? Is it worth putting up with the disruption for what amounts to a perceived view that the world will be a better place if we move a bunch of dirt and take out a dam?"

Missoula decided it was.

But Stash had been right about one thing. With her cause almost lost, she appealed to Missoula's altruism—or something—regarding the disposal of Milltown's sediments. "I would encourage people to really think about where it's going," she said, "how long it's going to take and how it's going to get there. There's been a total lack of discussion about that topic . . . But I can guarantee you they are not going to be welcome in . . . Anaconda–Deer Lodge County."

You might have thought Sandy Stash knew something nobody else knew.

⸸

The sediments were not welcomed in Anaconda–Deer Lodge. "That whole side of the story is my one big regret," Stone-Manning told me over coffee at Catalyst. "That we didn't see, that *I* didn't see that backlash coming. Because it happened fast, and it happened behind closed doors. It was a business decision."

What happened is that the Environmental Protection Agency, in 2003, released its proposal for the Milltown cleanup. The battle was over and ARCO had lost. The dam would come out. Per protocol, EPA had considered multiple options for disposing of the waste. The Opportunity Ponds were considered, but due to the cost of shipping the sediments a hundred miles upstream, the agency ultimately recommended that they be removed to a repository yet to be built at Bandmann Flats—named for Missoula's famous thespian and apple entrepreneur—on a bench above the floodplain in what had become East Missoula.

Even as Clark Fork Coalition staffers popped champagne to celebrate a hard-fought victory, ARCO was already advocating tweaks. Where EPA suggested dredging the sediments from the bottom of the still-wet reservoir and depositing them at Bandmann Flats before removing the dam, ARCO decided it would rather drain the reservoir and dig up the sediments "in the dry" and ship them by rail upstream to the Opportunity Ponds instead. Max Baucus, the senior U.S. senator from Montana, threw his weight behind the ARCO addenda as well. By the time EPA's long-researched proposal was presented for public comment, the tide had turned on Opportunity.

Comments arrived fast and furious via e-mail, postcard, and letter, almost unanimously praising the plan to take the dam out, and almost as unanimously insisting that the sediments go anywhere but East Missoula.

"The proposed Bandmann Flats site," wrote one, "would seem to have a higher and better use than a dump site," the inference being that Opportunity had no such higher and better use. Opportunity's ponds, wrote another, are "a perfect place to deposit these sediments because [they are] all ready [*sic*] contaminated." Shipping the sediments upstream would "permit long term positive development of the Bandmann Flat area to benefit Montana, Missoula County and the Bonner School District."

Canyon River Development LLC, which later built the Canyon River golf course community on Bandmann Flats, commented that it had "not formed an opinion on removal of the dam, but one thing is certain—if it must be removed, move the waste to the Anaconda [Opportunity] Repository that has already been designed for it."

"All the waste material should be taken back to where it came from," read another, typically enthusiastic, and typically confused about the river's history of human use. "They put it in the river, they should take it back."

Exactly three comments said no to the Opportunity solution.

The sediments had not come from Opportunity. An estimated 85 percent of the well-poisoning arsenic in Milltown Reservoir had come from Butte, with another 15 percent attributed to mining operations in Philipsburg, via Clark Fork tributary Flint Creek. Ninety-eight percent of the fish-killing copper in the reservoir had blown downstream from Butte. It would not be going home. Butte was by this time a town of some 26,000 voting-age souls, urban by Montana standards, and an old-school Democratic stronghold in an otherwise red, rural state. Butte was already staggering under a century's accumulated toxic waste from the mining that had turned its dun-colored hills inside out and left entrails scattered across the landscape. A few irreverent environmentalists, offering a rare combination of logic and humor, suggested dumping Milltown's sediments into the simmering Berkeley Pit—as close to a true source as they'd ever be likely to get—but, despite the prospect of poetic justice enacted at an unprecedentedly grand scale, no one seemed to take that idea seriously.

The Opportunity solution was a more practical sell, with a logic that proved irresistible, especially to Missoulians. To store the wastes at Bandmann Flats would require construction of a brand-new repository on otherwise unspoiled and potentially developable land near an urban center that prizes green space, whereas shipping the spoil to Opportunity would sock it away largely out of sight in an existing repository, where Missoulians would never have to see it. Besides, the Opportunity Ponds, as one commenter succinctly put it, were "already ruined."

The Opportunity plan made even more sense to ARCO, which already owned the Opportunity Ponds site and wasn't eager to create a second perpetual management nightmare near Missoula.

Despite its initial recommendations, EPA was convinced. The agency seems even to have agreed with the most wishful of ARCO's premises: that the well-poisoning Milltown sediments, a human health hazard requiring expenditures in the hundreds of millions of dollars near Missoula, would somehow transform itself into topsoil once dried out and spread on eight hundred acres of Opportunity's ponds. ARCO was already under a mandate to cap those ponds— a four-thousand-acre expanse—with "growth medium" sufficient to support the plant life needed to anchor the century's worth of toxic dust that had already been dumped there. Windstorms regularly blew that dust onto Opportunity's yards, across its streets, and through its windows.

If ARCO was going to have to get the sediments out of Milltown, and it had become clear that ARCO was, then they might as well be put to good use. Topsoil is expensive to buy, expensive to haul, and hard to find in quantities sufficient to cover hundreds of acres. The Milltown sediments were a start. (By comparison, the same sediments dumped on downtown Missoula would have buried the little metropolis under more than seventy feet of gunk.)

Moving the Milltown sediments to Opportunity would at least get them out of Missoula's backyard. If they solved part of Opportunity's dust problem, that would be two birds with one stone and cream gravy on top.

Keith Large, the state's Superfund manager at Milltown, said that the impact of three to four million cubic yards of Milltown waste spread out on the Opportunity Ponds would be "insignificant," and suggested the possibility, later transformed in media reports to a near certainty, that the suddenly "organic material" could "conceivably save us money on the Anaconda [Opportunity] cleanup."

The only problem, which proved surmountable, was that Opportunity wasn't buying it.

The train-bound transformation from poison to potting soil became known around Opportunity as the "magic carpet ride."

"It became this horrible, falsely portrayed thing as an environmental justice story," Stone-Manning told me later. "Which is just a crock of shit. It didn't exacerbate the problem in Opportunity. Opportunity is in a world of hurt already, and this is literally inches added to the world of hurt."

Environmental justice is an ethical inquiry into the equitable distribution of burdens—things like four-thousand-acre plots of toxic waste—resulting from endeavors that produce waste, which is to say industrial economies.

By any measure, Opportunity seemed a fertile field for the study of environmental justice. I took Tracy to be saying that as a landscape so burdened, Opportunity was already off the charts anyhow, that an additional burden was effectively no burden at all.

"Exactly," she says. "It's a horrible thing to say, but it's really true."

The several hundred citizens of Opportunity, on the other hand, were having a hard time seeing it that way, and in retrospect, Stone-Manning says now, her regret roosts in the presentation.

"There was a meeting in Opportunity about the Milltown cleanup, and they used the exact same presentation they used in Missoula and Bonner. They did not tailor it for the community. Right down to the very last slide on the PowerPoint. It was a pretty picture of what the two rivers [the Clark Fork and Blackfoot] could look like. Right? Close on the pretty. Someone raised their hand and they said, 'Where's *our* pretty picture?' It's that simple. They rightfully want their community to be fixed, and there we're doing this dog-and-pony show about how we're going to put all these people to work in Missoula and how we're going to clean up and get the pretty picture and you're going to get the sediments . . . Everyone else got a vision."

I asked Tracy if she could envision a Milltown-style solution for Opportunity, and her answer was blunt.

"No. What do you do? You dig it up and you take it somewhere else? Some other community? Like the Berkeley Pit, it's sort of a testament to how badly we can screw up as humans. We screwed up really badly, and now, making amends in those areas, there's no A-plus answer."

⊶⊷

Of all the things Bob ever said to me, the one I remember most precisely, and the one that's haunted me, is, "I just want you to be perfect." I was probably twelve. He said it in a car, angrily, in self-justification for an outburst of disapproval over some long-forgotten failure of mine. Never mind the precise definition of perfect—it had something to do with King Arthur—here was a bar I could fall short of.

The fatally efficient beauty of the statement was that it set an expectation designed to disappoint us both: he, who probably wanted nothing more than that his son should embody a remedy for the inevitable disappointments of his own life, and me, who wanted, as sons do, to earn his approval.

It hasn't escaped me that the lasting impact of that single seven-word sentence may have influenced, for better and worse, my choice of career. There was the very definition of the power of words. He loathed that word: "very." He had grammatical opinions, as a first-generation college graduate might be expected to. He said "very" provided an emphasis that was too often unearned, that it added no useful information to the adjective it modified. For a long time after I stopped listening, I agreed with that verdict, adopted the preference, and enforced it reflexively. It's only since he died that I've moderated to the saner position that while "very" is indeed overused, and could profitably be thinned from much speech and writing, sometimes it's *precisely* the right word. Sometimes unearned emphasis is the effect you're going for.

I suspect, in retrospect, that Bob was a frustrated writer himself, and that his disapproval of me was born in resentment of an opportunity he'd never had—an opportunity he gave to me but felt I hadn't earned.

During our estrangements when I was in high school—born of garden-variety disagreements over the appropriateness of harboring a Sex Pistols album in *his* house—I wrote him letters full of overheated teenage rhetoric, claiming independence, and, as I saw it, pushing back against the weight of his expectations. He returned them riddled with corrections.

"I will try to express the way I see things, because I have a strong feeling that you do not understand me or my thinking," I wrote him. I was seventeen.

"Too strongly stated—emotional," he wrote in the margin in red ink.

I'd later learn that he'd done the same thing to a family genealogy he'd compiled, notating his judgments on family members in the margins. My aunt, his sister, has the only copy, and she refuses to show it to me. I don't know what harm she thinks it could do at this point. I've already internalized his compulsive editor's insistence on corrections. I already know he found me illogical, sentimental, and trite. I've inherited his dismay at my worst attributes.

I learned from Bob how to be disappointed, and how to parse imperfection. I still argue with him, and he's been dead almost a decade. There's a voice in my head that sounds like his. It says that Opportunity's story isn't even worth telling.

There was one person, more than Senator Baucus, more than the EPA, more even than collective Missoula, for whom the Opportunity solution was, in fact, close to perfect. A Spokane native and Missoula son, number sixty on *Forbes* magazine's 2012 list of the four hundred wealthiest Americans, his name is Dennis Washington. Among dozens of corporate properties under the umbrella of the Washington Companies, he owns Envirocon, the remediation contractor hired by ARCO to remove the Milltown Dam and dredge the toxic sediments out of Milltown Reservoir. Washington also owns Montana Rail Link, the railroad line hired to freight the Milltown sediments to Opportunity. It is of purely poetic resonance, though hardly coincidental, that Dennis Washington also owns Montana Resources, the company currently mining copper and molybdenum from Butte's Continental Pit strip mine, adjacent to the old Berkeley Pit—property he purchased from ARCO in 1986, after ARCO shut down the mines. Washington makes money mining copper. He makes money cleaning up copper mining waste. He makes money moving that waste to Opportunity.

He's Montana's modern-day copper king, vertically integrated and vastly diversified in the mold of William A. Clark and Marcus Daly, and sharing traits seemingly cherry-picked from each man's biography.

From Daly he may have learned the value of relating to the common man, and what of his sketchy biography has been publicly released emphasizes humble beginnings on the wrong side of tracks he would eventually own in Missoula's working-class Northside neighborhood. Washington's education never progressed beyond his graduation from Missoula County High School, class of 1952, but, having escaped personal privation, he created the Dennis and Phyllis Washington Foundation in 1988 to support mostly education-related charitable causes. He has donated a 64,000-acre ranch in Oregon to the Christian youth ministry Young Life. After being awarded the Horatio Alger Award in 1995, Washington became a patron of the Horatio Alger Association, funding fifty students annually through scholarships at the University of Montana, where the football team plays in Washington-Grizzly Stadium.

From Clark he may have learned the value of close control: the Washington Companies are privately held, and the man himself is notoriously press-shy. I contacted his old friend and confidant Mike Halligan, a longtime lobbyist for the Washington Companies who now runs the Dennis and Phyllis Washington Foundation, seeking to broker an interview. I wanted to ask Washington about the copper kings, and his memories of the Clark Fork. I wanted to ask him about Opportunity. Halligan made it clear that Mr. Washington would almost certainly decline.

Despite maintaining a home in Missoula, "He doesn't spend much time in Montana anymore," Halligan told me. Plus, "He just doesn't do interviews." I pointed out that Washington had recently flown a reporter to Vancouver for an exclusive tour of his freshly refurbished yacht, *Attessa IV.* Halligan corrected himself: "Except *Forbes.*"

Dennis Washington was born in 1934. At the onset of World War II, his parents went to work in a Bremerton, Washington, naval shipyard, and the family lived in government housing, where Dennis contracted polio at age eight. He was sent to an experimental treatment facility in Seattle, and then to his grandmother's home in Missoula to recover. When his parents divorced after the war, Dennis moved among relatives in California, Washington, and Montana, spending his final two years of high school in Missoula. His Washington Companies biography claims Dennis had become self-sufficient by age fourteen, working as a grocery boxer, newspaper delivery boy, service station mechanic, and railroad depot shoe shiner.

After graduation he moved to Ketchikan, Alaska, to work construction as a crane operator, returning to Montana two years later to do similar work for an uncle. At twenty-nine, he married 1962 University of Montana homecoming queen Phyllis Jean Peterson, took out a $30,000 loan from a Caterpillar dealer, bought a bulldozer and a motor grader on credit, and went into business on his own, competing with his father, Roy, from whom he'd been estranged as a young man. Roy went bankrupt. Dennis gave him a job. "I got where I called him Pops again," Washington told a reporter from *USA Today*—his only known non-*Forbes* press concession—in 1997.

Along the way he burnished a reputation as a tough guy, spending nights in Missoula's basement jail and losing teeth in bar fights. One altercation with Missoula bar owner Sonny Llewellyn ended with $12,000 in damage to Llewellyn's Thunderbird Motel bar. Washington paid off the debt in installments.

One of Washington's first government contracts was a job building a parking lot in Glacier National Park. A specialty in Forest Service contracts led to more federal work, including interstate highway construction, and by 1969 Washington Construction was the largest contractor in Montana. He branched into mining in the early 1970s, but doesn't seem to have made a mark until 1986, when the Butte mines caught his eye.

ARCO had lost more than $100 million on its ill-advised take-over of the Butte mines in 1977, and by 1985, with the price of copper stalled at sixty-seven cents a pound, the oil company was looking for a way out. Washington initially expressed interest in buying the property's mining equipment for scrap, but a former Anaconda executive convinced him the mines could be profitable even at fifty cents a pound, if only the union could be broken.

Washington broke it. The Anaconda branch of the United Steelworkers of America had been out of work for three years, and had little fight left. Washington tendered a lowball offer reported as $13.5 million for the properties ARCO had acquired for $700 million just eight years earlier.

ARCO was so eager to get out from under its Anaconda acquisition that the company sweetened the pot with 38,000 acres of undeveloped recreational land the Anaconda Company had stockpiled, and another 12,000 acres of mining land. He also got the Butte Water Company and its $4 million in annual revenues. He quickly sold off a sliver of the land for development, netting $8 million, and just like that, without mining an ounce, Washington's purchase price was essentially covered. What Washington did not buy was ARCO's environmental liability for the old Anaconda Company.

Water rights to Silver Lake, the reservoir just down the road from my idyllic Montana cabin, were owned by Dennis Washington until the mid-1990s, when ownership was transferred to Butte–Silver Bow County. Montana governor Brian Schweitzer's Georgetown Lake mansion sits on former ARCO land purchased from Dennis Washington. The Stuart Mill Bay fishing access site where I've flailed at fly-fishing was donated from the same Washington windfall. Much of my Montana dream wilderness, it turns out, is a subsidiary of Dennis Washington's leftovers.

Like Daly's, Washington's timing was uncanny. In 1986, desperate over Montana's depressed economy, the state loaned him $5 million to reopen the mines, and Butte gratefully dispensed 80 percent tax abatements. By 1989 the price of copper had doubled to $1.40 a pound, and the company Washington renamed Montana Resources had already cleared $100 million on his $20 million investment. As a privately held company, Montana Resources doesn't report earnings, but in 2012 the price of copper on the London Exchange is just over $3.50 a pound. Two wars have helped to keep the price high.

The Butte mines were Washington's big score, and funded his expansion into dam-building, railroads, and shipping. In 1987 he took another step in the tracks of Clark and Daly by purchasing the Burlington Northern Railroad's southern Montana line— a thousand miles of track from Huntley, Montana, to Spokane, Washington—for a reported $160 million. He renamed it Montana Rail Link.

A year later he formed Envirocon to leverage his construction expertise into the growing market for environmental remediation services, securing contracts for cleanup work at Hanford, Washington, the most contaminated nuclear site in the United States, and elsewhere.

In 1996 Washington Construction paid $380 million for the storied but bankrupt Boise, Idaho, construction firm Morrison-Knudson—builders of Hoover Dam and the San Francisco Bay Bridge—and went on to acquire parts of Westinghouse and Raytheon to form Washington Group International (WGI). The Raytheon acquisition sent WGI into bankruptcy in 2001, whence it emerged with a sweetheart deal exempting the company from federal taxes on $80 million in annual operating profits for the following decade. Washington sold WGI in 2007 for $2.6 billion to the San Francisco-based URS Corporation and relinquished any role in the company, but not before it had earned $931 million between 2003 and 2006 with Department of Defense contracts for rebuilding Afghanistan and Iraq.

Today the Washington Companies include a Seattle-based manufacturer of fuel-efficiency equipment called Aviation Partners Inc., an international retailer of heavy equipment called Modern Machinery, the Southern Railway of British Columbia, two real estate development companies, and Seaspan Marine Corporation, an association of Canadian shipbuilders, ferries, and tug companies, including a $5 billion joint venture with the Carlyle Group to service the Asian maritime market, where, incidentally, the entirety of Butte's current copper output is sold.

Along the way Washington has managed to quietly change the face of Missoula. The Washington Companies' unobtrusive office sits at the corner of International Way and Reserve Street, the locally unpopular but guiltily indispensable big box store corridor developed and in part managed by Washington's Gateway Limited Partnership. His private Pullman car sits on a siding at the old depot that heads Missoula's main drag, Higgins Avenue, next to the site of the Saturday morning farmers' markets, whence it occasionally fires up to ferry underprivileged children down the tracks for free onboard dental exams.

Washington himself, meanwhile, is rarely seen. Though he owns a home in Missoula's Rattlesnake neighborhood, reputedly framed in steel in deference to corporate disputes with a lumber company, he spends most of his time at his home in Palm Springs, or at his ninety-acre estate on Stuart Island north of Vancouver (where *USA Today* reported that Washington "trains a floodlight on churning black waters where hundreds of sharks—their eyes luminous gold—feed on shrimp"), or the $19 million, nineteenth-floor condo at New York City's Plaza that he purchased in 2008. He owns a Gulfstream II jet, a helicopter, and, shades of Daly, a stable of Arabian thoroughbreds. He recently finished a four-year renovation of the 332-foot *Attessa IV*, his latest fixer-upper yacht. That accomplishment inspired Washington's latest concession to publicity, in which he flew a starstruck *Forbes* reporter across the country for a tour of the boat's five floors of 18-karat gold walls, marble staircases, twelve-seat theater, $500,000 onboard tender boat, helicopter deck, and antique fireplaces. Washington bought his own shipyard to accomplish the retrofit, and employed a crew of 224 full-time for three and a half years. Estimated cost, purchase plus rehab: $250 million.

"He is dressed more like a deckhand than the mining and construction magnate he is," the reporter writes. "Jeans, and untucked oxford shirt, a black baseball cap and white socks (no street shoes are allowed onboard; his white Prada sneakers are in a box below)."

Starstruck to the point of nonsense is probably the reasonable response to wealth on this scale, but this is the kind of toady journalism that makes my skin crawl. What the hell sort of deckhand shuffles about in white socks while his Pradas are stashed in his fabric-ceilinged bedroom belowdecks?

I don't have anything against Dennis Washington. As billionaires go, he seems like a relatively laudable sort, philanthropic and hard-working, without the apparent mean streak of a William A. Clark, or the reprehensible politics of a Koch brother. Like everyone else, I can hardly look away from the trappings of incomprehensible wealth, but the sight sparks more suspicion than ambition. Can this really be the Randian hero ascended on the strength of his own good work and iron will, unassisted by irreproducible happenstance and favor? Is this mountain of dollars not dug out of a growing depression somewhere else?

When I worked at Missoula's *Independent*, the publisher—my boss, himself a locally formidable financial light—told me that he would consider the weekly newspaper well and truly established when Dennis Washington deigned to grant the paper an interview. We saw our chance in 2004 when Washington held a bash for his seventieth birthday at the old Northern Pacific Depot. The man who told *USA Today*, "I don't have room for big shots. I'm not one and I don't want them around me," invited 250 guests to the celebration, Oprah Winfrey and Arnold Schwarzenegger among them.

Leading up to the event, the city's daily paper ran a page-one story announcing the impending birthday, failing to name the date, along with a curiously placed plea from spokesman Mike Halligan. "It's a private function with some invited guests, and we'd like to respect their privacy," Halligan told the *Missoulian*. "Dennis is not one to seek press coverage, or to make public something private."

To date, neither the *Indy* nor I have scored that interview. If I were wearing Dennis Washington's Pradas, I wouldn't give it to us either.

✝

In February 1994, in response to growing concerns about the fairness of concentrating the nation's hazardous waste in the country's poorest communities, President Bill Clinton signed Executive Order 12898, directing federal agencies including EPA to "make achieving environmental justice part of its mission by identifying and addressing, as appropriate, disproportionately high and adverse human health or environmental effects of its programs, policies, and activities on minority populations and low-income populations."

I wanted to know why EPA had changed its mind about storing the Milltown sediments in East Missoula, and decided instead to dump them on Opportunity, not just in spite of the fact that Opportunity had already been dumped on, but apparently *because* Opportunity had already been dumped on. Four parties know the reason: EPA, ARCO, Max Baucus, and Dennis Washington. Only ARCO and Washington had money in the game. None are talking.

It was April 2003 when EPA released its proposal to remove Milltown Dam, dig the reservoir sediments out of the floodplain, and store them in a waste repository to be constructed in East Missoula. A public comment period was set for April 15 to June 20.

On May 5, 2003, Baucus, chairman of the powerful Senate Finance Committee, announced that he wanted Missoula's toxic sediments stored not at Bandmann Flats, as EPA had recommended, but at the Opportunity Ponds. Baucus's advice arrived in the form of a letter to EPA's Milltown site manager, Russ Forba.

"I believe this option is superior to EPA's proposal in several respects," Baucus wrote. "First, it would allow EPA to coordinate and manage in one place the contaminated materials and sediments from Milltown, Silver Bow Creek and the Upper Clark Fork. This will greatly simplify long-term monitoring requirements for future generations." In other words, keep all the rats in one trap.

"Second, moving the sediments to Opportunity Ponds will also remove any constraints on the size of the EPA's proposed repository [at Bandmann Flats]. Additional research during the design and implementation phase of EPA's cleanup efforts at Milltown may reveal that additional sediments will need to come out. Choosing Opportunity Ponds as the recommended repository will allow EPA to be flexible as it moves forward with its proposal to clean up Milltown." If the cleanup's disposal needs were to balloon, Baucus wanted them to balloon in Opportunity, not Missoula.

"I understand," Baucus wrote, "that there are significant costs associated with removing the contaminated sediments to Opportunity Ponds. However, I firmly believe that the long-term benefits to Montana and the environment far outweigh these potential costs. I also pledge to work closely with the interested parties to help negotiate a way to reduce the costs associated with hauling contaminated sediments to Opportunity Ponds.

The interested parties were ARCO and Dennis Washington's Montana Rail Link.

Butte's *Montana Standard* reported that Baucus was already "working to bring the parties together to make using Opportunity Ponds a viable option."

"The senator's contact at Montana Rail Link," meanwhile, "did not return a telephone message." The paper paraphrased EPA's Russ Forba saying that "the settlement negotiations are secret" and "not open for discussion."

A secret deal was struck. ARCO would pay Dennis Washington's Envirocon an undisclosed sum to remove the dam and dredge up the reservoir. ARCO would pay Washington's Montana Rail Link to freight the waste upstream and deliver it to Opportunity's ponds. Max Baucus would bask in the gratitude of a substantial downstream constituency that didn't want the poison stored in its backyard, and vote-scarce Opportunity could lump it.

In other words, Senator Baucus, Washington, and ARCO conspired privately to override the EPA's recommended disposal of Missoula's cleanup wastes in a manner that specifically benefited Washington's company at Opportunity's un-consulted expense. EPA rolled over.

By June 2004, even Tracy Stone-Manning and the Clark Fork Coalition had sent their own letter to the EPA: "Enclosed please find comments from 558 citizens about the amended proposed cleanup plan for Milltown Reservoir and dam. These comments urge you to release a final decision that calls for dam removal and sediment removal, with the contaminants being hauled by rail to Opportunity Ponds."

That's what happened. Missoula got its way. In the midnight bedrooms of Opportunity, they could hear the trains coming.

—┼—

Matt Fine came to Missoula from Seattle in 2004, hired by Envirocon specifically to manage the Milltown Dam removal and reservoir cleanup. What he found was both a challenge and a greased wheel. Years of Superfund experience as an engineer, geologist, and MBA had accustomed him to the multiyear delays, hidden agendas, and ax-grindings endemic to the process, but by 2004, that was no longer the case at Milltown.

"As far as the environmental aspect, there was nobody against it, which is pretty amazing. My experience in these things is they're very controversial, and there's very loud groups on both sides."

Not just the populace was on board, but the agencies as well. The Federal Energy Regulatory Commission fast-tracked the normally complex retirement of Milltown's dam license. The state whipped into action to reinforce bridge abutments that suddenly running water would otherwise have washed out. EPA allowed Envirocon to start the work in stages, even as construction designs were still being drawn up; typically, full plans would be completed and approved before ground could be broken. Years were saved.

"The project had a lot of momentum," Fine told me. "People wanted it gone. The real driver is the fact that, I think, there was this political momentum to get this done. I don't know all the backwater stuff that was going on"—I think he meant "backroom"—"I tried not to get involved in that, but it was clear that people had made commitments. It was 'figure out a way to make this happen, quickly.'"

ARCO and EPA signed a consent decree—the legal contract resolving Superfund liability and specifying cleanup—by which ARCO agreed to remove the dam and repair the site. ARCO then purchased a policy from insurance supergiant AIG insuring against cost overruns. (The Milltown cleanup ultimately cost in the neighborhood of $75 million.) Though the specifics of ARCO's deal with AIG are confidential, AIG started signing the checks, most of which went to Envirocon, which had been contracted by ARCO to perform the actual remediation. Should the remediation not take—should Milltown's groundwater remain contaminated with arsenic—it's the AIG policy that will pay for additional remediation. Fine won't say how high the policy goes, but he says it's high enough.

"You couldn't *spend* that amount of money in the local area," he says.

Though the EPA had originally recommended storing the Milltown contaminants just downstream at Bandmann Flats, that plan "had some problems," Fine said. "People didn't like it, was the biggest one."

The idea of hauling the lake bottom to Opportunity instead came from ARCO, as Fine remembers it.

"They knew they needed quite a bit of material to cover those tailings impoundments, and material to do that in that area of Anaconda is hard to come by. I think the lightbulb went off and they said, 'Well, what if we just use this material and haul it up there?'"

The missing link was rail. Envirocon's sister company, Montana Rail Link, operates a line running almost a straight shot from Milltown to Opportunity. Dennis Washington's Envirocon contracted with Dennis Washington's Montana Rail Link to lay about 2,500 feet of new connector track down into the floodplain and haul the sediments to Opportunity.

"There was certainly some coordination at very high levels to make it happen," Fine says, "because that was the big piece. That really was the key to the project."

First Envirocon opened the dam's floodgates, drawing down the water behind it. Then the company installed two dewatering wells hard against the interstate and dug a new channel, lined with clean rock, for the Clark Fork's temporary home. With the reservoir dried and the river skirting the site, the dam and powerhouse were dismantled and removed. Then the earthmovers went to work, GPS-controlled excavating equipment loaded with a computerized topographic model of the floodplain's contaminated elevations telling them how deep to dig. Sawn stumps on the original river bottom marked the sedimentary baseline. At the state's request, Envirocon left the stumps there. "It helps in roughing the floodplain and capturing fine-grained sediment," Fine explained, "and providing places for critters to live, the whole ecosystem thing."

On the morning of October 2, 2007, and every morning for the next two years, Montana Rail Link left forty-five empty cars on the loading siding. Every evening, Envirocon left forty-five cars filled with a hundred tons per car of sediments infused with heavy metals. Every night for two years, Montana Rail Link ran the trains to Opportunity, where Envirocon excavators transferred the dirt to dump trucks, drove them to an eight-hundred-acre patch of the Opportunity Ponds, and spread them two feet thick on the ground.

Before I left the break room where Matt Fine and I had talked, he offered to show me his office. The building we were in was Dennis Washington's original Missoula headquarters; Envirocon had been moved back in while the Washington Companies' newer digs out on Reserve Street were being renovated. Fine gave me his card and told me to feel free to follow up. He'd been generous with his time and knowledge, and I felt bad for noting the bumper stickers tacked to his wall with distaste. "Earth First: We'll Mine the Other Planets Later," one read. Another said, "Strip Mines Prevent Forest Fires."

The company name Envirocon always read wrong to me. I see "environmental con." When Washington's Continental Pit in Butte eventually becomes unprofitable and Montana Resources Inc. walks away, it could very well be Dennis Washington's sons, running Dennis Washington's companies, called in to clean up the mess. It looks like good work if you can rig it.

I'd been off the Clark Fork for a year. It started snowing at my cabin in early November, and I'd hung my canoe from the side of the porch with bungee cords and huddled up for the winter. When the new year came I took a temporary job teaching rudimentary writing skills to high school kids in rural eastern Oregon that took me away from Montana for two months.

When I got back, the snow had already started to thaw, and it kept thawing, in a quick and steady melt-off that turned Missoula's rivers to boiling mud.

There are several sorts of spring, water-wise. High-altitude temperatures can remain cold and the ice pack frozen well into what's supposed to be spring, delaying the front end of canoeing season, or the thaw can come fast and furious, melting everything at once, flash-flooding the rivers and flushing out in a matter of days. The latter means a short rush of too-dangerous deluge followed by a long summer of low water. The thaw can also start early and pace itself in sustained release, which means a long spring and decent chunk of summer when the water is just right for boating.

The water in the spring of 2011 was sustained, and it was high, but the twisty little upper Clark Fork, all sharp turns and undercuts, isn't anyone's idea of whitewater fun. That water is narrow enough to pin a tree trunk from bank to bank, and canoeing full-to-the-banks, pushy water, with nowhere to turn and a woody sieve between you and your destination is a good way to die an unpleasant death.

Instead I paddled a rocky section of the cold Blackfoot at 10,000 cfs—3,000 is more what I'm used to. I joined friends for a high-water float on the wider Clark Fork in Missoula, below the dam site, traveling in twenty minutes what usually takes an hour. We took out at the rock beach below the Finn & Porter restaurant (the water was too turbid to draw the otherwise de rigueur fly fisher), and walked up to the porch for a beer. Missoula's nice like that.

Long as it was, water-wise, spring turned into summer with seeming suddenness. Four full seasons cramp each other, no matter how you slice them. I took a few more trips down the Blackfoot, and a few on the Clark Fork through downtown. On a whim, I decided one day to float a section of the Bitterroot. I was sitting still in the middle of a wide spot in the river when a robin swooped upriver and landed on my head. I was surprised, and my fluster flustered the bird, which took off as soon as it realized where it was. I guess I looked like a log.

In mid-July I went with Quinlan and his wife, Jori, to the Canadian border and spent three days spinning down the North Fork of the Flathead River, the western borderline of Glacier National Park. We've done that every July for six years now and I look forward to it like I used to look forward to Christmas.

For Labor Day weekend I joined friends on an overnight on the main Flathead, below Flathead Lake, through Flathead Indian Reservation lands. We did nothing but drift, eating shore lunches of fresh-caught smallmouth bass fried in cornmeal and drizzled with lemon.

It was early October, after a month of trying and failing to interest a shuttle-driving second to join me, before I strapped the canoe on the truck and went back to the river I'd come for. I put in at the Arrow Stone Park in Deer Lodge, the county seat, where I'd taken out at the end of my last float the fall before. The sign at the road carries a cutout of an arrowhead almost exactly like the one the Anaconda Company used as its corporate logo. A couple of hundred yards downstream, someone had propped a sheet of plywood on an upturned crate to make a ramp for launching bicycles *Jackass*-style into the river's adjacent pool.

The first two miles sneak through the town of Deer Lodge and behind Montana's mothballed territorial prison, established in 1871, just a year after William A. Clark moved here to launch his banking career. Clark would later fund construction of a thousand-seat theater in the prison, just as he would build an amusement park in Butte called Columbia Gardens, where miners and their families rode Clark's trolley to congregate on weekends for roller-coaster rides and popcorn. Clark seems to have had almost a fetish for keeping the serfs entertained.

The old prison at Deer Lodge was closed in 1979 and was re-incarnated as a modern facility five miles west and farther from the river. The defunct original eats up two city blocks, a redbrick, inmate-built inner sanctum surrounded by a perimeter wall of sandstone four and a half feet thick, cornered with turrets that make it look like a medieval castle. Today the complex is a museum with a split personality, dedicated in equal parts to tours of the old stone fortress, now separated from Main Street by nothing but a sidewalk, and to an incongruous collection of classic cars accumulated by Sherm Anderson, who makes his hobby money operating Sun Mountain Lumber, a lumber mill just across the river from the old prison's back wall.

I pass between banks striated with rusty chemical orange slumping over eroded undercuts and nudge my way past glossy pillows of water hiding grassy root balls under the surface. Downwind of the lumber mill, with thousands of cut and trimmed logs stacked just back from the bank, the smell of sawn wood asserts itself and lingers around the next bend. On one bank a retired orange-and-black locomotive stands static on an isolated spur. On the other, edging a junkyard profusion of abandoned car parts and rusting construction equipment, a psychedelic school bus rots behind a barn. After I pass an RV park hosting a white-haired man looking at a laptop outside his Storm model travel trailer, I am out of town.

It's a blue-sky day with what Bob liked to call photographers' clouds and a tailwind pushing the canoe perpendicular to the banks. I spend a lot of time trying to pry myself straight with the paddle. There are too many shallow spots to just drift sideways. I glide over a chunk of white corrugated fiberglass paneling and past a corroded gas tank half-buried on shore and come to the river's first literal warning sign, in red and white lettering on a black and white background, stuck into the soil and framed with weeds blowing in the breeze.

HEALTH WARNING
HAZARDOUS MINE WASTE MATERIALS PRESENT
Ingestion, inhalation, or physical contact
with mine waste soils located next to the
Clark Fork River may be harmful to your
health. Avoid contact or, during high winds,
inhalation of any exposed sand-like soils
near the River that have little vegetation
or contain a white, blue, or green salt
appearance on the surface. For more
information please contact the
National Park Service at (406) 846–2070.

"Sand-like." I am standing in just such a slicken as the sign describes in a strong downstream wind. This slicken is an acre or so. Opportunity sits next door to four thousand of these.

This modest dead zone, more stunted than truly lifeless, probably owes its warning labels to its presence on the Grant-Kohrs Ranch, a 1,600-acre national historic site operated by the National Park Service on Deer Lodge's outskirts. In its heyday, the ranch's ten-million-acre empire skirted nothing; mere townships skirted it. Today it's a working ranch and interpretive site. The Park Service, unlike other entities up and down the river, has a budget for signs. I'll pass two more before I'm done for the day, and a couple more unsigned slickens, with their familiar blue and green pimples, forming raw gullies where runoff sluices into the river. A few feature wooden stakes flagged with pink nylon ribbon, presumably to direct the crews that will be following me downstream over the next several years, digging the bad patches out.

I also pass ducks, a goose, a plenitude of splashing fish, a deer, and what is likely either a mink or an otter. I hear him slide and I see the mud he trails cloud the water at the bottom of the bank. Later I scare two giant bald eagles off their perch in a lone cottonwood and watch them soar off downstream.

It's becoming easier to take the poison part for granted and ignore it in favor of the more immediate sensory experience. The distinct but conjoined sounds of rippling water and wind gusting dry grass is momentarily exquisite. The hills, starting to close in here at the tail end of the valley, are arranged in soft undulations and shadowed with the contours of weathered mudslides. Bright light gives depth and volume to their monochromatic swell, and for a minute I entertain the fancy that I could grab the hills' skin like the hem of a bedspread and unfurl it into the sky, snapping off the slickened soil and toppling the dwarfish pinyons, and let it waft back to rest refreshed.

Take away the fences, the concrete rubble, the mine waste, and the occasional noise blown over from the interstate and I could almost convince myself that I'm paddling through virgin Montana prairie, but then I don't know what virgin prairie would look like. The pinyons that look to me to be stunted by mine waste could just be the offspring of a naturally dry microclimate, growing exactly the way nature intended. The relative lack of river-bottom cottonwoods may be nothing more than the spotty expression of thin and naturally alkaline soils. Whatever "natural state" means, there's no sorting it out now.

Around another bend a four-cow crew of Black Anguses panics at my approach, deciding for some reason they'd feel safer on the other side of the river. They crash from their low beach across a shallow spot and up onto a high bench, lowing at me with what sounds like menace and probably would be, if they knew about the open bag of jerky between my knees.

Another couple of meanders and I'm at my takeout, a fishing access site off the feeder road called Kohrs Bend. The place was empty when I hid my bike in the bushes four hours earlier, but there's a bright red Ford truck parked there now, and I pass its owner on my approach to the sandy spit where I'm beaching the canoe. He's fishing from shore and I give him as wide a berth as the river allows, apologizing for disturbing his water.

He waves me off with the self-deprecation I've come to expect from fishers almost anywhere but Texas: "I'm not catching anything anyway."

I paddle the canoe up onto the sand and feel the abrasive grind shiver through the thin hull and up my thighs. I get out and walk into the river, just standing there, chilling my ankles and stiff knees, and watch the baldy I've chased downstream cruise the jittery gusts over the highway.

# PART V

# OPPORTUNITY

*It is narcissistic, vain, egotistical, unrealistic, selfish,*
*and hateful to assume emotional ownership*
*of a town or a word. It is also essential.*

—RICHARD HUGO, "The Triggering Town"

In the bicentennial year of 1976, a hundred years after Utah's Walker brothers sent Marcus Daly to inspect Butte's Alice mine, a group of DIY heritage buffs called the Deer Lodge County History Group compiled *Under the Shadow of Mt. Haggin: The Story of Anaconda and Deer Lodge County from 1863–1976.* It's one of a vanishingly few titles in the Anaconda public library that includes specific reference to Opportunity. The mention comes in the recollections of one Lorene Frigaard, who writes: "I don't think anyone very famous came from Opportunity, that is to my knowledge, like a president or a movie star. I think I can understand that."

I'd love to know what Lorene meant by that last part. What about a place precludes or predicts the spawning of greatness? There's nothing about nearby Deer Lodge, for instance, that would predict the birth there of Chicago Bulls and Los Angeles Lakers coach Phil Jackson (who now owns resort property on northwestern Montana's Flathead Lake, far from the former smelter's zone of influence). A peripatetic youth spent partly in Anaconda didn't keep Lucille Ball, daughter of an Anaconda Copper telephone lineman, from developing a sense of humor.

Opportunity had its best shot at glory in 1967, the year I was born. An underdog took the swing.

Brawling Roger Rouse was a bar fighter, NCAA boxing champion, and 1956 Olympian from what *Sports Illustrated* called the "hopefully named town in Montana." His dad, Jim, worked as a foreman at the Anaconda smelter's zinc-casting operation. Roger's own periodic stints at the smelter tended to end without two weeks' notice. Roger and his four brothers preferred to tie several on and tear shit up in the thirty-seven bars that then served Anaconda's twelve thousand citizens. *Sports Illustrated* profiled Rouse in November 1967, on the eve of his first world light-heavyweight title bout, challenging Biafran champion Dick Tiger, and the reporter couldn't resist asking Rouse about the origins of his hometown's name.

Rouse replied: "Somebody was trying to be funny, I guess."

With Montana governor Tim Babcock in attendance, Rouse fought a close fight in Las Vegas's convention center on November 17, scoring with quick jabs, but Tiger's heavy left hand eventually wore him down. After getting knocked to the mat for mandatory eight-counts in the ninth, tenth, and twelfth rounds, Rouse emerged the loser on a technical knockout. He was standing, bloodied, shaking his head no when the fight was called.

✝

Opportunity isn't much to look at. I was driving from Missoula to Butte the first time I saw the highway sign just before the ramp off of Interstate 90 at exit 208. Opportunity, Montana, sounded bucolic. It sounded good to say. I wanted to see what a place with that name looked like.

It looked pleasant enough that first brief drive-by, an uncrowded collection of modest homes, mostly single-story, many on plots of several acres. The lots were green and sometimes treed, and several housed horses in small pastures, or hayfields, or sprouted rows of steel-sided storage sheds for rent.

Opportunity isn't incorporated, and as far as the U.S. Postal Service and Census Bureau are concerned, it's of a piece with Anaconda, another five miles down Montana State Highway 1. Estimates of Opportunity's population run from three hundred on the low end to five hundred tops. The entire community amounts to some five hundred acres and sixteen streets, many little more than lanes stretching a country block or two, each named for a Montana governor up to John E. Erickson, elected in 1925. Montana continued to elect governors after 1925, but Opportunity didn't continue to grow.

Country Club Lane, bypassing residential Opportunity, accesses the Anaconda Country Club, a semi-dilapidated course built in 1918, largely segregated from Opportunity's residential streets by tiny Mill Creek, winding toward its junction with channelized Willow Creek, and then beneath I-90 into the Mill-Willow Bypass. Trees still cluster around the ribbon of Mill Creek.

Browsing deer shared the fairways with a couple of late-season hackers when I drove through that first fall day and I wondered at the weirdness of the dead-end amenity in such an out-of-the-way spot. It got odder driving down Stewart Street, Opportunity's spine and home to Solan's Grocery, a ramshackle corner store built in 1952 to replace an earlier version that had burned to the ground, Opportunity's sole retail establishment unless you count the resident who's converted his side lawn to a concrete yard-art emporium of pale birdbaths and garden trolls. The sign on the latter's chain-link fence said OPEN, but the place didn't look it.

That's not where I saw the man in the white hazmat suit, walking out from behind a garage; I might have passed it off as a cement artist's tool of the trade. This was at the other end of Stewart, unaccompanied by vehicles or obvious activity. Just one man out of doors, casually strolling down a driveway wearing what might as well have been a moon suit. I couldn't invent a reason for it.

I also couldn't really get a grip on the geography of Opportunity, concise as it seemed, until I pulled it up on Google Maps. At satellite scale, the pieces begin to connect. There's a tilting witch's hat formed by Interstate 90 on the east, Highway 1 running diagonally on the south, and Highway 48 running diagonally on the north. In the southeastern quarter of the hat is a pocket of green, transected at its eastern extremity by Silver Bow Creek, its barren floodplain stained tan. That pocket of green is Opportunity.

The northern half of the hat is an immense expanse of bleached white crust crisscrossed with rusty washes and gray roadbed. Zoom in and you can see patches of soil colored bright aqua with copper sulfate and, at almost dead center, a small heart-shaped recess filled with Caribbean-hued water. If you could airlift that blue charm 130 miles by helicopter, it might look right at home as one of Yellowstone's hot springs. These four thousand acres of bermed cells and piled plateaus are collectively the Opportunity Ponds.

They're called ponds not because the entire area, Opportunity included, was originally a creek-threaded wetland, which it was, but because the Anaconda Copper Company, having filled those wetlands with tailings and waste from the Anaconda smelter upstream, for decades kept them covered with water, both to settle metals out and to contain the dust. Largely dry, much of the ponds are now a vast, pocked plain of more or less loose, acidic, metallic dust, up to fifty feet deep. At the center of each cell is a depression designed to keep water from running off the mounds. From the sky the ponds look like a scab, partially stubbled with ingrown hairs of stunted vegetation. Zoom out and you can see how the deformed triangle overlays the delta spilling out of the mountains and across the valley, stretching toward the Clark Fork.

Deer Lodge Valley is the site of one of the first environmental lawsuits in the nation. For years before the big still-standing stack was built, the Anaconda Company's Old Works and Lower Works smelters had been carpeting the valley with a near-constant cloud of arsenic, sulfur, and lead. Downwind farmers started to complain about withered crops and of horses dropped dead in the fields with chemical holes burned through their muzzles. It was brought to President Teddy Roosevelt's attention that the smelter plume was also killing off large swaths of federal forest.

The plaintiffs of the resultant suit were mocked in company-owned newspapers as "smoke farmers," trying to milk a buck from the company with phony damage claims.

The company effectively outwaited Roosevelt, and settled its Deer Lodge problem by buying out valley landowners. It was their land now, and the company was unlikely to prosecute itself for polluting.

On a portion of that land, the company directed its own Deer Lodge Valley Farms subsidiary to develop Opportunity. Drain tiles—underground culverts—were installed to dry the swamp.

The land was platted into five- and ten-acre lots. Company man Henry C. Gardiner was installed to encourage the carefully engineered conclusion that Opportunity's air, soil, and water were not the least bit compromised. Opportunity was born as a fake garden community carved from a carcass of repossessed ranchlands, cheaper to destroy than to save.

The plots were sold at a discount to smelter workers and promoted with the promise of a healthful country life removed from the urban bustle of industrial Anaconda.

Early property deeds specified that if a deed-holding husband were to die before dispatching the mortgage, the company would forgive the remainder of the debt—a powerful mollification in a community riddled with early widows. Still, a typical deed, dated April 15, 1916, reserved certain tellingly particular rights to the company: "The flowage or deposition upon any of the above-described lands, of tailings, slimes and other debris, from or carried by, the Deer Lodge [Clark Fork] River, or the waters thereof, and subject to any and all rights now existing, to pollute or flow with slimes, tailings, chemicals or other debris, the waters of the Deer Lodge River; and the above premises and lands are hereby conveyed and taken and accepted by the grantee, subject to any injury or damage which may hereafter be caused thereto from the waters of the Deer Lodge River."

You could buy the company's land, but it would only partly be yours. One of the biggest, dirtiest industrial concerns of the twentieth century retained the right to shit in your yard.

In 1989, ARCO commissioned a "Cultural Resource Inventory and Assessment of the Opportunity Tailings Ponds" as part of the Superfund administrative record, and appended it to EPA's "Smelter Hill Remedial Investigation/Feasibility Study Operable Unit Work Plan." There have been millions of pages of documents like this generated over the course of the past thirty years, and no single human has read a fraction of them. Just the list of stakeholding and offshoot agencies—the Environmental Protection Agency, the Montana Department of Environmental Quality, the state Natural Resource Damage Program, the Army Corps of Engineers, the Bureau of Reclamation, the Clark Fork Council, the Clark Fork Task Force, the Clark Fork Technical Assistance Committee, etc.— makes a headache sound appealing. The collected paperwork was stored at the Hearst Free Library in Anaconda—Phoebe Hearst's vestigial philanthropy—until the collection outgrew the space. Now it's all filed in an office downtown, perusable by appointment. A librarian told me no one ever asked to see it anyway.

I haven't tried to read it all, but I did read the "Cultural Resource Inventory," which was undertaken to determine whether the erstwhile ponds contained sites that might require protection— from remediation—on the National Register of Historic Places. It turns out that history can't survive a four-thousand-acre blanketing of industrial refuse—surveyors found nothing much of note— but the document did prove the best accounting I'd found of the ponds themselves.

The Anaconda Company operated the Opportunity Tailings Ponds for tailings disposal from 1910 until 1972. The company built Pond 1, an expansion, in 1947, and Pond 2, another expansion, in 1955. From 1963 to 1985, the town of Anaconda used part of the site as a sewage dump. The survey covered the original ponds and Ponds 1 and 2, plus a seven-hundred-acre slag dump— 3,700 acres in total. The company regularly rebuilt and expanded the earthen dikes containing the ponds, and "consequently, many of the features that could be associated with the tailings ponds as historically significant have been buried or removed in the course of routine maintenance."

Indian projectile points, scrapers, cairns, and hearths dating to ten thousand years ago were found just south of the ponds, especially on the divide between Mill Creek and Deep Creek, where a chert quarry with two hundred hand-dug pits was operated between 1000 BC and AD 300. Just east of Anaconda is a prehistoric buffalo jump, and the surrounding area is littered with stone tipi rings and wooden wickiups in the forest. The valley was well watered and well traveled by prehistoric people, for much the same reasons, on an infinitely smaller scale, that drew Daly.

White prospectors arrived in the 1860s, followed by pioneers like Gwenllian Evans, Montana's first recorded female homesteader (and mother of the Anaconda Company's land agent Morgan Evans), in 1870, and Daniel Murphy, a placer-mining Irishman who settled in pre-Opportunity in 1871.

The first dikes were built in 1899, six years after Daly's first smelter fired up, and construction of the ponds proper began eleven years later. In 1914, the A Pond was constructed. Just three years later the Anaconda Company commissioned a study of what had already become a tailings disposal problem. The smelter was producing 12,860 tons of solid waste daily. Four more berm-dammed ponds were built to hold the crush. In a prescient echo of current restoration work on the Clark Fork, the dikes were strengthened with brush and log riprap to discourage erosion. The ponds averaged three feet deep, and were watered with diversions from Warm Springs Creek. Two new 2,080-acre ponds were built in 1919 as others were filled and abandoned. The company kept sixteen men on the payroll to operate the site.

In 1942, with advances in smelter technology and a wartime spike in copper prices, the company estimated it could recover seventeen million pounds of copper from the 800,000 tons of waste then in the ponds, but plans were abandoned when World War II ended in 1945, undermining demand. The leftover copper is still there, hundreds of millions of dollars' worth, along with the Indian projectile points and the buried remains of Gwenllian Evans's ranch, never to be seen again.

What's the difference between *The Lord of the Rings* and *Atlas Shrugged*? One takes place in a fantasy world, leaving its readers emotionally stunted and devoid of all capability for normal social interaction; the other is about Hobbits.

The third novel Bob gave me to read was *The Lord of the Rings*. Tolkien's trilogy was more comprehensible than Rand, but if Bob wanted me to follow in Aragorn's footsteps, he kept it to himself. It must surely have been the sense of quest he wanted to impart. He wanted me to have a meaningful life. Curiously, he must have wanted me to have it without reliance on any accomplishment of his; if there's a common theme connecting the heroes of *The Sword*

*in the Stone, Atlas Shrugged,* and *The Lord of the Rings,* it's that their
father figures are not, in fact, their fathers.

I'm hardly the first person who's been put in mind of Tolkien
while driving Interstate 90 past exit 208. Excepting blizzard conditions, or dust storms blowing off Opportunity's ponds, you can't
miss the Washoe smelter stack. It looms over the sparse landscape
like something spawned in Mordor. The smelter itself is three decades gone, but this last of its progressively taller chimneys still
stands sentinel on top of a low hill about five miles off the interstate, built of hand-laid bricks, reaching over seventy stories into
the sky. Its builders did handstands in the high winds on its rim,
wide enough to park a bus on. When the smelter was decommissioned in 1980, as ARCO buried or salvaged the infrastructure that
fed it, plans were made to tear the stack down. Anacondans pro-
tested. Anacondans are proud of their stack. They like to say that it
helped win two world wars, and it did.

In Tolkien's Middle Earth, the dark towers were citadels of evil,
the bad side of a good war. It's no longer possible in the American
West to see industry as the benevolent victory machine that drove
the mid-century imagination. Today, even from the interstate, the
despoliation dominates.

*The Lord of the Rings* is an almost perfect reversal of Arthurian
legend. Arthur becomes king when he pulls a sword from a stone,
wresting metal from rock. The ruler of men is a smelterman. Frodo's task, on the other hand, is to take a ring, the pinnacle of Middle
Earth's metallurgical art, corrosive in the hands of mortals, and un-
make it, de-refine it, return it to its elemental pre-smelted state.
Frodo's quest is to put metal *back in the mountain.* When he does,
Sauron's evil edifice falls, making the world safe again for layabout.

It's curious to remember that Tolkien wrote his trilogy at least
partly in response to the environmental degradations of the same
World War I that Anaconda copper helped the Allies win.

☿

Armed with nothing but sheer presumption, I applied for access to
the restricted cores of the Anaconda-Opportunity Superfund complex. Charlie Coleman, the Anaconda project manager with EPA's

Region 8 office in Helena, agreed to spend a few hours showing me around. I met him in the McDonald's parking lot in Anaconda.

I asked him to show me the places I couldn't get to on my own, the places with no public access, the places I'd be arrested for trespassing if I just went walking around. That led immediately to the Anaconda smelter stack.

The smelter itself was dismantled and buried or sold for scrap in the mid-1980s, and ARCO donated the land beneath the stack to the state, which designated it Anaconda Smoke Stack State Park. Only it's closed to visitors. The stack site has yet to be reclaimed.

The signs at its base warn of falling brick. Coleman told me that's liability-driven overcaution, that the structure is actually pretty sturdy. Still, I was required to wear a hard hat. The wind blew so hard that my voice recorder picked up only howl. I tried not to think about what a hard hat could and could not do against a brick with 585.5 feet of gravity-fed momentum behind it.

With the stack at your back you look north, up the Deer Lodge valley. The Clark Fork runs downstream away from you. The mountain of black slag in the foreground is half a mile long. The Opportunity Ponds in the relative distance cover more than six square miles.

Daly's engineers had struck an entirely elegant solution with their final smelter's location. Raw ore from Butte was freighted on trains to the top of Smelter Hill and dumped into the massive Rube Goldberg machine that was the reduction works, moving from one step of the process to another, following gravity downhill. The final products, metal ingots, were loaded on trains at the bottom and shipped to Great Falls for further refining. Anything that wasn't converted to money—un-retrieved metals, waste stone, chemicals, acids—was funneled downhill the same way, by gravity, into the Opportunity Ponds. The system, from hilltop to wetland, had been almost riverine.

We followed the waste downhill and up onto a dirt berm. The Opportunity Ponds are actually piles of dirt in various stages of rehabilitation: clean imported dirt in piles, odd thicknesses of mixed dirt carpeting dirty dirt beneath. There was no telling the difference with a naked eye. We passed a storage site for fill dirt and surfactant. Fill dirt, or "donor soil," is brought in from up and down the Clark Fork cleanup, or anywhere else ARCO or the state can find it, and tilled into contaminated soil, with maybe some manure and lime as well, depending on how contaminated it is. The surfactant is a gluey liquid acrylic polymer called "rhino snot" that, properly and frequently applied, helps prevent the dust of thousands of acres of bare dirt from flying into the windows and lungs of Opportunity. Contractors were in the process of seeding the site, rooted plants being the best way to keep the soil from running off and dust from blowing around.

This is called "treatment-in-place," and it's all the remediation the Opportunity Ponds are ever going to get.

About the only things vertical on the landscape were a dozen scattered "decanting towers." These are concentrated in the lower sections of the ponds, portions of which are, at least in terms of elevation, more or less original wetlands. They haven't been filled in. The abandoned towers once contained pumps to move pond water uphill to the smelter for industrial use, even as the depressions left behind were filled with industrial by-product. The decanting towers have vertical scaffolding so the water pump could be raised within the framework as each pond filled in and solidified. In the filled-in portions of the ponds, you can see the towers' metal tops poking out of the ground; you can only imagine the wetlands they once tapped.

The ponds are organized into "cells"—A, B, C and D—that roughly stair-step downgrade across the valley toward the Clark Fork. At the repository's eastern edge, an "interception trench" stalls and filters groundwater seeping out of the buried ponds. The muddy reddish stain is iron. The blue water immediately beyond is "wetland." Then there's Montana Rail Link's track, hard up on Interstate 90, where the semis pass. The blue water beyond I-90 is Warm Springs Ponds, full of the same toxic tailings.

This is as accurate a picture of the headwaters of the Clark Fork River as you're ever likely to see: filled, paved, and pinched between ponds full of poison.

⊹

The public face of Opportunity, to the dismay of some of his neighbors, is George Niland. He's fifty-six, with a wife and grandkids and dogs. He likes hunting and hot rods, and his blog posts tend to revel in the idea of their own political incorrectness, which is mild but distinct. When reporters need a quote about Opportunity, they generally call George.

I meet him at the twenty-four-hour Copper Bowl Cafe and Lanes in Anaconda. That's about five miles up the road from Opportunity, past the mile-and-a-half-long flat-topped grass pyramid of the Anaconda Tailings Pond and the half-mile-square, twenty-five-million-ton black slag heap and the decommissioned stack that decorate this stretch of Montana State Highway 1. There's no commercial establishment in Opportunity where we could meet.

Niland is rough around the edges, with a bit of the hangdog about him. This afternoon he looked a little like an inland pirate, with his ragged Fu Manchu mustache and green Carhartt overshirt, a camo-patterned do-rag clinging to his head. He looked at me over rectangular-framed glasses, refrained from smoking, and drank black coffee for two hours while we talked. I tried to match him cup for cup. When we parted company, I was shaking.

He was born in Anaconda's hospital and raised in Opportunity, in the house on two acres that his mother, eighty-one and healthy when he and I spoke, purchased in the early 1950s for $2,000. As a younger man, he had worked on the railroad and as a guard at the Anaconda smelter. Now he's on disability and repairs computers as a hobby. His three children and six grandchildren are scattered in Great Falls, Anaconda, and Bozeman. A brother-in-law works for Jordan Contracting in Anaconda, driving trucks across the ponds, part of the mini jobs boom generated by the Clark Fork's cleanup. George says he'd leave Opportunity if it weren't for his mother, but she's not going anywhere.

He attended school through sixth grade in the whitewashed Beaver Dam schoolhouse the Anaconda Company built for the community in 1914. The school was closed, on the heels of the smelter, in 1981.

Niland remembers the Clark Fork running either tobacco-colored or green from the mine tailings flushing out of the concentrator upstream at Butte when he was growing up. He called it Shit Creek. Neighbor kids played King of the Hill on the slag pile at the end of Stewart Street—the same slag spread as deicer on Opportunity's winter streets. The glossy black of it attracts snow-melting heat, and its glassy jaggedness provides bite on the ice.

Two of George's sisters died of cancer. Two of his mom's dogs died of cancer. He says he could name fifteen neighbors in Opportunity who have died of the disease. When he was forty-nine, George himself was diagnosed with a cancerous tumor on his spine. The doctors who removed it gave him a 70 percent chance of emerging a quadriplegic. He didn't.

It's almost pointless to try to quantify the direct health effects of living surrounded by so much metal. At least that's what everyone seems to have concluded, since no comprehensive health survey has ever been done. In a community of hundreds, or even thousands, the sampling populations are too small, and the factors too varied, to draw definitive conclusions. A decade ago, when Niland and a few others were starting to make noise about Opportunity's dilemma, activist Lois Gibbs—the woman who blew the whistle on New York's Love Canal to usher in the Superfund era—came to meet with the group. Niland says she told them not to bother trying to prove they were dying. It's incredibly hard to prove you weren't going to die anyway.

Even in Butte, with its larger population and localized exposure, no systematic study of environmental mortality rates was done until 2012, when University of Montana interdisciplinary studies doctoral student Stacie Barry presented a dissertation titled "Coming to the Surface: The Environment, Health, and Culture in Butte, Montana, 1950–2010."

"The Community does not track disease rates," Barry found, "and has never performed a longitudinal epidemiology study. . . . This study showed that the majority of mortality rates in Butte are greater than the state of Montana and United States rates for all disease groups, and that mortality rates fluctuate over time but are consistently elevated."

More tellingly, Barry's study showed that neither EPA nor ARCO *wants* the mining center's mortality rates specified. Both sought—and failed—to have Barry's study, and the data on which it was based, classified as confidential.

EPA's standard for earthbound arsenic in Opportunity is 250 parts per million. According to Niland, EPA tests of his yard came back at 167 ppm. Niland doesn't trust the results. EPA approves of ARCO's test methods, which involve taking multiple two-inch surface samples, mixing them, and then testing the mix to arrive at an average. If arsenic is found in the sample at a concentration of 250 ppm or above, the soil is further sampled to a depth of eighteen inches, and the contaminated portion of the yard is dug up, hauled away, and replaced. If the averaged concentrations in the top two inches are below 250 ppm, the yard is considered clean, and ARCO is done.

If the EPA took four samples, and three tested at 50 ppm arsenic, and the fourth—from a hot spot beneath a swing set, say—tested 500 ppm, he'd get a result much like the one he got. Safe. Not actionable.

Niland has a habit of asking unanswerable questions. Why was the downstream Superfund stretch cleaned up before the upstream work, which will continue sluicing poisons downstream? Why concentrate all the restoration wastes in Opportunity, so close to the headwaters?

I ask him a question of my own: What should be done?

Niland says that if he were in charge, he'd make ARCO buy Opportunity out, like it did in the 1980s with the smelter-centric community of Mill Creek, just across Highway 1. Move the residents and raze the houses.

But Opportunity lacks leverage. The Opportunity Citizens Protection Association (OCPA), an organization Niland helped found to watchdog ARCO and EPA, is idled now. When the Clark Fork Coalition showed up at the last OCPA-sponsored "Opportunity Days" picnic with four hundred pounds of barbecue and found no one there to eat with, OCPA stopped hosting the previously annual event. The group has dwindled from seven official members to four, and George has lost more friends than that over his advocacy. They say he's dragging property values down, as if his blog posts about "Toxitunity" were the only sign of what happened here.

"We got tired," George told me at the Copper Bowl. "We don't know what to do next."

⸙

It was December but hadn't yet snowed when I tagged along with University of Montana professor Robin Saha's environmental justice class to Opportunity. Saha is the man who led the fight to change the formal name of the Opportunity Ponds to BP/ARCO Waste Repository. His class was sampling the community's dust for heavy metals. They were looking for arsenic, cadmium, and lead. Nobody else was.

Dust sampling is harder than it sounds. First you have to find community members willing to invite you into unclean corners of their homes. Then you have to use a finicky little vacuum to collect samples in intricately labeled little jars. Then you have to pay to have the samples analyzed. Finally, with luck, you'll have an unaccredited sliver of evidence (the students aren't certified on the machinery, and so whatever they find isn't really officially admissible) that's at least measured in the kind of units that can be compared and contrasted with EPA standards.

This year's dusting is a follow-up to last year's dusting, which unfortunately employed a measuring technology that delivers results in milligrams per kilogram. EPA uses parts per million (ppm), and the math between the two is apparently insurmountable. This year the class is borrowing equipment from environmental consultant Jim Kuipers and Associates that yields ppm measurements. Now, if anyone wants to, they'll be able to compare at least a little bit of data on Anaconda's airborne dust exposure to what the EPA says, or may in the future determine, is a safe level.

Aside from the groundwater—the wells aren't known to be contaminated yet—dust is Opportunity's biggest current health concern. The Milltown sediments were supposed to anchor it with roots, but they failed to grow anything.

The students tested the interior and exterior of the Opportunity Community Center, one private residence, and Solan's corner grocery. They left flyers and published a press release in the *Anaconda Leader* inviting more participation. They'll return the following Saturday, if no snow falls, to try to hit another seven houses.

When you look at all the ought-to-be-basic things that need to get done in Opportunity, you'd think that a reasonably systematic analysis of the most obvious potential health threats in the homes of Opportunity would be near the top of the list. Start there. Noting the absence of such information, you have to wonder how badly anybody really wants to know. Any further findings could and probably would cost EPA and ARCO more time and money. There is no news that's likely to save any of either. What's the use of identifying a harm that's too big to do anything about? It'd just rile up the Nilands.

┼

The last smelterman on the Anaconda hill volunteers in a basement now. His name is Jerry Moran Hansen, and when I met him he was eighty-one years old.

The Marcus Daly Historical Society lives underground in Anaconda's old city hall, a compactly ornate redbrick structure built in 1896. The ground floor houses the Copper Village Museum and Arts Center, where the local quilting club meets, and a small hair salon. The second floor, structurally unsound, is unoccupied.

Jerry basically *is* the Marcus Daly Historical Society. There's no staff and no budget, just Jerry and his memory and his smelter salvage and whatever attic-cleaning locals might bring in to donate. The small space is a maze of radiator-sized copper ingots, parade sashes, and Ancient Order of Hibernians pins. Jerry holds court there a couple of days a week, when he feels well enough.

I kept arriving when he wasn't feeling well. I called for weeks trying to set up an appointment, but could never find him in. The woman who answered the phone upstairs finally gave me Jerry's room number at the Community Hospital of Anaconda, and I arranged to meet him there. He somehow looked dapper in blue-and-white print pajamas. He's got a sharp face and a standing shock of white hair that makes him look like a kind-eyed Samuel Beckett. The first thing he did was correct me. I liked him immediately.

"Probably a few things that you don't understand and don't know," he told me, "and most people don't know: This was not a copper smelter. This was the world's largest copper *reduction works.* Not a smelter. A smelter smelts concentrates. The reduction works creates concentrates *and* smelts them. It may have also been the world's largest manganese reduction works, because we did at one time produce 90 percent of the manganese concentrates in the world. This is not in stone, but it's fairly reasonable. It was also one of the largest zinc reduction works in the United States too. It was a large one, let's say that. It was a phosphate reduction works. It's also a ferromanganese smelter. I don't think that happened until near or after World War II."

Forty years later the reduction works themselves were reduced.

"They started laying people off . . . this is hard to remember, because they did it piecemeal. For one thing, they shut down the phosphate plant, which was a huge plant, and when you shut down the phosphate plant, you shut down the acid plant, and the acid plant produces acids for other things besides the phosphate plant. And there was the zinc plant . . . I'm not sure which went down first, but they shut down one, and then they shut down the other, then they reopened both and we went back to work for a while."

Eventually the re-openings stopped, and Jerry, who had performed nearly every job on offer at the Anaconda Reduction Works since going to work in the ferromanganese plant when he was eighteen, became a pensioner, first of ARCO and then of British Petroleum, which absorbed ARCO in 2002.

"I was the last smelterman off there," he told me, insisting that he meant it literally, "and I thought, this is too much to lose. So I was packing off every picture, blueprint, drawing, photograph, document—whatever I could lay my hands on—and giving it to a lady by the name of Alice Finnegan who organized our historical society in 1976. I have irritated her horribly. She called it the Anaconda–Deer Lodge County Historical Society, and I did change it to the Marcus Daly Historical Society, and she hasn't been too happy with me since, and there's a story in itself."

It was hard not to think of Grandpa Simpson wearing an onion tied to his belt—"which was the style at the time"—but I meant no disrespect in thinking it.

"We had the second-smallest railroad in the United States and the busiest," he continued. "There could be as many as thirteen ore trains a day into Anaconda, plus passenger service." That wasn't counting race days, when two special trains a day delivered horse-racing fans to the Anaconda track. "Daly's horse-racing track here was the finest in the West," Jerry affirmed. I asked if it was even finer than the one in Butte, where Daly had also built a track.

"Butte likes to claim all sorts of things," Jerry sniffed.

Trying to straighten his eyeglass frames on a bedside stand, he said, "I've been sleeping on them. They're no good like this." He finally put the glasses away.

"My grandfather, John Francis Moran, was a Molly Maguire," Jerry said. His hands rattled and he took in my confusion with what looked like resignation. "You don't know a Molly Maguire—those were the Irish coal miners who started the union movement in the United States, and he was one of them. He did not have to be one here, because Daly was a man who never forgot his roots. My grandfather, the Molly Maguire, he was dead twenty-two years when I was born, but my family was steeped in the union movement. I don't know when they first got here. The thing is, they were Irish revolutionaries, and my great-grandfather had to get the hell out of Ireland by the dark of the moon, and he left my great-grandmother and I think all his kids in Ireland, and he didn't stop till he got to Fort Benton. Then he went down to, uh—why the hell am I dropping all these things all of a sudden? He was just trying to get out of Ireland. It was the second capital of Montana."

"Virginia City?" I ask.

Yes. "My grandmother was born there in 1872. He then went from Virginia City to Meaderville, in Butte.

"There's one thing you have to understand about the Irish," Jerry says. "They don't talk a hell of a lot about themselves. They'll talk about everything else, but themselves not so much."

Jerry, for instance, would rather talk about Marcus Daly, a man who died thirty-one years before Jerry was born. "He was an ardent Democrat, and there was another Irishman here by the name of Jack Morris, and Morris had a saloon over around Front Street someplace. Morris was some sort of a socialist, and Daly was a Democrat. So he went into Morris's saloon one night and tried to talk some sense into Jack, and it wasn't very good, and finally Daly blew his cork and he just chewed the rear end out of Morris in front of everybody, and of course the joint was packed, they all were, and he really reamed him out. And Daly went back the next night and he says, 'Jack, I had no right to scream at you as I did, and I apologize.' And that's one of the most powerful men in the West apologizing to a saloon keeper.

"I've had people come in and interview me"—Jerry has served as a consulting historian for numerous books and documentaries— "and one guy said one time, he says, 'Everybody speaks of Daly as if he was a saint.' I said, 'He was!'"

Daly was long gone by the time Jerry signed on at the reduction works, but the great man's stamp, he says, was still on the place even half a century after his death. Jerry was there long enough to see the stamp fade.

"Problem was, it wasn't being run by somebody whose mind, spirit, and heart were in the operation."

I ask if he means ARCO.

"Well, even before . . . it was being run by bean counters who weren't really interested in producing. There was a time, at least from what I understand of industrial America, corporations were run by people who founded them, who wanted to produce aircraft, machine bolts, whatever. That was what they were interested in. These other people with the lawyers, the bean counters, they just produced *stuff* . . . and I think maybe this is something that has kind of thrown a wet towel over American industry, because it's money, it's profit, it's not product. I think that's the problem, and this damn near happened to us."

Jerry goes on: "There was a valve company that wanted us, and I want to say Nibco, but I'm not sure that it was Nibco. What they were going to do was buy the company and sell off all its profits. No pensions, nothing, and we were shit out of luck. The guy who was head of the Anaconda Company at the time, he sold it to ARCO, he said that he held the company back from Nibco—I don't think it *was* Nibco—because they were not going to guarantee pensions. Timco wanted Anaconda too, and he wouldn't sell it to Timco. He sold it to the corporation who guaranteed the pensions, which—bless that fellow. I think you can go on and say 'bless BP' too, because they guaranteed pensions after they bought it."

Jerry isn't one to indulge knee-jerk reactions against "the Company," but he does acknowledge that Anaconda's story has turned the corner from industrial fable to environmental cautionary tale. Even so, he doesn't think that story has been properly comprehended either.

"I don't think enough people understand what happened here.

I assume you understand that arsenic is a horrible thing. Well, I'll tell you one thing about arsenic. It's *delicious*. I got a mouthful one night and, oh, it was good. It's sweet. I've never smoked in my life, but I used to hear everybody else who smoked complaining about arsenic making their cigarettes taste sweet. So that one night, it was night shift, going in to work in a boiler, I looked up like that." He cranes his face skyward. "Opened my mouth, *plop*, and I thought 'oh boy.' But not even a stomach ache."

Jerry fiddles with his glasses again and asks when I think I can come back. He'd like to meet me in the basement archive, where his memories are more accessible. "They've been telling me for eighteen days I'll be out tomorrow, so I don't know when, but give me a call next week and maybe we can make arrangements to talk. Maybe I can add a little coherence to it."

On my way out the door I ask him what he's in for.

"I think it's my kidneys. All of a sudden my calves swole up like that, turned purple, and they were telling my family they thought I was going to lose my legs, but I knew I wasn't. My grandfather John Francis Barry died, and it was his kidneys. This seems to be an Irish thing. My mother told me one time that the doctors told him it was because he chewed tobacco. Perhaps. But I run into an awful lot of that. My great-grandmother Barry died of it. John Francis Moran died of it. My mother died of it, and I had a couple of uncles die or come close to it. And just going through the old newspapers researching, there's a lot of Irish died of kidney failure."

Even low levels of exposure to arsenic in drinking water have been linked to increased incidence of kidney disease.

"I may have just escaped it," he tells me. "I could be out, oh, maybe Monday or Tuesday."

I call Jerry at home the following week, but he's still in the hospital. A week later I try again, and this time he's home. He's not feeling well, though, and doesn't know when he might make it back to his basement post. He sounds grumpy, and though I've called only when he's asked me to, I don't want to keep bothering him. I give him my number again and ask if he'll call me later when he's feeling better.

"It's not about feeling better," he barks back at me. "It's about *being* better."

꩜

On December 16, 2011, I was one of a couple hundred history-conscious Missoulians who walked out onto a snow-covered bluff above the old Milltown Dam abutment to see something you almost never get to see: a river tangibly restored. Below us, the Clark Fork began to spill down its reconstructed streambed, joining the also-undammed Blackfoot River in free flow for the first time since the dam was built in 1908. We took pictures, though the visuals weren't dramatic. A wall of water crashing down the valley would have looked much cooler.

At first, as earthmovers upstream breached the embankment that kept the river in its temporary bypass, the restoring confluence was just a trickle you could step across—not that anyone was allowed down there to do that. By the end of the day, it had washed out its mouth and was flowing full bore in its new custom-made bed. Now it's a river. Parks are planned, and the banks have been planted, but the confluence won't be open to through-going canoeists for another couple of years.

Just two days before standing on that bluff and watching the new confluence, I'd gone to Anaconda for a town hall meeting with EPA. It was twenty degrees Fahrenheit and blowing snow that night, and I was one of about thirty people sitting on benches in the main courtroom of the county courthouse. EPA's Charlie Coleman was there, along with a representative of the Clark Fork River Technical Assistance Committee. ARCO was not. The update concerned the Opportunity Ponds.

The first speaker, consultant Gunnar Emilsson, referred repeatedly to "the Opportunity Ponds" until a man in back raised his hand and asked if Emilsson was aware that the name of the site had been changed. Some Opportunity residents would just as soon disclaim naming rights to the poisoned perpetuity next door, and had successfully petitioned to change the site's name to better reflect its management and function. It was one of Opportunity's few victories. Emilsson didn't know what the man was talking about.

"What's it called now?"

"BP/ARCO Waste Repository," he was told.

"Okay," Emilsson said, sighing. "Well, the site's official name is Opportunity Ponds, as reflected in the Record of Decision [EPA's guiding document for site management], but you can call it whatever you want."

Emilsson gamely stumbled over the new name two or three times and then reverted to "Opportunity Ponds." Everybody does, even the newspapers, which ought to know better. I do too. The landscape has already been stripped of integrity. Why deny it this perverse poetry?

BP/ARCO had been faced with two concurrently pressing problems. First, the company needed someplace to remove the Milltown sediment to. Second, upstream at Opportunity, it needed topsoil. The predictably bad news, formally admitted for the first time at the town hall meeting, is that the toxic sediments made for poor topsoil. The Milltown waste had been shipped and prepped and spread and planted on a portion of Opportunity's ponds, but nothing had grown on it. We saw slides of shriveled roots.

Everything that Opportunity had been told was false. ARCO had gotten what it wanted: the Milltown sediments disposed of. Dennis Washington had gotten what he wanted: a fat contract to haul the spoil. Max Baucus had gotten what he wanted: a press release lauding his helping hand in restoring Missoula's confluence of historic rivers. Missoula had gotten what it wanted: the Milltown wastes gone. All Opportunity got was lied to.

When the Milltown Dam came down and the trains started rumbling the dredge toward Opportunity, resident Connie Ternes-Daniels had told reporters, "This is a good thing, but some are paying the costs. We're sacrificing for everyone else." Opportunity had been assured that the toxic sediments were nothing to worry about. It had repeatedly been reported that the Milltown sediments—a tiny fraction of the waste that had already transformed Opportunity's ponds into low plateaus—were in any case less toxic than what was already there.

That also turned out to be false. Dennis Neuman, a Bozeman-based reclamation specialist and EPA adviser, informed the crowd that contrary to projections, tests showed that the new cap of Milltown dirt is up to five times *more* toxic than the toxic dirt it covers. Since the entire purpose of the project was to keep unsecured toxic dust from flying across the community's windowsills, importing the Milltown sediments had only made the problem worse.

A woman up front raised her hand and said, "Everybody here is feeling really betrayed. You guys have had information that we didn't have."

Opportunity's residents seemed to have a hard time grasping the full blatancy of what they had just been told. One man at the meeting insisted that the Milltown waste be "sent back to Missoula" since it hadn't worked as advertised. Another asked, "Any more secret stuff we ought to know about?" The crowd laughed. Coleman, the EPA's much-abused but well-liked project manager and spokesman, said, "We are learning new stuff all the time."

It's a fact worth noting, though I'd never heard it mentioned before that meeting, that the Milltown sediments were never studied for their suitability as topsoil in Opportunity. Why wouldn't you study that? Because it didn't matter. The Milltown sediments weren't imported to Opportunity to cap the ponds. The Milltown sediments were imported to Opportunity because ARCO needed someplace to dump them. If they somehow worked as topsoil too, then ARCO saved the expense of buying and hauling clean new dirt from elsewhere. Regardless, the waste had to go somewhere. Waste always does. It doesn't disappear. It just gets kicked down the road.

EPA exercises approval and oversight of ARCO's remediation responsibility. At that December 14 meeting, EPA said ARCO had until spring to come up with a viable plan for providing six to eighteen inches of functional soil—in which plants could grow—on top of Opportunity's Milltown mess. Come May, EPA extended the deadline. ARCO's dilemma, EPA had been persuaded, is the kind of thing that requires further study.

☨

In December 2011, the state's crews were working, atypically late into the season, on Silver Bow Creek as it winds past Opportunity, between the ponds and the interstate. I pulled over at the little bridge crossing where I'd first launched my canoe the year before. The pullout pad was fenced off now, and the muddy slope where I'd slipped my boat into the water was buried under a uniform spread of gray-white rocks. Looking upstream, what had been a gentle arc was now purposefully serpentine, lined on one side with a new fabric mat retainer. The creek itself was still running even in mid-December, but constrained to a third its width by creeping bank ice. On river left, a stack of ice shards a foot thick and as big as a kitchen table had been stacked on a bend, busted out of the freezing creek to create access to the shore. On river right, a yellow John Deere excavator was scooping contaminated soil into a pile a hundred yards back from the bank. Dump trucks raced up and down a dirt road, loading portions of the pile and ferrying them back across Highway 1 to the Opportunity Ponds. A stork-like tripod of blue pipe levered an elevated nozzle over the road, where it could water the contents of the passing trucks to tamp down dust, but on this day at least the trucks didn't stop and the nozzle didn't dispense.

George Niland's dog wanders over to meet me when I pull into his drive. Niland's house is blue-sided, single-storied, and low-ceilinged. The property is unfenced, and George says someone's called Anaconda Animal Control to complain. It can't be his neighbors, he says, because his dog doesn't leave the property. If he has a suspicion, he doesn't say, but he knows more than a few people in the valley have grown tired of him. Those are the people—the majority of them, he says—who "don't *want* to know."

Out Niland's front windows, across the street, is the ribbon of green following Mill Creek through the Anaconda Country Club's golf course. Beyond the golf course, the greenery abruptly turns to a patchwork of gray and brown where Opportunity's streets dead-end into ARCO's gated holdings at Country Club Road. Four thousand feet beyond Country Club Road begins the blistered, treeless expanse of the Opportunity Ponds. When the dust rolls in off the ponds, it first rolls over Niland, his wife, and his dog.

That's one reason Niland fought to finally have an airborne dust monitor installed two years ago, a quarter of a century after the property was listed as a Superfund site. He drives me out to the site to show me where the mobile monitor sat until six months ago, when EPA cut the funding it feeds to Anaconda–Deer Lodge County, leading the county to cut the air-monitoring program. The road dead-ends at a gate, behind which the dirt track continues to a still-wet pond behind a scrim of cottonwoods. When Niland was a kid, the gate wasn't there. He'd walk the road on hot summer days to swim in the "slum ponds."

The county government, preoccupied with the relative population centers of Anaconda and Deer Lodge, treats Opportunity like a redheaded stepchild, in George's opinion. We drive by a case in point: the new Beaver Dam Park, "established 2011." The park's centerpiece is the Beaver Dam School, built by the Anaconda Copper Mining Company to educate the children of the company's newly landed employees. The building has sat empty since its closure, along with the remains of the company that founded it, in 1981. Niland attended elementary school there, and he'd like to see it restored as some sort of interpretive center or historical society.

Niland and a few neighbors had to fight just to keep the school standing, though two back wings were demolished. The structure, like many its age, is riddled with asbestos insulation and fireproofing, making rehab an expensive proposition. The county, Niland says, wanted to raze it. Niland has applied to put the property on the National Register of Historic Places. For now the old schoolhouse is mothballed, its windows boarded up, doors padlocked, the whole thing painted ghostly white and surrounded by an eight-foot-high wire-topped chain-link fence. It looks like a tomb anchoring 9.52 acres featuring a pavilion, a small playground, a pickup baseball field, and a blacktop track lit with lights mounted to poles modeled on a style commonly cast at the old Anaconda Foundry Fabrication Company. Eventually, Beaver Dam Park will serve as the trailhead of a greenbelt slated to follow Silver Bow Creek all the way upstream to Butte. Of all the trails in Montana, it's hard to imagine this one seeing much traffic.

EPA standards allow for higher levels of soil-bound arsenic in the park than in, say, a residential yard, on the theory that a park receives only periodic use. Still, contractors had to remove and replace eighteen inches of contaminated soil from the site, at Opportunity's northern edge, to meet safety standards. Niland lives just a few blocks west. His yard, EPA keeps telling him, is fine.

We continue our Opportunity tour past the new communal cow pasture ARCO donated to the community, past the old communal cow pasture that ARCO has closed off for reclamation, and past another gated dirt road into the ponds, behind which the remains of a corral and the foundation of the old Gwenllian Evans ranch—Gwendale—are still visible. We cross a ribbon of water that George calls "the yellow ditch." He says it was used as overflow for excess tailings when the Butte mines worked overtime and Silver Bow Creek couldn't handle the load. The yellow ditch runs straight into the ponds along Opportunity's western edge. It was remediated by ARCO last summer, while I was canoeing Silver Bow, but not restored. The banks hold no vegetation but weeds. Its surface is stiff with milky blue ice.

We pass low pits in the fields, "borrow areas" where ARCO has poached piles of soil to move somewhere else that soil is needed, and then out onto Highway 1, beneath the empty space where a wooden flume once funneled smelter waste overhead, across the road, from Smelter Hill down to the ponds.

We cross the highway and head southwest onto Mill Creek Road, in the literal shadow of Smelter Hill. Somewhere under that upslope soil, lined vaults entomb too-dangerous-to-move industrial poisons. Beryllium is the one everyone in the neighborhood whispers about. It was used to make an experimental copper alloy, the strongest of the copper alloys, and a useful toolmaking metal in industrial applications because it doesn't spark. Beryllium-copper tools protected smelter workers on the hill, but the liquid form, the sort buried in drums up there, is a Category 1 carcinogen.

Niland recalls the story of a tractor driver, working the ponds after the smelter shut down, who uncovered a stash of buried beryllium. The uncomfirmable rumor was that the tractor driver died within weeks. The beryllium was moved to a repository on Smelter Hill. Later, Anaconda planners were celebrating the redevelopment of an urban plot at the foot of Smelter Hill just as contractors breaking ground for a new Bi-Rite grocery store uncovered more barrels of beryllium. Bi-Rite pulled out. Nobody wants anything to do with the stuff.

We drive past the former community of Mill Creek, where dozens of homes hugged the neighborhood's eponymous waterway a mile southwest of Opportunity. When the smelter shut down, ARCO razed the homes and paid to relocate the residents. We turn back east on Willow Glen Road, where dump trucks and earthmovers have been busy scraping toxic soil from the landscape. Willow Glen is directly downwind of Smelter Hill, and directly upslope and upstream of Opportunity. Niland tells me that aside from the dust, he's less worried about metals in the Opportunity ponds, downstream of his home, than about metals in Willow Glen, upstream. Sampling has detected a huge arsenic plume in the groundwater beneath Willow Glen. The plume appears to spill downslope toward the river, but scientists say it stops right at Highway 1, just upstream of Opportunity. Nobody was quite sure why until a hydrologist discovered that the old Anaconda Company had built an underground dewatering ditch just across the highway from Opportunity. The ditch diverts the upstream plume of water into Willow Creek, and thence untreated into the Clark Fork. So far the ditch has protected Opportunity's wells, but there's no contingency for maintaining the century-old system, and it will eventually, inevitably, fail.

We cross I-90 to the old dirt Eastside Road running alongside the Warm Springs Ponds. The terrain is elevated here and we look down on acres of recently groomed soil where ARCO remediators have cannibalized clean fill from the recently remediated fields, shuttling remediated dirt from one place to dilute dirty dirt at another. I learned that's what was going on only later. George didn't know. "They don't keep us informed at all."

Driving back through Opportunity to Niland's house, I tell him the story of my first impression of Opportunity, the man coming out of his garage in the white hazmat suit. Turns out George knows the guy. He works at the Montana Resources molybdenum plant in Butte, where they have access to disposable white Tyvek coveralls. He brings them home and wears them while mowing his yard to keep his clothes clean.

Accurate assumptions in Opportunity are hard to come by.

George worked for Montana Resources too, for eleven years. He worked on the crusher and in the flotation unit. For a while he drove a haul truck. His dad, a crane man with the Anaconda Company, died of kidney failure at thirty-two.

George hunts elk in the mountains around Opportunity and smokes his own sausage. He's built a little man cave out back with a woodstove in the corner, where he can smoke his Marlboro Reds out of the weather and tinker with computers, but what he's most proud of he saves for the end of our visit. It's parked in the garage, a 1969 purple Plymouth Satellite with a rare flower power "mod top." He bought it used in 1976 and has restored it to mint if not entirely original condition over the last few years. There's a bank of speaker boxes where the back seat should be. Its back axle is up on blocks in the garage while the rear end is being rebuilt. It hasn't been out in a while, and it's collecting dust.

I look a little too long at the dust. We've driven a full circle around Opportunity, from one remediation site to another, the ponds due north, Smelter Hill due west, Mill Creek and Willow Glen due south, Silver Bow Creek and the Eastside Road due east. George Niland and his Plymouth and his family are the supposedly exempt doughnut hole at the eye of the Superfund storm.

"This cleanup has been going on for twenty years," he tells me. "It's completely surrounded this community. It's all around us. But we're clean?"

George Niland is an idiot. That's what Don Wyant thinks, and Don Wyant thinks he should know. He's known the neighbor he calls "Georgie" since he was "this long"—his use of the word "long" instead of "tall" telling you everything you need to know about how many years he's known Georgie Niland. Don used to be hunting buddies with George's dad, and used to salvage scrap iron with him from the long-defunct smelter site on the north side of the valley when the southside smelter that replaced it was shut down with strikes. The scrap iron brought them $8 a ton, which was a long day's haul, but in the 1950s a day's wage at the smelter was only $11.11.

"You're talking to a guy that's bitter," Don tells me. "Against ARCO. His dad died. His dad had Blight's disease or something like that"—"Bright's disease" is an antiquated term for a range of kidney diseases—"he died down here. So Georgie lost two sisters down here. His sister died of brain cancer or something, you know. If it was caused by arsenic in our water, we'd all be dead by now. We all been using it all these years. I been down here since 1950.

My wife died, but she didn't necessarily die of cancer. She had bad kidneys. Sure as hell wasn't from drinking the water or I'd have been dead. I'm eighty-four, hadn't hurt me. I'm still working."

The logical fallacy at play here is called proof by anecdote: the presumption that one's personal experience has descriptive and predictive powers applicable to broad populations. It's a useful presumption for writers, less so for doctors.

George Niland had suggested I go see Don for a different perspective. It was Sunday afternoon and Don was in his shop, a pack rat's warren dense with metal tools hung from hooks, separated from his house by a fenced yard full of molded concrete lawn ornaments for sale. He sat next to a massive iron woodstove, spray-painting an indeterminate trinket black. He wore blue jeans, rainbow suspenders, a green, flannel-lined work shirt, and an orange-and-black camo-patterned hunter's cap over a thatch of white hair. His hand, when I shook it, was gnarled and hard.

Don was born and raised in Anaconda, moved with his family to North Dakota, entered the Marine Corps, and moved back to Opportunity when he got out of the service. His dad still owned a house in Anaconda, but "we didn't see eye to eye anyway," and he came back more for a brother and for the work. Don is a pipefitter. He worked at the smelter for thirty-two years, and when the smelter shut down he started commuting to the concentrator at Butte. He retired in 1987 and started collecting the pension checks he still gets in the mail every month: $540. To make up the difference between his pension and the cost of living, he built a shop and repaired washers, dryers, and refrigerators until his Social Security kicked in at sixty-two. When the shop burned down he bought an inventory and went into the lawn ornament business, selling to anyone who might care to buy.

"I don't advertise. Once in a while somebody'll come in and want something. It ain't no good for a winter business," he says.

Don is of two minds about the cleanup. On one hand, he thinks that ARCO has done an excellent job.

"I do. I got no bitches against them. I worked and raised nine kids when I worked for 'em all those years. They always treated me fine, and if I didn't like it I'd have got the hell out of here. If I felt like some people feel, I wouldn't stick around—if I thought my kids was being bothered." As for the Opportunity Ponds, he says, "I think they're a hundred percent better than they were. We got grass growing over there, we got moose over there, we got antelope over there, we got deer over there. We never had them before. No, I think they've done wonderful."

On the other hand, he thinks money is being wasted, just because ARCO is compelled to pay.

"All they're doing is taking the dirt from there and moving it to someplace else. I think that, oh, it might take a hundred, two hundred, three hundred years, but I think the earth heals itself anyway. They should've left the creek alone. You see that piece across from the overpass that they're working on now? That was sagebrush. In the fifties it was all sagebrush. I don't know why they tore that up. There was no smelter over there."

Don's got no patience with "Georgie's" sentimentality about the old Beaver Dam School. The mention of it makes him raise his voice.

"The schoolhouse! Why put two million dollars into that when later on the kids'll get doped up and they'll go down and rip the damned thing apart? They should've leveled that out and planted grass and forgot it, the schoolhouse right with it. Why certainly that's a waste of money. Who the hell's gonna use that park? *I'll* never use it! We've only got a few people down here. We used to have lots of kids. I had nine of 'em myself down here. They're all still living except the two. One was born with a bad heart, and the other was in a car wreck down here. That isn't nothing to do with pollution."

Which is not to say that there was no pollution.

"The company, they had everything up in that damn place, they had stuff you couldn't live around, and we worked on it all the time. I bet you they used to dump four or five train cars of acid a day up on the high line, up by the stack, and that went into the system for flotation to recover the copper. They used some awful stuff, they used cyanide, barrels and barrels of cyanide, and they mixed it up at—they called it the Dead Horse. And this cyanide was skull and crossbones on the cans that you dumped. A friend of mine, Owen Miller, used to run the Dead Horse, he used to mix all that stuff up there. See, the hill, when it was laid out, they dumped the ore way up high, then it went through all the crusher systems, then it come down and went through the mills, then it went through the flotation to get the copper off of it after it was crushed and the tailings went out here." Don points toward the Opportunity Ponds.

Don tells me the same story George had told me about the worker who uncovered a stash of fifty-five-gallon beryllium barrels buried in the ponds and "didn't live very long afterwards."

"The only thing I didn't agree with," he tells me, "is they took all this beryllium that they had over here and they dug it up and they hauled all that up the hill again. They put that plastic lining up there by the smelter, up by the stack someplace. These weren't concrete—they just had it lined with plastic. That's a real bad stuff, beryllium. I would think it'd been better to take it and dump it in one of the old mines or something, some place where they're not going to ever use it."

Butte's Berkeley Pit, for example? "Why not? It's contaminated beyond repair. They'll never clean it, not in a million years. I worked around it. I know."

Don does not seem bothered that this is exactly the logic behind the designation of the Opportunity Ponds as the waste repository for the entirety of the Clark Fork cleanup. He's not particularly worried about it. The ponds are downslope of Opportunity, and what's downslope flows, if it flows, away.

What concerns him more is upstream, above Butte, the Yankee Doodle Tailings Ponds filling what used to be Yankee Doodle Gulch, impounded behind one of the largest earthen dams in the world and growing by 250-ton truckloads every day. "That's what worries me," Don tells me. "If someday all of that mud breaks loose, it's gonna cover Butte. It's gonna go down in the flats. It was moving here about thirty years ago. They were worried about that dam, 'cause it was moving downhill."

In the meantime, he thinks, Opportunity is healing itself. The horses in his neighbor's pastures are proof.

"When I first come here, I bought me a horse in '51," he says. "It wasn't even two years and he was running into the side of the barn. Arsenic ate the roof out of his mouth, toward his brain, from eating that arsenic close to the ground, eating that grass." Don calls the affliction "the blind staggers."

"There was arsenic on top of the ground fifty years ago. You couldn't keep a horse out in the pasture. It'd die in two or three years."

Cows were a different story, he says. They don't browse so close to the ground, and so don't ingest as much arsenic as grazing horses.

That's in the past anyway. The smelter has stopped spewing since then, and three decades of time and rain and snow and ice have filtered the arsenic into the soil, diluting it and washing it downstream. "It goes down into the ground, and it's out of our reach. It don't come back up! Water goes north from here. I know that from digging big holes. Throw a leaf in it, I don't care if there's no wind, it'll go north! Always has down here. Dig a fence post and you watch the water, you can see it moving. It's downhill all the way."

We've been talking for several hours and it's getting late in the day. I thank Don for his time, and put on my coat to leave. He doesn't seem to want to let me go. He's asked and knows I'm from Texas, so he tells me about one of his sons who's in the air force there, retiring this year after thirty years of service, building himself a house near Houston, Don thinks, or close to the Dallas Cowboys stadium, he's not sure. Then, as I creak the heavy shop door open into the wind, he asks me: "Are you thinking about moving to this area?"

"Somewhere up or down the river," I tell him, though this is a lie. I wouldn't touch title to property in Opportunity with a ten-foot pole. It's not exactly what I came to Montana for. It's exactly not what I came to Montana for.

Leaving town, I detour off Stewart Street down a dirt road that dead-ends into the overpass abutment of Highway 1. I want to get a closer look at the excavator at work down there, loading the parade of dump trucks with fresh fill for Opportunity's ponds. I take a few pictures, turn around, and drive back toward Stewart Street to head home. Just past the little bridge crossing, a worker holding a road sign reading "Stop" on one side and "Slow" on the other flags me down. I stop and a clean-cut man steps out of an Envirocon truck and walks up to my window. He'd been watching me. He is polite.

"Would you mind not driving down that road again?" he asks. "That's private property. It belongs to ARCO, and it's contaminated."

┼

What does it mean to be contaminated? Is Opportunity a safe place to live? I've asked everyone. Everyone has an opinion, and nobody knows. Everyone tells me to talk with Jim Kuipers.

Kuipers doesn't know either, but he has a pretty good guess. In a moment of frustration, he once made a suggestion to John Wardell, the then-director of Montana EPA, whom Kuipers admires. "I should get a bunch of dump trucks and go to everybody's yard in Helena that works for EPA," he told Wardell, "and let's put the same soils there that you're leaving in place in here. I'm going to spread it on all of *your* yards."

Wardell, who subsequently died in a mountain-climbing accident in 2009, hadn't taken the needling between friends lightly.

"I was told," Kuipers recalls, " 'If you do that again, that will be taken as a threat toward a federal government official. I will have you thrown in jail if you even threaten that again.'

"My point is, they should be living in this community, not doing their things here, giving us the runaround, and then driving back to Helena. If you really think it's clean, bring your family here, prove to us that you would put your own family in the same circumstance you're asking everyone else to live with here. And you know what I've been told? 'Hell, no, I wouldn't, but that's beside the point, Jim.' "

Kuipers keeps business hours in Butte and in Anaconda, where I meet him in an office lined with cheap veneer bookcases filled with thick white binders of environmental-impact statements and mine-site assessments. He lives sixty miles from the Superfund zone, in Wisdom, near the Big Hole River. Kuipers can afford to choose, and he chooses safe over sorry.

"The problem is we don't know."

The problem isn't just that no one knows, but that thirty years after the community became the epicenter of a Superfund site designated in response to apparently imminent environmental health threats, nobody has bothered to find out. I had assumed that must be EPA's job. The public perception of EPA, especially in years of Republican anti-regulation rhetoric, is of a fire-breathing enforcement agency in jackboots, grinding its heel into the gasping neck of American industry. Not in Anaconda.

By Superfund law, ARCO, having assumed the lead role in cleaning up Anaconda and Opportunity, gets to do its own tests and propose its own "remedies." EPA gets to approve ARCO's science and plans or, if they prefer the prospect of drawn-out litigation, send them back to the drawing board. ARCO rarely gets sent back to the drawing board.

EPA is outgunned. That's what Kuipers thinks, and he would know. He's worked both sides.

Kuipers was born in Butte and raised by educator parents in central Utah, spending summers in Cook City, Montana, drilling and blasting and mucking a small claim with his grandfather.

"My parents fed me a steady diet of Edward Abbey and my grandfather fed me a steady diet of Ayn Rand," he says, "and needless to say those two aren't really the same."

Kuipers won the Utah state tennis championships as a high school junior and was on track to attend the University of California, Berkeley on a tennis scholarship when his miner grandfather—disapproving of young Jim's lengthening hair and antiauthoritarian attitude—waylaid him into Butte's Montana College of Mineral Science and Technology.

The cure seemed to take. He graduated in 1983 with a BS in mineral engineering, well "indoctrinated," he says, into mining life. He became a mill superintendent at twenty-six—half the typical age for that job—and was managing a New Mexico mine at thirty-one. At thirty-three he started handling corporate acquisitions for Anglo American, one of the largest mining companies in the world.

Still, in the back of his mind, he had questions.

"Why aren't we doing things better? Why do we sit there at public meetings and say we're doing everything we can possibly do when I know damn well that's a lie? A bald-faced lie. We just sat in the boardroom and strategized yesterday to make sure we didn't put on the table what we know the answer is, because it might cost us a little more money."

By 1995 he was conflicted enough, and wealthy enough, to take off a year to hike around the world with his wife. When he came back, Montana environmentalists were in the middle of a campaign for an initiative that would have increased the state's water quality standards. The mining industry was calling the proposal impossible. Kuipers got in touch with friends at the Montana Wilderness Association and the Clark Fork Coalition.

"I said, 'How'd you like to have a mining engineer work for you?' It enraged me as a technical person, as a scientist, that people would have the brazenness to say we couldn't do it."

The groups gave Kuipers $1,500 to write a paper and deliver ten educational presentations around the state. It was a pay cut.

"I figured honestly I owed it," he says now. "I destroyed enough of the land. I dirtied enough of the water that it was my turn to pay for that."

In 1996 Kuipers took on his second client, Montana Trout Unlimited, working against a proposed gold mine at the headwaters of the Blackfoot River. The next year he hired on as an advisor with the Clark Fork River Technical Assistance Committee, a Superfund-enabled organization charged with providing independent information to Superfund-citizens. Kuipers still has that job, which is ultimately funded by ARCO, today. He works for EPA as well, helping write the agency's national mining reclamation enclosure rules. He also works for Anaconda–Deer Lodge County. They pay him with EPA-funneled funds appropriated to enable the county a modicum of engagement in its own destiny. The county pays Kuipers to test the county's soil and water. At least it has in the past.

When John Wardell died in 2009, the county was getting $1.2 million a year to coordinate cleanups with new development projects and test wells and watchdog the entrenched Superfund tag-team of ARCO and EPA.

"He dies, the next year the budget goes down to $900,000. Now it's $550,000. They're telling the county next year it's $350,000."

George Niland's dust monitors got cut. The county still has the portable X-ray fluorescence machine that susses out subsurface soil contamination, but there's no longer funding to use it. "Citizens or the county out there collecting data? That's scary," Kuipers mocks. "We might actually find out the real deal."

Kuipers had in fact begun to discover the real deal, which is that ARCO, under EPA's watchful eye, had vastly and by appearances knowingly underreported the extent of contamination in Deer Lodge Valley.

"I've never seen a site that was more incompetently done in my career, and I don't mind being on the record on that," Kuipers says. "Anaconda is the worst Superfund site in the country for mining. They did little or nothing right here."

Not least of what's wrong is EPA's arbitrary-seeming standard for safe levels of arsenic in Opportunity. George Niland's reading of 167 ppm would spark a very different reaction in, say, Denver, where citizens near a defunct refining plant were able to request soil removal and replacement if their yards tested higher than a mere 28 ppm arsenic—an average background reading. Butte and Anaconda–Deer Lodge County have the highest arsenic action level in the country. Even ranchers on the lower Clark Fork get their soils replaced at 200 ppm.

Why Anaconda and Opportunity should be treated differently, if there is a reason, is muddy.

"What you'll be told," Kuipers tells me, "is that our arsenic is different. Our arsenic is *special* arsenic. It's not as 'bioavailable.'"

Everyone I'd talked with had mentioned ARCO's "bioavailability" studies, not once without a smirk.

"They took three samples," says Kuipers. "Where, what they represent, nobody can tell me. You take the soils and you feed them to pigs, and then you take everything they excrete and gather that up, and then you do a mass balance. I fed them one gram of arsenic; how many grams of arsenic did they excrete? If they excrete .97 grams, that means there's only 3 percent uptake. What they've come back with is that there is not a high level of uptake from this arsenic here. My question is, what arsenic? What samples were these representing? Did they take a tailings sample? A slag sample? I've gone to these folks and said, 'can you provide that additional information?' Nobody can tell me where these samples came from, upon which these suppositions have been made. In fact, it's more like 'You need to quit talking about this, we're not going to question that, it's a decision made long ago.'"

Never mind that arsenic changes forms.

"What may have been in 1983 an insoluble form of arsenic, if it's oxidized since then, it's no longer bound with sulfur; it is now more available to become soluble and go into the environment. What about when the arsenic goes to plants, the plant dies, the arsenic now becomes a different form of arsenic? Are we talking about arsenic trioxide or arsenic pentoxide? Arsenic trioxide is much more lethal. These are all things that we should have answers to."

It has become clear to Kuipers that Superfund law, designed to address relatively discrete chemical spills like Love Canal, was ill-designed for mining "legacy" sites like that left by the sprawling Anaconda Company.

"What's different for mining sites is we don't clean it up, we cover it up. Just the use of the word 'cleanup' is the wrong connotation. Mining sites are covered up, and then you have to manage them in perpetuity."

The Opportunity Ponds are a case in point.

Acid mine waste is the single largest source of environmental poison from abandoned mine sites. Opportunity's tailings ponds are full of sulfide minerals—iron pyrite, copper pyrite—whose common trait is their association with sulfur. Add air, water, and a ubiquitous species of bacteria and the sulfides oxidize, shedding their sulfur. The process can produce relatively inert sulfates or, if they're not neutralized with pH-balancing amendments, acids. When the pH drops, the metals become soluble, generating acidic water full of dissolved metals. On the slicken-striated banks of the Clark Fork, the reddish soils on top are oxidizing. The gray soils layered below are sulfides. The necessary bacteria are everywhere. As rainwater drains from the slightly concave pond surface into the groundwater below, suction pulls oxygen down into the soil. The acid water, when it comes, will drain into the Clark Fork. Whether the drainage will carry metal concentrations harmful to human health or the environment is what Donald Rumsfeld would call a known unknown.

At Montana's Golden Sunlight open-pit gold mine, a model of modern reclamation techniques near Butte, "we know exactly what the water is below their tailings," Kuipers says. "We know exactly what the tailings look like. The state has predicted they'll go acid in thirty years and we'll have to treat them forever. Did we do the same thing at a Superfund site with 600 million tons of tailings sitting next to the Clark Fork River? No. We've got this big thing sitting here, and we're not doing anything about it. We've just crossed our fingers."

Meanwhile, what *has* been done, in the yards of Anaconda and Opportunity, turns out to be entirely too little. Before mine waste can be covered up, it has to be found, and Kuipers found it where it wasn't supposed to be.

"Everywhere I'm digging around here, in my first six months, below that two inches—that was the guy's *grass*—the contamination is right there if I go where there's not grass. Go in the backyard where the dog's digging in the dirt."

Kuipers began uncovering arsenic contamination at concentrations higher than EPA's action levels, where ARCO had assured that the soil was clean. Deeper than the two-inch testing cutoff, arsenic was actually plentiful. It had dusted the valley aerially, from the smelter stack's emissions, but it had also been imported with truckloads of tailings, donated to Opportunity residents as fill for swampy driveways. As Kuipers knew was common in mining communities, smelter workers had "borrowed" company leftovers. The plumbing in many of Anaconda's older homes is piecemealed out of one-foot lengths of copper pipe stamped "ACM"—a mine company corollary to Johnny Cash's lunchbox-Cadillac epic "One Piece at a Time." Basement rec rooms and fences were painted with pilfered gallons of company paint, manufactured to fireproof wooden mine staves and composed of an unheard of 8 percent lead.

That lead was another problem. Though lead hadn't been even an afterthought of EPA's original cleanup plan in 1996, Kuipers found it all over town.

What's the harm? One old-school environmentalist friend of mine, happily ensconced in Helena, responds to the question with a directive to "just take a walk through the Anaconda Safeway." The preponderance of palsied shuffles is all the evidence he needs to counter the claims of a Don Wyant or a Jerry Hansen, that, hell, they're still here. No environmental poisoning has killed them yet. Death, though, is hardly the only negative outcome.

"We don't talk about their quality of life," Kuipers says. "And they would say, 'Well, my life's been fine,' and I wouldn't want to be the one to say it hasn't. But what I can tell you is there's a reason you don't see any new businesses here, there's a reason you don't see a vibrant young or even middle-aged adult community."

The reason is that vibrant young people tend to move away from home for better opportunities elsewhere, and that long-term exposure to heavy metals, especially as a child, doesn't foster vibrancy.

While acute exposure to heavy metals can cause acute illness or even death, chronic low-level exposure is more likely to affect health in chronic, low-level ways, especially in the early stages of human development.

"This is a very important part of it that I think most people don't understand," Kuipers says. "[For] growing people, when they're exposed to contaminants, it has much different effects than once we're already grown. It can affect your immune system, your brain. Now once we're adult, those things are done, and now if I'm exposed to arsenic or this or that, the chance that it'll lead to developmental issues is much lower. So when we do assessments of contaminants, we really look at that pregnant-woman-through-about-seven-year-old population. That's the at-risk population for these types of things. With arsenic and lead we see diminished brain capacity. You'll basically see a drop in IQ."

Kuipers continues: "This is the kind of thing that people don't like to hear, and I'm always very hesitant to say it, but Anaconda's not a very smart community. What's the reason? The same population smokes and drinks a lot. We do know that we seem to have a population that has a depressed IQ, and we have clusters of cancers and things. Unfortunately the science isn't there, and that's the hardest thing about this."

When I talked to Kuipers in Anaconda, the county was even then negotiating with EPA and ARCO over a second round of yard removals and cleanup to encompass the newly discovered lead problem. ARCO had indicated a willingness to clean up the lead if doing so took the company off the hook for any additional arsenic mop-ups. Kuipers and the county wanted both.

"So there's a fight going on," Kuipers told me. "If this county chose today to take on the battle that I would like them to take on, they'd get trashed by ARCO, their golf course would get shut down, EPA would abandon them. Personally I think they ought to go ahead and compromise. Do I think they have any choice? Hell, no, because EPA doesn't have the guts to do what they know needs to be done. I just don't want anything to do with it, personally. I'm not going to be part of telling people they're safe when they're not safe, that things are cleaned up when they're not cleaned up."

Being an in-demand private contractor, Kuipers can afford to stand on principle and advocate for what he says needs to be done: a complete redo on the community's inadequate arsenic cleanup, and additional cleanup for lead. EPA, he understands, doesn't have that same luxury.

"As a regulatory agency, it would be really hard for them to say, 'We made a mistake in '96 when we agreed to this other remedy.' I think they would tell you that pushing the issues that I would push might delay a decision. They also would simply not get an agreement. They'd have to go do the work themselves and sue ARCO for recovery of the costs. To some extent I can understand it, but it's not my job to sympathize with them."

It's not just EPA that has a hard time admitting fault. Aside from a few increasingly marginalized voices, the residents of Opportunity and Anaconda seem disinclined to question the future that EPA and ARCO are mapping out for them. Questioning the future requires assessing the past, and there's no such rush to judgment in a company town. As Kuipers describes the dynamic, "If you say 'We harmed somebody,' everybody who worked up there had a hand in it. It's very difficult in my experience for us, as people who were involved in mining, to turn around and say we were wrong. That's invalidating an entire life, a culture. You're almost condemning people for having made a living, having done what they did without the knowledge, and nobody really wants to put themselves in that situation. Very few people can be self-introspective that way, or want to be."

"It would be really hard for them to admit they made a mistake." That sentence makes me think of Bob. He was either the least introspective person I've ever known, or the most reflexively self-protective. His wife of twenty years, my mother, finally gathered the courage to escape his constant criticisms after my sister Cameron and I were mostly grown. Cameron disowned him in college after suffering his stereotypical lack of interest in the legacies available via a daughter. His sister, my aunt, ceased communication with him after he made it clear one too many times that he considered her teaching career a mark of subpar intellect and ambition. His own elderly parents stopped speaking to him after his apparently monomaniacal therapy sessions convinced Bob to try to persuade them that they, after fifty years of marriage, had never really loved each other, and should divorce. Then there was me, trying to wring some meaning out of his interminable disappointments until I finally gave up too.

There was something wrong with all of us. There could be no cause in the common denominator. In his eyes, his parents were incapable of self-reflection. His sister was jealous. His wife was disloyal. His daughter was overly influenced by his wife. His son was ungrateful and selfish.

"What if," he'd written me during our estrangement, "I do have good judgment, and my attitudes about you, though poorly expressed, are basically insightful? If so, then your resistance to me is in truth a resistance to face your own need to change."

Then he died. I'd answered his question the only way I could, in the negative, but I knew that would never satisfy him. Nothing but acquiescence would have, and I didn't have that to give.

⁜

When I visit Becky Guay in her office at the Anaconda Courthouse, the building's restoration is only recently completed. Before we start, Guay wants to know if I'm funded in any way by BP. She laughs, but she asks.

Then Guay answers my question about EPA's efficacy in overseeing the cleanup of Anaconda–Deer Lodge County, which encompasses both Anaconda and Opportunity, and of which she is the chief executive officer: "It's been thirty years. That's all I need to say, right?"

Becky was working in Southern California, on a twenty-three-year hiatus from the town of Anaconda, where she was born, and where her parents still live, when EPA set the safety threshold for her county's special arsenic at the record high of 250 and allowed ARCO to perform its testing as an average on just two inches of sod. "Don't get me started," she tells me, and proceeds to stretch her lunch hour to three hours, recounting the county's travails.

"I remember as a kid, if the wind blew from the east, the sulfur taste would keep you from playing outside, and if it was bad enough the leaves would turn yellow and fall off the trees, but you just lived with it." High school geology teachers led field trips to toxic tailings piles on the hills above town.

"Tailings pretty much underlie everything," she tells me. "They're in the streets, they're under people's garages and houses, they're under the sidewalks. It compacted really well, it was a great material. Unfortunately it's a bad material. Even places where we didn't believe there would have been contamination . . . for example, the hospital did an expansion and added a new clinic down on Pennsylvania Street; there was really no reason to believe that there'd be tailings there—but there were."

Guay returned to Anaconda just as EPA agreed to fund the county independently of ARCO, enabling it to educate itself, hire Jim Kuipers, and "flex its muscles a little bit."

"When you're so tied to ARCO for the funding, you can't risk being aggressive or having a good strong opinion, because then they just don't pay."

The county and ARCO do have different agendas. ARCO is "spending money that they're not getting any return on, essentially, so they're not really in a hurry to have to do that, and they would rather not do extra things, or things that would be good but aren't absolutely required. The county's on the side that we want our community cleaned up. We want to be able to say we're not a Superfund site, we're clean, we're healthy."

As for EPA: "I've got to be delicate here, but I think that this site suffered somewhat from EPA's own employees taking the path of least resistance. The only expertise they had coming to them was from ARCO. By law, ARCO's allowed to do the studies, they're allowed to do the testing, they're allowed to propose the plans, they're allowed to implement the plans, and essentially EPA's role is oversight. Well, in a vacuum, where they don't have access to the kinds of expertise that ARCO does, the consultants and such, they tend to take the path of least resistance, and they don't have information telling them 'no, that's not right.' They only have ARCO's side. There isn't anybody on the other side saying 'but we don't think that's gonna work.'"

EPA is also gun-shy about the prospect of litigating against the best lawyers that BP can buy.

"I've seen that many times," Guay tells me. "They'll say, 'We're going to do this!'" Becky pounds her hand on her desk for emphasis. "And then they go meet with ARCO and come back and say, 'Well, we're not really.'"

Guay adds, "Because it's such a big site—such a long-term, ongoing, never-see-the-end kind of site—frankly I don't know that it got as much attention from headquarters as it should have. I think the folks in Montana were just left to struggle along the best that they could."

One example is Charlie Coleman, the remediation project manager assigned to Anaconda since 1994—the same who gave me a tour of Smelter Hill and the Opportunity Ponds, and the same who told residents of Opportunity that the Milltown sediments would magically transform themselves into topsoil on the train ride from Missoula. Coleman is the man who approved EPA's initial "remedy."

"Here you are in 2011," Guay says, "and you've implemented that thing and the problem really isn't fixed. If you're the one that was here in 1994 and said, 'That's going to work,' it's pretty rough for you to go back and say, 'Maybe I was wrong.'"

Of Coleman she says, "I think he's been here too long. These are the people that have been signing off on all of the agreements in Anaconda forever, for the last thirty years, and I personally think that Anaconda has been used as a bargaining chip in a lot of other places. 'Oh ARCO, if you'll help take out the Milltown Dam, we'll give you a pass on Anaconda. We won't look quite so hard at your remedy on the ponds that we know isn't going to work forever. We'll just kind of look the other way.'"

Why would her county be the pawn, I ask, and not, say, Missoula County?

"Have you looked at Anaconda? Some of it's a matter of constituency, some of it's that Anaconda's population tends to be much less educated, tends to be on a way-lower socioeconomic scale, much higher poverty rates. EPA and Atlantic Richfield, all of them, thought the community wouldn't notice, and also, for many years, and still to this day, though it's starting to diminish, this community isn't one to put up much of a fight. I tried. I tried really hard the first couple of years I was here to rally the community, get this 250-ppm standard changed, and a lot of the community says, 'Well, ARCO was good to us; they paid our paychecks.'"

A lot of people, Guay says, are still afraid of the company: "'Oh, they're gonna cut off my retirement.' I think that because it was a company town, because of the fear that a lot of folks here have of ARCO and what they could do to them personally, it was pretty easy for ARCO to say, 'Trade off Anaconda—they won't squeak.' I think some of it's an environmental justice issue, I really do. The community is more uneducated than farther downstream, it's poorer, it's older, and all of those things conspire."

They conspired most dramatically in Anaconda's Old Works Golf Course, planted on the valley floor of the Superfund site where the Anaconda Copper Company's original smelters used to sit. It's an incongruously green carpet at the foot of dun hills dotted with toppled bricks. The sand traps are filled with repurposed "sland"—the glassy, black, granular slag produced by the reduction works. Warm Springs Creek, which meanders through the course, is extensively engineered with subterranean treatment features to steer rainwater and runoff away from the site's buried poisons, and allow them to exit the course clean. The ribbon was cut in 1997 to environmental-success-story acclaim.

In fact it's just a green bandage, and a hammer in ARCO's negotiations with the county.

Has it proved a good solution? "No," Guay says. "Not only was the golf course going to act as a community resource, it was going to generate untold millions to do restoration work and remediation work. It was going to return enough money that the county was going to have this big honking economic development fund. We'll have hotels developed around the golf course, and executive housing developed around the golf course. We'll have so much money we'll be able to go in and do additional tailings removals over areas that were just capped. It was just going to rain greenbacks, you know? Well, it didn't happen. They're not breaking even. They are not acquiring any funds toward maintenance of the golf course as a Superfund structure. Contractually, the county assumed responsibility for paying for that, through the proceeds of the golf course. Well, there have been no proceeds from the golf course."

So far, ARCO has forgiven several lines of credit to keep the course solvent, but there's no long-term plan in place to maintain the site as long as is required, which is forever.

"They got off incredibly cheap," Guay says of ARCO. "Good public relations. I think ARCO looks at it as: 'That's what Anaconda got. You guys got a golf course. We're done.' And part of that is then you have to accept what we do for soils, you have to accept what we do for Opportunity Ponds, you have to accept all of that. 'Here's your bone.'"

"And poor little Opportunity. Between you and me and a rock, the stuff has to go somewhere, right? It's there. The big-picture environmentalist part of me says, 'Wouldn't it be tragic to take this stuff somewhere else in Missoula County, put it on virgin ground, and have to put up another fence around another piece of ground that could be used for something else?' So bringing the material back to a place that's already contaminated, will *always* be contaminated, makes some logical sense. It really does. Two problems with it. One, the community was not in my opinion fairly compensated for taking back that waste, all of the waste; it was just shoved on them; and number two, the fact that we were absolutely sold a bill of goods: 'We're doing you guys a favor. We're bringing you material that's going to grow stuff. It's going to be wonderful.' I believe, and I will believe until the end of my days, that scientists, at least, absolutely knew that the material they were bringing up here was very ill characterized. No one ever did any kind of studies in a laboratory before it got here. You give ARCO a whole year with toilet paper tubes and plant seedlings just to see what they can get to grow on it, but the community didn't have the benefit of any kind of study or anything."

Guay understands that the material had to go somewhere, but she thinks that "it should have come here in a studied manner, it should have been well characterized and understood. The community shouldn't have been told, 'Oh, it's good stuff.' They should have been told, 'Yeah, it's just more of the same crap that's already out there, and since we're bringing it back we're going to compensate you in some way that the community feels good about, and let's all be honest and up-front about it.'"

$$\dashv$$

On November 8, 2011, Connie Ternes-Daniels totaled her Buick Rendezvous on a bull moose. That's how she knows that things in Opportunity, slowly but surely, are getting better. She tells me about it over lunch at Donivan's Family Dining in Anaconda. Connie orders a salad. I have the Miner Burger—a cheeseburger with a slice of ham on top. Donivan's also features an "Opportunity Omelet" on its all-day breakfast menu, filled with sausage and drenched in cream gravy. Connie says she's never tried it.

Connie, the Anaconda–Deer Lodge County planning director, was driving east on Montana State Highway 1, heading from a commissioners' meeting in Anaconda to the thirty-acre homestead she shares with her husband in Opportunity. The meeting had ended at 7:00 p.m. and the road had already grown dark. She had just passed the turnoff to Mill Creek Road, but not yet reached the railroad tracks, when the moose materialized out of nowhere. She was traveling about 65 miles per hour in the 70 mph zone and yanked the steering wheel trying to avoid the animal. The Buick's passenger side plowed into it, knocking it dead into the ditch between the eastbound and westbound lanes. The impact shattered her windshield, but Connie wasn't hurt. The son of Anaconda's sole auto dealer and his girlfriend were driving behind her, thinking about passing, when they saw Connie swerve. They let her wait with them in their truck, out of the cold, while her husband came to pick her up.

A week later, another local resident ran into an elk on the road, and several weeks after that a pilot flying into nearby Bowman Field radioed in a moose browsing in the middle of his runway.

Connie felt terrible about killing the moose.

"It's sort of interesting that all of the remediation has really enhanced wildlife," she told me. "I just don't want to run into them."

Connie was born in Deer Lodge Valley and left to attend Montana State University in Bozeman and then Montana Tech in Butte, before going to graduate school at the University of Montana in Missoula. She's lived in Opportunity since 1982, when her husband—an Opportunity native and an electrical engineer on Smelter Hill until it closed down in 1980—inherited property from his grandfather, who had purchased one of the community's original ten-acre tracts from the Anaconda Company's Deer Lodge Valley Farms development arm. Now they operate a small hobby farm, with some cows and horses and hay, and Connie raises miniature horses.

"There's always been agricultural use in Opportunity," she tells me. "That was the whole purpose of it from the beginning. It was to show that you could have little agricultural operations under the plume of the big stack."

You could and you couldn't. The local rumor is that the Anaconda Company raised livestock on the upwind side of Smelter Hill, importing healthy animals to Opportunity fairs for show. Now that the stack produces no plume, Connie hasn't noticed any problem.

Gold, her palomino Tennessee Walking Horse, is thirty-four years old. "He eats the grass and drinks the water. My vet says he's one of the oldest horses he's ever seen, and the horse has lived in Opportunity since he was nine years old"—that was seven years after the smelter shut down.

Which is not to say that Connie thinks everything is peaches and cream in Opportunity. She knows better. She served two terms on the county commission before going to work for U.S. senator Jon Tester as his Butte field director. She left that job to come work for Becky Guay as the county's planning director.

"Jon's state director offered me more money to stay. I took a pay cut from what I was making to come over here. I like projects, and I like being able to say, 'Yeah, see what you can do when you work together?'"

She knows what it's like when you don't. Connie was on the county commission on May 5, 2003, when Butte's *Montana Standard* announced that Senator Baucus wanted to send Milltown's toxic lakebed to Opportunity.

Connie read about Baucus's proposal in the newspaper like everyone else.

"There wasn't a discussion here about that. It was announced in the newspaper and there was no discussion with any public official at the time. We read about it. I was irate about it. I have no proof, but I have to believe that Dennis Washington had a discussion with Senator Baucus and said, 'This means jobs.'" Jobs, that is, for Washington's Montana Rail Link, which would ship the wastes to Opportunity.

"I firmly believe that that decision was a political decision that influenced the EPA," Connie says.

To add insult to injury, two years later Baucus announced that he had secured a $5-million congressional appropriation to help redevelop the Superfund-affected communities with parks and trail systems. This time Connie got the news directly from Baucus's state director, Jim Foley.

"I'll never forget that call," Connie told me. "He said, 'Max has got five million dollars for redevelopment. Four point eight million is going to go to Missoula and two hundred thousand is going to go to you.' I think my statement was, 'Over my dead body.' I was incensed. We have had to scrap and fight for every little pittance. What the hell are we going to do with that? I mean seriously."

Ultimately Connie fought and scrapped and got the appropriation halved between Missoula and Anaconda–Deer Lodge County; $1.3 million went to remediation and redevelopment of Opportunity's Beaver Dam Park.

Beaver Dam Park is named for the fenced-off Beaver Dam School, where George Niland went. The Beaver Dam School itself was named for the valley's once prodigious beavers. The water-slowing dams they built meant that more mine tailings settled out here, on the valley floor, than anywhere else in the watershed.

Connie is happy about the park. She fought for years to get it. It's something. If nothing else, it cleaned up a contaminated and blighted block. "The fact remains," she says, "if it wasn't used as a school or park ground, it would have reverted back to Atlantic Richfield. There are lots of reversionary clauses on a lot of company ground. If it wasn't used for its original intention, then it would revert back."

Even once Connie secured the money for the park, she had to fight to get the property's soil tested before construction began. EPA and ARCO were willing to presume the ground was nontoxic enough for Opportunity's children. It wasn't. Contractors conducted a removal action—stripping contaminated soil and replacing it with clean donor soil—before work could begin.

Some of the donor soil came from the Stewart Street "borrow area" on the other side of the interstate, across from Opportunity, but there's not much soil left there.

Nine months after EPA's initial deadline, EPA and ARCO finally announced a plan to cap the Milltown section of the Opportunity Ponds. The compromise calls for twelve inches of new "vegetative growth medium"—topsoil, that is—on top of the Milltown sediments. The county had wanted eighteen inches. The modern national standard for reclaimed mining sites is three to four feet. If forced to find more dirt, ARCO publicly threatened, the company would dig up the grassy, tree-crowded buffer strip that partially obscures the treeless ponds from Opportunity's view. It's company property, after all.

In short, ARCO, with EPA approval, is digging up dirty dirt, diluting it, calling it clean dirt, and mixing it into more dirty dirt to dilute that. Require anything more thorough and the company stands ready to cannibalize this "garden community" of a company town for dump cover. It boggles Daniels's mind.

"Anyway—"

Connie Daniels says "anyway" a lot, usually as a way to trail a thought off, sometimes apologetically, as if she's gone on too long. It's an enormously confusing patchwork of projects to keep track of, and she has developed pet peeves, but she doesn't want to dwell on her frustrations.

"I don't think running around screaming about 'it's contaminated' and blah blah, and going on about every negative thing under the sun is ever going to get you out of it," she says, in oblique reference to George Niland, who has made himself a thorn in the county's side. "I would rather focus my personal energies, and my professional energies, on trying to do something constructive and positive to make some sort of an impact to change things to some degree, to the best of our abilities."

What Connie wants to change is what Opportunity has already become: a ghost town whose ghosts haven't left yet. She is encouraged by the new START—Sanction, Treatment, Assessment, Revocation, and Transition—adult correctional facility recently constructed just across Highway 48 from the ponds, and the Anaconda credit union's new office in the old company train yard, and the newish $200 million NorthWestern Energy power plant and transfer station just up Mill Creek Road, each of which required pre-construction soil remediation. But she knows that's not enough. Neither is the park.

"The park is wonderful, it's a great little thing, but really, for this community to recover, it needs a lot more. I think you need to put something back here. People still live here, there are still businesses here, so what can we do to help them? I've lived here my entire life and I can do things every single season of the year. I was out cross-country skiing yesterday, I horseback ride in the summer, you can go to Georgetown Lake. There needs to be some investment back in it to help these areas recover. I think it's only fair."

Connie is one of the few people I've talked with who seems comfortable speaking about Opportunity in terms of bald fairness. It is conceivably logical to dump an entire river restoration's waste at an already dumped-upon site, but is it fair?

Is it fair that the EPA's national safety standard for arsenic in soil is 150 ppm, while the standard applied in Anaconda and Opportunity is 250 ppm? Is it fair that ARCO's thousands of acres of dump site are taxed as agricultural land, the state's lowest tax bracket? Is it fair that in calculating the resources lost to the state through a century's worth of mining and mining waste, the state Natural Resource Damage Program discounted Anaconda–Deer Lodge County and the Opportunity Ponds entirely, never to be compensated for? The place was too fucked-up to make amends. Connie has tried to find out who made that decision, but no one will say.

Is it fair that Missoula gets it river cleaned up at Opportunity's expense?

"Do you think for one second that Missoula would take one drop of contaminated soil from this area down there?" Connie asks me. "Absolutely not." She's finished her salad, and periodically checks her watch. Her mother has been ill, and she's expecting an update from her brother. I've told her that I've felt almost guilty, as a Missoulian, at the way Opportunity has been steamrolled, the way it's been taken out of the equation.

"Don't think we haven't noticed," she says. "It's really hard for a little town like this with pretty limited resources to fight this. It is a community. It's a great little community. It has survived the smelter closure. It has survived all these things. I don't have any regrets. I don't want the legacy of this community to be the waste repository of the Clark Fork, and that's it. I live here. I don't have any plans on moving. Maybe that's part of our generational attachment here. Our son is fourth generation on his [father's] side of the family, and I'm second. I like Missoula, but I'm not moving down there."

The last time I checked in on Opportunity, Jim Kuipers was still hanging on at the county, waiting to see how hard a compromise the community might be forced into. Becky Guay had resigned mid-term as Anaconda–Deer Lodge County's CEO to take a job as city manager in West Yellowstone, nearly two hundred miles away, on the border of Yellowstone National Park. Connie Ternes-Daniels was still raising miniature horses in Opportunity, and had been named interim executive director of Anaconda–Deer Lodge County when Guay left. George Niland was recovering from shoulder surgery. Don Wyant was still tinkering in his shop. Jerry Hansen was still showing up when he could to oversee the basement archives of the Marcus Daly Historical Society. His environment hadn't killed him yet.

There's a voice that says: So what? Who cares? A little out-of-the-way town got shat upon. Opportunity's fate is logical, politically convenient, and advantageous to several generations of billionaires. The world has bigger problems. Massacres, genocides, and epidemics. Collapsing economies and murderous fundamentalisms. East European sex slavery and Mexican drug violence. China rises and America flails. The oil is running out. The sun will explode. So what if one little Montana backwater gets thrown under the bus. Besides, big good did come of it. Industry, wealth and convenience, lives extended and improved by mineral-aided comfort, communication, and speed. That would be Bob's take: a necessary sacrifice. There are harsher fates in the world than a quiet life in Opportunity, worrying, or not, about dust in your lungs, the dirt in your yard, and the water in your well. Those who live here aren't rich. They might not be the sharpest knives in the drawer. They aren't contributing much. Where's the crime, right?

As crimes go, the cleanup of the Clark Fork, the failure to fix Anaconda, and the sacrifice of Opportunity belong firmly in the category of First World Problems. I remember describing the story to a fellow journalist, an opposition reporter in Russia, a woman whose closest colleagues had been murdered for speaking truth to power. She looked at me for a long time, trying to gauge if I was serious. When she realized I was, she said, of my country, "you are so far ahead of us."

Is it really an injustice? Does an injustice require someone to blame? Who do we blame for Opportunity? The mining company that helped industrialize a nation and collaterally despoiled a landscape, or the state of Montana that rolled over for it? Blame ARCO, which has done almost nothing about the site but spend money, however variably effective? Do we acknowledge that the residents of Opportunity are fully accessory to the crime? Men who raised families in Opportunity worked on the smelter in Anaconda. They produced the copper and they produced the poison. They drove company trucks to tailings dumps and poached the stuff to fill low spots in their yards and muddy driveways. Theirs was no paradise lost.

Maybe Opportunity is just a cost of doing business. Something we had to do. Something we chose to do and wouldn't, on balance, choose to undo.

The concept of necessary sacrifice strikes at the core of the deal that modern America—and the increasingly modern world—has made with itself: we'll write this one off, and we'll move along, not looking back. It's the deal that meat eaters make with themselves even after they've toured the abattoir. It's the deal that dedicated smokers make even after the cancer has been diagnosed. It's the deal that love-it-or-leave-it patriots make to embrace American exceptionalism without regard to the global sweatshop that supports it. It's the deal William A. Clark struck when he conflated personal profit with American dominion and left future generations to fend for themselves.

It's self-imposed blindness, failure to recognize, the discomfort of acknowledgement, that's erasing Opportunity. EPA, the state department of environmental quality, and the Clark Fork Coalition have all published maps of the Superfund stretch from Butte to Missoula. Not one of them marks Opportunity.

The country's largest Superfund site proffers no shortage of hooks upon which to hang complaints. Industry has too little motivation to do the right thing, and too much power to be forced to. Cleanup of the watershed has been enacted out of any logical order, downstream first, exhibiting political favoritism toward the already relatively powerful. It's taking entirely too long—three decades in, Butte doesn't even have an encompassing Record of Decision governing the work still to be done. If you believe Jim Kiupers and others, even the revised remedies in Anaconda are inadequate. Nothing has been done to prepare for the day when the Opportunity Ponds turn acidic and start pumping heavy metals into the river, potentially undoing hundreds of millions of dollars' worth of restoration already accomplished.

Opportunity is a sacrificial landscape that allowed America to become what it is, and that is now enabling the restoration of a river and the betterment of Missoula. The Clark Fork's total restoration bill will come in around $1.3 billion—a dollar for every man, woman and child in China. Opportunity got 0.01 percent of that—$1.3 million—for a mothballed schoolhouse in a token park. Residential Opportunity will always be next door to four thousand acres of tailings piles.

Waste doesn't just disappear. Excepting an eruption of the Yellowstone caldera that would vaporize much of the Rocky Mountain West, it cannot be made to go away.

We carry our disappointments, the failures we've inherited, with us. We are uneasy with those we owe, so we look away. I owe Bob, but I don't know how to acknowledge him. Blaming him is too easy, forgiveness seems disingenuous, and he's no longer around to allow the possibility of making things right. Better perhaps to just bury the debt under four feet of clean, fenced-off soil and walk away. You can't save everything.

Yet we owe Opportunity something. You could argue that we owe Opportunity everything. The least a beneficiary can do, and more than we've done, is say thanks.

# PART VI

# REVIVAL

*Even a devastated place is sacred. If we know what it once was, we may begin to understand what its possibilities are.*

—EMMET GOWIN

The language loves a do-over: remediation, reclamation, redevelopment, redemption. People love a good comeback story. It affirms their faith in technology to repair the damages that technology wreaks. It assuages liberal guilt and absolves corporate apologists. Everyone wins.

F. Scott Fitzgerald gets frequently quoted on the dearth of second acts in American life, never mind American landscapes, but the quote is usually misunderstood. Second acts aren't synonymous with second chances. The second act—and Fitzgerald the screenwriter knew it—is the three-act play's meaty, messy middle, where quests become complicated and outcomes tarred with doubt before resolution finally parts the clouds in Act III. What Fitzgerald really meant, I bet, is that Americans have no patience for uncertainty and setback. Give us inciting incidents and cathartic climax. Skip the confusion.

It's important to be precise with all those "re" words. They mean different things and fall under distinct purviews. Remediation is removing or neutralizing threats to human health. In terms of a Superfund cleanup, that's the full extent of EPA's mandate. Restoration is re-creating or at least approximating the original preindustrial resource, whether it be a 120-mile stretch of river or an

179

urban brownfield. Redevelopment, Superfund communities hope, will follow successful remediation and restoration. That which was dead will come back to life.

￼

Montana isn't my first mining outpost. It was 1995, and I was twenty-seven. I took a trip to the Big Bend country of Far West Texas, an eleven-hour drive from Houston, and the closest thing around to an unspoiled wilderness. The gateway to Big Bend National Park is a tiny non-town called Terlingua, where an assortment of sun-dried dropouts had colonized the stone-and-adobe remnants of an abandoned prewar mercury mining camp. On the porch of the trading post one day, drinking cans of cold beer and trying to act local, I found a bulletin-board note card advertising a small stone earth shelter for rent in the cactus-dotted backcountry, four miles off the pavement, with solar electric, propane water heater, tin-roofed porch, and a stone-rimmed fire circle, at $285 a month. Three months later I lived there.

The real estate boomlet that has since turned Terlingua into a scattered trailer court of subdivided ranchettes had yet to hit, and the area's only economies were a struggling school serving kids from a hundred miles around and a whitewater rafting outfitter doing slim business on the nearby Rio Grande. I hadn't become obsessed with rivers yet, but I was growing interested. My place was sunk into the side of a small hill overlooking a maze of ravines just a few hundred yards from Terlingua Creek. The creek was dry most of the year, harboring a few tinajas of stagnant clear water just deep enough for a hot afternoon dunk, but when it rained over the expansive and hard-packed watershed—sometimes too far away to see, even with forty-mile visibility—the creek would rise from nothing into a wall of boiling red mud. A pamphlet produced by the national park warned visitors, "Do not camp in arroyos or washes, they may become raging rivers while you sleep." From half a mile away I could feel the rumble underfoot as the water came down the draw, and I knew I could never outrun it.

Flash floods like that were spectacles to watch from a safe distance. While I was there a local high school girl and her friends sat on a dirt cliff to watch such a flood roar past below. The current undercut her perch, washing her into the water, where she drowned, devastating her single-parent dad and sending the far-flung but tight-knit community into a deep funk. It was best not to get too close. It was better, and safer, when just wind came whistling through the sandstone corridors. You could hear it before it arrived and close your eyes before the airborne abrasive hit.

The first time I ever overnighted in a canoe, paddling through the days and camping on river banks, I was living in Terlingua. Bob and I were corresponding, trying to come to some sort of detente over the distance. He was living alone by then, divorced from my mother and estranged from his daughter. He was awfully alone, and I was his only grudging family contact. The letters were probably his therapist's idea. At least they read like they were. They tended to begin with throat-clearing session talk like, "I got your letter today, and I feel especially good about it." Not that my letters were encouraging. I had him over a barrel: I was his last family gasp, and I knew it. I could be as shitty as I wanted to be and he had to take it if he wanted to keep any shred of contact. After he died I found the correspondence in a manila file folder in his office drawer in Humble. He'd saved copies of his letters to me, and the letters I sent in return.

One such was a terse postcard that read, "Dad—Got your letter. Curious to see that you ignored mine. What's up with that? Baffled, Brad." It shames me, without excusing him, to read it now.

It was in one of those letters that he suggested driving out from Houston for Thanksgiving. He would rent a canoe and hire a shuttle driver and we would spend three days canoeing the Rio Grande through Boquillas Canyon, a famously scenic stretch of river traversing the remote Big Bend. My first thought was of spending three straight days in Bob's judgmental company, but I finally decided that the real effort being expended was his. If he wanted to invest in quality time with a surly son, I wasn't ready to tell him he couldn't. I never got beyond a feeling that I owed him at least a chance, even if the chance I offered wasn't much of one, even if I wasn't convinced he deserved it. He just wanted me to be perfect. I didn't have to like it. He probably wasn't going to like it either. Liking it, liking each other even, was beside the point.

He wasn't going to have another son, and I wasn't going to have another dad. There were no A-plus answers. We were stuck with each other.

He arrived bearing two Cornish hens in an ice chest and an assortment of boxed and canned trimmings that we heated on the shelter's propane stove for our holiday dinner. The next morning we met the driver he'd hired, a man I knew in passing from the bar in the ghost town, who drove us and a canoe to a small boat ramp at a campground called Rio Grande Village and dropped us off. He would meet us again three days later at a decommissioned bridge thirty-six miles downriver. In the meantime we would be as alone together as we'd ever been.

Aside from hazy recollections of the views, I remember three things about that trip. The first is lunch on the first day. Bob had brought Styrofoam cups of dehydrated soup mix, and several hours in we pulled off at a high sandbar to light the little propane camp stove and heat water. I didn't like the looks of the little black squiggles in my mix and waited until Bob had slurped down several bites before I pointed them out. Weevils. We tossed the soup and ate bananas with peanut butter and never said a word about the weevils, though we both knew he'd eaten them. I wondered at his inobservance. He doubtless wondered at my delayed warning.

My second recollection is of arguing about nuclear energy. Neither one of us was involved nor even much engaged in the issue. In retrospect, I suspect it was just a handy divide to disagree across.

For a man so attuned to the problems of waste—whether municipal sewage or wastrel offspring—Bob was weirdly insensitive to what I saw as the nuclear issue's central conundrum: what to do with the poisonous by-product. Until that problem got solved, I figured, arguments about the "cheap and clean" advantages of nuclear energy were so much radioactive dust in the wind. Not Bob. Taking an attitude I've since heard echoed by engineering types and seen foreshadowed in the pollution-control efforts of early-twentieth-century Anaconda Company technicians, he viewed nuclear waste as a detail that science would inevitably catch up to and render moot. Yes, we'll have to deal with that later, but we'll deal with it. They must teach technological optimism in engineering school. To me it sounded like blind arrogance.

He took the opportunity of forced proximity to make me an offer: he would help offset the cost of my reeducation, as an engineer, by employing me as an assistant in his otherwise one-man business, which consisted of manufacturing, selling, and installing aeration diffusers for municipal wastewater treatment plants. Eventually, he intimated, I could take over the family business. At twenty-seven I was keeping my head above water as a freelance journalist. He thought he was doing me a favor.

The last thing I remember about our Boquillas trip is how it ended. The canyon is famous for headwinds, and Bob had neglected to bring a map, so we had no way of knowing how far we'd traveled each day. To meet our shuttle on time, we planned to paddle the thirty-six miles in a reasonable two and a half days. By midmorning of our second day on the water Bob had decided that we were hopelessly behind schedule. He was driving from the stern, of course, and made it clear that while his primary job was steering, mine was the provision of motive muscle.

He may as well have been beating a galley drum back there. We did not stop to explore Boquillas's gorgeous side canyons. There was no question of breaking out the camp stove for a hot lunch. We paddled like fugitives until dusk blurred the water. We beached the boat, raised the tent by flashlight, and passed out like beaten dogs.

The next morning we got up before the sun, choked down clots of instant oatmeal, loaded the canoe, and paddled two hundred yards around a bend—to the takeout. We'd ruined one day on the river and voided the next one. We raised the tent again, because what the hell else was there to do, and spent six hours huddled out of the wind, waiting for our ride to show up, sore and stewing in silence. I have never since seen any wisdom to hurrying anywhere in a boat.

After he went home, I wrote another angry letter. Instead of thanking him for the trip, I punished him for his effrontery.

"Your suggestion, or, as you may have it, your offer regarding the possibilities of a career in engineering was insensitive and rude, and your attempt, upon noticing my defensiveness, to recast the insult as a compliment was either facile or total bullshit," I wrote, steam whistling out my ears. "The whole thing makes me so mad I can't tell which."

"Dear Brad," he wrote back: "I agree that the things I said about re-training to be an engineer were insensitive, thoughtless and rude. I apologize and hope that you will forgive me." Still, "We agree that society is not currently compensating you well for your efforts as a writer."

We went back and forth like that.

┼

I meet Joel Chavez at the new rest area just off Montana State Highway 1 headed into Anaconda. Chavez, the man at the Clark Fork Symposium who described the Opportunity Ponds as a suitable single trap into which to put all the Clark Fork's rats, is the lead Montana Department of Environmental Quality (DEQ) official overseeing the state's portion of the Clark Fork cleanup. Since ARCO volunteered to take on the Milltown cleanup downstream, Chavez's purview is Silver Bow Creek upstream of the Warm Springs Ponds, and the Clark Fork downstream another fifty or so miles to Garrison Junction—an old railroad stop, now nothing but an exit sign—near Deer Lodge. I wanted to meet the man who'd been given the job of rebuilding a river.

I expected a Ford F-350 or some similarly heavy-duty contractor's truck, but Chavez arrived in his state vehicle, a dark Toyota Prius that he claimed to enjoy, aside from not being allowed to smoke his American Spirit cigarettes inside. I climbed in and we were off for a Silver Bow Creek restoration tour.

Chavez is from Idaho, and he began his career as a geologist in mining exploration. Performing a one-man microcosm of the transforming economy of the American West, he got laid off from his job finding new veins to tap and found new employment reclaiming old mines in Montana. In 1999 he started rebuilding Silver Bow Creek in Butte, and he's been working his way downstream ever since.

He filled me in on the background as we drove.

To fix a broken river, you first define your terms.

First: "river." It's not just the ribbon of water that's poisoned. To varying degrees, the entire valley is contaminated. In the case of the Clark Fork's course through the Deer Lodge valley, the floodplain is expansive. The bank-spilling flood of 1908, preeminent among the floods that have made the Clark Fork the mess it is today, deposited a layer of toxic tailings anywhere from one to three feet deep along the river's upper reaches. Some of that deposit is exposed as the salt-rimed slickens I explored from my canoe. The vaster portion is buried beneath more recent sediments, invisible, but seeping into groundwater and the river nonetheless. Much of this, slickens and buried deposits both, is far from the riverbank, at inland oxbows and orphan channels. Additionally, for a hundred years, the valley's farmers and ranchers have irrigated their fields with water drawn from the Clark Fork, spreading suspended heavy metals and fine sediments far and wide over the shallow valley floor.

Second: "broken." Heavy metals in the soil and water threaten human health. Poisoned banks deter vegetation, and banks with no vegetation can't hold the river. Fish populations are stunted.

Third: "fix." That one is more complicated. The sole purview and target of Superfund remediation is human health. The minewaste heavy metals embedded in the valley floor over a century of discharge—copper, cadmium, nickel, arsenic, and lead—can make people sick. Depending on the method and extent of exposure, acute or chronic or both, they cause cancer and lesser ailments at a rate marginally higher than these same ailments are found in the general population. EPA determines threshold levels of "safe" exposure, and individual states often determine their own standards. Such standards differ from place to place based on an array of factors, including land use, likelihood of exposure, regularity of exposure, method of exposure (skin contact? oral ingestion?) and, not least, the feasibility and expense of reducing exposure to below the established threshold levels.

For example, EPA's "arsenic risk concentration levels" for the soil and water along the Clark Fork near Deer Lodge, close to the end of what remediators have labeled "Stretch A," are as follows:

150 ppm for residents in their yards
620 ppm for farmers and ranchers working their fields
680 ppm for children playing in public playgrounds or the county's Arrow Stone Park
1,600 ppm for fishers, swimmers, and inner-tubers wading and floating the river itself.

The thresholds are lower for activities repeated regularly over the course of years, and higher for activities presumed to take place infrequently.

EPA is charged with removing—i.e., remediating—the threat to human health. Get the ppms down to acceptable concentration levels, and as far as EPA is concerned, the river is no longer broken. They're done. Superfund has done its job.

But there is much more wrong with the Clark Fork than the threat it poses to human health. There's the land's diminished agricultural capacity, the water's diminished trout population, the river's diminished ability to perpetuate itself due to erosion and other factors, and the state's diminished enjoyment of the economic benefits of a healthy, tourist-attracting ecosystem. These may pose no threat to human health, but they are damages nonetheless, and they're referred to as "lost resources": attributes and benefits that but for the by-products of mining *should* have been here, and once *were* here, but are here no longer.

In 1983, the state of Montana filed suit against ARCO for the restoration of such lost resources. In 1999 ARCO settled, handing $12 million to the Confederated Salish and Kootenai Tribes (whose treaty rights to the river gave them a stake in the settlement), $86 million to Chavez's DEQ for cleanup of Silver Bow Creek, and $129 million for restoration of lost resources in the upper Clark Fork basin. In 1990, the state of Montana inaugurated an office called the Natural Resource Damage Program (NRDP) to spend that money repairing the river, or, in cases where repair is impossible, replacing the lost resource through the purchase of new state lands. A second settlement in 2008 saddled ARCO with $169 million in liability for remediation of the upper Clark Fork, Butte, and Anaconda's Smelter Hill.

The state's money has been invested, earning 7.5 percent interest for twenty years. Much of the cleanup that's occurred so far has been paid for out of the interest.

NRDP is a different pot of money from Superfund money, and it's spent, at the governor's discretion, on different goals. Where Superfund money is for remediation of health hazards, NRDP money is for restoration. It's the NRDP component of the Clark Fork cleanup that adds orders of magnitude to the task's complexity, requiring intricate coordination and buy-in between multiple parties with multiple and sometimes conflicting agendas.

The Superfund complex, like a complicated medical procedure, is divided into "operable units." There are dozens of them. At some, including the Milltown Dam and Reservoir, urban Anaconda, and the old smelter site, ARCO has taken on remediation work in-house. ARCO's books aren't open to the public, so nobody knows what the company is spending.

Other operable units, including the Streamside Tailings Unit from Butte to Warm Springs Ponds, and the Clark Fork Tailings from Warm Springs downriver to Garrison Junction, are the state's bailiwick. DEQ does the cleanup work out of its own budget, with some additional restoration work funded by the Natural Resource Damage Program pot.

In all of these operable units, there are two kinds of waste: that which will be treated to one degree or another "in place," and that which will be dug up and dumped on the Opportunity Ponds.

The process goes like this. The state first gets consent from the landowner, which might be a private rancher, ARCO, or the state itself, to which ARCO has offloaded a fair amount of its liability property. Next, state scientists study the site, identifying and prioritizing contamination areas for treatment; construction plans and specifications are drawn up, usually by private-sector consultants; and contracts are put out for public bid. Then, assuming a thumbs-up from Montana's governor, who personally controls the NRDP's purse strings, and weather permitting, the earthmovers move in.

The river is rebuilt a couple of miles at a time, in chunks costing $10 million or less, to minimize simultaneous disturbances of the river.

Chavez shows me an illustration at our first stop. It's a small two-lane bridge over Silver Bow Creek on a county road upstream from Opportunity, not far from the Fairmont Hot Springs Resort. Chavez's crews replaced five thousand linear feet of heavily contaminated streambank winding beneath the bridge just last fall; two thousand feet of it washed away in high spring water. His crews will be back out to rebuild it again next week. It happens.

"It's not science," Chavez tells me. "It's kind of art. Everybody's an expert. Nobody likes anybody else's design."

You can't tell a river where to go, or how to behave, and expect it to listen. The river will spill its banks; that's why healthy river valleys are layered with fertile sediment and laced with oxbows. The engineer's job is to create an environment in which the river can "deform naturally" instead of destroying itself in a hydrological process called "unraveling." You build the banks wide and shallow to accommodate floods and peak flows. You re-create a grade that allows the river to move sediment downstream—a river's fundamental geological job—instead of clotting itself into stagnation.

The rebuilt river is not a permanent structure. I've heard the phrase "engineered failure" used to describe the design of geologic structures intended to last a while, making suggestions to the river, guiding it just long enough for the banks to stabilize and natural processes to take over, while the engineering dissolves into obscurity. The phrase always makes me think of a child-rearing strategy. You give advice and then you get out of the way. Bob wanted me to affirm his experience by mimicking it. He couldn't conceive of a contingency in which I might jump the banks. He took my meanderings as a personal affront.

"You shouldn't play God with this stuff," Chavez says. "We're not equipped for it. People want an idyllic babbling brook, but you don't get that on day one."

So far he's moved more than four million cubic yards of contaminated sediments from Silver Bow Creek to Opportunity's ponds, including a five-mile section completed five years ago that was a solid corridor of slickened floodplain two thousand feet wide. Silver Bow, Chavez says, is 90 percent rebuilt, and barring bad weather and do-overs, should be complete by 2013.

Today his crews are working on a two-mile stretch of Silver Bow through Durant Canyon, a narrow constriction occupied by a railroad track threading the base of steep stone walls. DEQ has twenty men working the site, plus another sixty or so contractors. The stretch is budgeted at $5.5 million. The fresh-cut roads are muddy from recent rains, and at a trailer serving as site HQ we pile into a foreman's 4x4 for the last part of the drive, using a walkie-talkie to make sure the skinny road is clear of outgoing dump trucks before we proceed.

This is the first time I've actually seen a river undergoing surgery.

It looks like an abandoned railroad grade in negative relief. I can see where the river went, where a river ought to be, but there's no river there. It's been disassembled. The river—the water, anyway—has been diverted into a tiny ditch at the butt of the berm elevating the railroad track, which can't be moved. (Closer to Butte, Chavez tells me, he had to put Silver Bow into a pipe with a capacity of 70 cfs during spring work, and hope that it didn't rain.)

The riverbed, shed of its water, is naked and uncannily neat. The contaminated soil has already been removed, up to thirteen feet deep in places, and replaced with donor soil stripped from a nearby ranch leased for that purpose.

There's no surfeit of good soil close by, and the dirt that DEQ buys is composted and amended with lime, which helps neutralize the pH, before the new banks are seeded. I ask Chavez where the lime comes from, wondering if it's mined. He tells me it's a by-product of sugar beet processing in Billings, 250 miles away.

A new watercourse has been wound through the canyon like an infinitely repeating S, all shallow bends and curves. The banks are low, defined with wavering golden tubes, two tubes to a side. The tubes are made of coconut matting imported from Sri Lanka. One is wrapped around stones, and stretched out at the bank's base. Another is wrapped around packed soil and placed on top of the tube full of stones.

Between these tube-lined banks, where the water will be, lies an alternation of bare dirt and sections of gleaming new white rock, where the ripples will be. Trout, absent from these waters for a hundred years, will soon fan their egg-filled redds into the rocky interstices. For now, the bed is dotted with bright yellow earth-moving equipment, establishing the gentle gradient that will keep the river moving downhill toward the Pacific.

There are still three miles of Silver Bow through Durant Canyon to rebuild, including a railroad bridge sacrificed to reconstruction that the state will have to replace, but when it's done the water will be steered back out of the ditch, which will be filled, and nature can start taking over again. The water will rise and fall, so stabilizing the new banks is key. Willows and native grasses are planted in the amended soil, and Chavez tells me that high-nutrient effluent flowing out of an inadequate sewage treatment plant in Butte, while threatening a long-term negative impact on water quality, actually helps plant life establish itself in the short term. The restoration of Shit Creek, it turns out, benefits from shit. Beavers will return first. Too soon, Chavez says. They eat the young vegetation before it roots.

Still, if his upstream experience is any guide, Durant Canyon will look like a natural creek to an untrained eye in a few short years. Ten years ago just two bird species could be found in the upper creek watershed. Today there are sixty-nine resident bird species, along with deer, elk, bear, and fox. The first trout returned to Silver Bow in 2008 after a century's absence.

"Get the poison out," Chavez says, "and it'll heal itself."

There are limits, of course. The poison is dispersed, and it's viable to remove only the heaviest concentrations. "Once you make these messes," he admits, "you're always going to live with some of it. You'd be digging to China to get all that zinc out of there."

There's also the issue of where the poison goes once it's gotten out. Where it goes—all of it—is Opportunity. Chavez shakes his head. He knows I'm going to ask.

"What am I going to do with this stuff? I can't shoot it to the sun."

Chavez's DEQ has dibs on a hundred acres of the 6.25-square-mile Opportunity Ponds site on which to dispose of every last molecule of poison excised from Silver Bow Creek and the Clark Fork. ARCO will be obligated to cap it with "growth medium," clean soil, so it doesn't blow back all over creation. Chavez wonders where they're going to get the dirt. He has a hard enough time finding the soil to rebuild a river, never mind to bury the river that's been un-built.

But that's ARCO's problem, not his, and Opportunity is collateral damage, existing damage, unfixable. Chavez's problem—rebuilding the Clark Fork—should be solved in a decade or so, on track and under budget.

It's what comes after that that worries him now, when the large agricultural landowners lining his restored river find themselves fronting a newly thriving trout fishery in the undiscovered middle of the last best place. Mining was the last century's greatest threat to the state's watersheds; development is this century's. What happens when the owners of those economically marginal family ranches realize they're sitting on recreational gold and start subdividing into five-acre mini ranches, each with its own unregulated well drawing down the aquifer, its private septic system spilling into the stream, and its log McMansion butted up against a bank freshly riprapped so its owner can enjoy a sundown Scotch overlooking the pretty river without worrying about it spreading out of its carefully constructed floodplain?

"By fixing this river," Chavez tells me, surprising me, "I'm probably destroying it."

Thanks to a 1984 Montana Supreme Court decision, the state has one of the country's most liberal stream access laws. The rivers—basically anything inside the high-water mark—belong to the citizens. We can wade them, fish them, paddle them, and otherwise putter to our heart's delight. Where cattle fencing and diversion dams create hazards, we can climb the banks and traipse private shores to go around without getting busted for trespassing. In a state where hunting and fishing are more commonly categorized as cold-dead-finger birthrights than mere recreational amenities, citizens cannot be denied access to running water.

The law has fielded challenges over the years, from over-zealous, property-rightist Republican legislatures and out-of-state landowners who don't understand why their purchase of sprawling trophy acreage doesn't include deed and title to the blue-ribbon trout streams running through them.

James Cox Kennedy, the Atlanta-based chairman and CEO of his grandfather's media conglomerate Cox Enterprises, which owns the *Atlanta Journal-Constitution* and the *Austin American-Statesman*, along with dozens of radio and television stations, is one such. Cox owns 3,200 acres of prime southwestern Montana real estate with almost ten miles of frontage on the meandering Ruby River, where he's established a lodge catering to out-of-state visitors with thousands to spend for a day of fly-fishing on the public Ruby and spring-creek tributaries that Kennedy advertises as "private access waters."

Kennedy first came to my attention when the University of Montana began soliciting donations for a new building for the journalism school, and approached Kennedy, a perennial flower on *Forbes* magazine's annual list of the richest Americans. Kennedy, a self-described conservationist, wrote UM's president back to complain that "many Montana residents are making it known that they are not happy with nonresident landowners in their state. In addition, stream and river access issues are also being raised. Until these issues are resolved and our presence in the state is more appreciated, we have decided not to make any further contributions in Montana."

The stiff-arm made news when the journalism school's dean went public with the letter and got a reprimand from the university president, who, it was revealed, had personally forwarded Kennedy's entitled gripe to the state's newly elected governor, Brian Schweitzer. The impression was of a university president happy to throw a cherished stream access law under the bus and carry an out-of-state billionaire's water all the way to the capitol in exchange for a donation to a J-school that the same university president had slapped on the wrist for doing what journalists do.

The access issue in question had arisen over Kennedy's use of barbed wire and electrical fencing to block foot traffic to the Ruby through the two county bridge easements that crossed the river on his property. Local fishers had gone apoplectic over the blockades and sued the county for failing to clear the paths. Access advocates and canoeists and rafters—who almost never used the Ruby anyway, given its distance from any population center where rafters and canoeists congregate—teamed up for a protest float one July Sunday in 2005. I was there, helping friends pass boats over Kennedy's fences to the Ruby's bank, drinking canned beer through hours of lazy bends, watching the Tobacco Root Mountains shimmer in the distance, and scarfing grilled hot dogs at the takeout park in Twin Bridges before driving home to Missoula. I didn't move to Montana to get fenced off a river.

Quasi-rocker Huey Lewis fenced one in for himself. A longtime landowner in the Bitterroot Valley south of Missoula, where his neighbors are Private Wealth Partners chairman Ken Siebel and drive-through investment broker Charles Schwab, Lewis fenced off a watercourse called Mitchell Slough and posted "No Trespass-ing" signs to ward off fishers and duck hunters. Lewis's argument, which a district court judge affirmed in 2006, was that the mu-sician's restorative investments in the stream had so transformed the landscape that it was "no longer a natural waterway," and thus not subject to Montana's stream access law, sending a precedential chill up the spines of river restoration specialists. It looked, for a moment, as if helping restore a river might translate to ownership for the restorer. Two years later the Montana Supreme Court over-turned the decision, reaffirming public access to the fifteen-mile tributary. A year after that, Lewis and his neighbors set out duck feeders along their properties in a backhanded effort to thwart hunters—it's illegal to shoot waterfowl where they're being baited. The slough's self-appointed gatekeepers have also recently de-clined to take their irrigation allotments out of the Bitterroot to feed the slough in winter, when fish are trying to spawn. Appar-ently they'd rather torch the trout they spent so much trying to bring back than share them.

You can't blame them for trying. When and where it's suited them, these have always been rich men's rivers.

Once overwhelmingly dominant, Montana's extractive resource industries—mining and timber mostly—today account for less than 5 percent of the state's economy. The shift has been seismic, throwing thousands of Montanans out of work and leaving the state government struggling to find replacements for the dwindling in-dustrial tax base. No single industry will fill mining's shoes. One patch promoted by Governor Schweitzer is the "restoration econ-omy." A 2009 study commissioned by the governor's office sug-gested that some 3,500 jobs had been created by the Milltown restoration. Casey Hackathorn's is one of those.

A former fishing guide in his early thirties, Hackathorn started full-time work at Trout Unlimited (TU) just six months before we spoke in 2011. With Milltown Dam removed and cleanup of the upper river commencing, TU is focusing attention on improving trout habitat in the tributaries that feed the Clark Fork. The tributaries sprout in the mountains, typically on Forest Service land, and traverse private, mostly agricultural land on their ways to the river. Some are topped with abandoned mines spilling acid wastewater downstream. Others are dammed or gated or diverted in ways that prevent spawning trout from swimming upstream, or fry from surviving the trip down.

TU's preferred fish are natives: westslope cutthroat, bull trout, and browns. Rainbows are pretty, but they hybridize, diluting native gene pools. One challenge facing restorationists as they reopen the branching pathways of a river's upland system is that some of the same blockages that prevent the watershed from full function as a fishery have also isolated valuable populations of genetically pure trout, which stand to suffer in a newly viable free-for-all.

It's Hackathorn's job to survey the tributaries, prioritize them in terms of potential bang for project buck, document and negotiate water rights to support in-stream flows, coordinate stakeholder support, and find and leverage money. There are a thousand water rights in the basin and four hundred "points of diversion." A typical project might involve an irrigation-canal-feeding weir dam that blows out in a spring flood. TU will try to replace the dam with stepped pools to accomplish the same purpose in a fish-friendly manner, or the organization might raise up to $4,000 per cfs to screen diversions to keep trout from losing their way in a maze of irrigation ditches. TU might work with Deer Lodge's Watershed Restoration Coalition or the Clark Fork Coalition to find dollars from the National Fish and Wildlife Foundation, fly-fishing outfitter Orvis, the EPA, one of two national forests, the National Park Service, or Montana Fish, Wildlife & Parks. The big pot of gold is the NRDP, with 39 percent slated for aquatic resource projects.

Because there's a risk of being perceived as improving fisheries for private landowners at least partially at taxpayer expense, TU also lobbies Montana's legislature in support of the state's liberal but perpetually besieged public access laws. Nobody wants to see money spent on something they can't use.

Hackathorn says the Clark Fork currently supports about 20 percent of the trout population it should, and that number should only improve. He hadn't had much optimism that cutthroat could be restored to a rebuilt Silver Bow Creek, but there they are, and remnant populations of browns appear to be thriving. Still, the nutrient loading from Butte's leaky sewage plant that has helped Joel Chavez reestablish vegetation on the banks of the creek remains a problem for trout revival. The nutrients send algae growth into overdrive, sucking oxygen out of the water and starving fish. The city is scheduled to update the antiquated plant in 2012. It's a job Bob would have bid for.

The ecology of an optimally functional fishery is a dance of fine balances. "What we know now," Hackathorn tells me, "will not be what we know in ten years, I guarantee you."

That's why TU and the rest of the "restoration community" prefer a long view and a slow go. The state, meanwhile, after a long dither, seems inclined to hurry up and spend. The state and its administrators have a legacy interest. They want accomplishments to trumpet now, before their successors in public office step in to take credit.

As a result, there's a risk, inherent to the process, of applying fixes to the river not because we know how to fix it, but because money is available.

Still, that's a problem the Clark Fork's restoration community is happy to have. Nowhere else in the nation is there such a confluence of environmental impairment and deep-pocketed, deeply hooked resources for repair.

There's no irony in Hackathorn's voice—and no call for any—when he describes this circumstance behind his job as "a huge opportunity."

✙

The Clark Fork may be a special case, but it's not an isolated one, and few men have worked harder to turn environmental tragedy to triumph than Pat Williams.

Williams, seventy-four, is old school now. Nobody still breathing remembers the zenith of Butte's interestingness—call it 1919—but Williams was a child there in the booming war years of the 1940s, when the mines were still bustling. Mining was still a thing men did underground, with shovels and explosives. He remembers the sound of a shift whistle and the tramp of boots on gravel as thousands of men marched to work and thousands more marched back home, or to uptown bars. He remembers taking Butte's inside-out landscape for granted, playing on barren brown hills—tailings mounds, he knows now—"that I thought God put there." He was there in 1955, when the Berkeley Pit began displacing underground hard-rock miners with giant ore-hauling trucks, and in 1973, when Columbia Gardens, the bucolic amusement park William A. Clark built in the early years of the century, burned to the ground overnight in what was widely considered a case of arson. Columbia Gardens was one of Butte's sentimental treasures, and the Anaconda Company had discovered new ore bodies beneath it. The embers were hardly cool before the expanding pit swallowed the site.

Pat Williams remembers going to Columbia Gardens and seeing a sign on a stake in a meadow threaded with tiny streams. The sign identified the trickles as the headwaters of the Clark Fork of the Columbia River.

He remembers going down the hill to Silver Bow Creek to play with Bob Knievel—later Evel—with whom he shared a grandmother and on occasion a home, and staining their bare legs green in the copper-soaked water. Pat's parents lived on Butte's West Side, ran a restaurant downtown, and kept a nearby apartment for weekend nights when they worked until the last customer left, sometimes at three in the morning. He remembers hanging around the restaurant all evening and walking home on those late nights, his mom holding one hand and his dad holding the other, lest he get swept away in the teeming streets.

Like everyone who grew up there, he's intensely proud of Butte. He's also intensely saddened by what it's become, as only those who've left Butte can afford to be.

He worked briefly in the mines as a nipper—a miner's assistant—and developed an admiration for hard work and unsanctioned smarts. He spent a couple of summers working at the smelter in Anaconda, stirring vats of melting copper with a long stick.

Williams lost two uncles and a best friend to the mines. Instead of following their footsteps, he went to the University of Montana and became a schoolteacher. In 1980, he was in his first year of nine consecutive two-year terms as a U.S. congressman from Montana when ARCO shut the mines.

He hadn't been expecting it. Earlier that year ARCO had told Montana's legislative delegation that it was exploring building a new smelter in Anaconda and a new refinery in Great Falls. So when ARCO called a meeting with the delegation in D.C., Williams and his fellow lawmakers anticipated good news to deliver back home. Instead, ARCO announced it was closing its Montana properties.

"When?" Williams asked.

"In the morning," the ARCO rep answered.

Williams retired from Congress in 1996 and he's lived in Missoula since, teaching at the university, writing guest columns, and holding positions at various think tanks. When we sit down for coffee at Bernice's Bakery in November 2011, he's adjusting to his first year of retirement from the university—the first year he hasn't worked since fourth grade. Even so, he still holds the title of senior fellow emeritus at the Center for the Rocky Mountain West.

As an officeholder, Williams introduced sixteen bills designating new and protecting established Montana wilderness areas, a category of nonindustrial land management enabled by the Wilderness Act of 1964. Williams's last effort passed Congress in 1988 but got pocket-vetoed by President Reagan, putting a two-decade-and-counting stake through the heart of efforts to preserve Montana's remaining wilderness.

Montana is no longer the extractive resource powerhouse that it was in 1919 or in 1940. The jobs that have replaced mining jobs are often poorly paid, seasonal, or have sprung up in a peculiar Montana service sector that caters to tourists and nature lovers. If Montana spent most of the last century as a resource colony for the American coasts, it's entering the twenty-first century largely as an environmental theme park for moneyed out-of-state visitors and pleasure seekers.

Williams has spent much of his post-political career coming to terms with that shift, and proposing plans to exploit it. He as much as anyone has given currency to the concept of a "restoration economy," an idea as intuitively simple as the pitch is difficult: putting people to work repairing damage done in the past. There are almost five thousand abandoned hard-rock mines in Montana, many of them leaking acidic mine water into the upland forest tributaries that feed the state's famous trout streams. Montana has 32,000 miles of logging roads, only 20 percent of which the Forest Service has enough money to maintain. The rest fall into disrepair, shedding sediment into streams and blocking fish at crossings. Williams has spent a decade trying to convince politicians to invest in restoring such scars.

He's had little luck. Landscape-scale restoration is expensive. State budgets are tight. Federal earmarks—a natural conduit for restoration-aimed funds, especially in the vote-thin West—have largely fallen victim to political excess and antigovernment rhetoric. The immediate-term jobs promised by restoration are too few, and too expensive. In Montana, funding for the federal Legacy Roads and Trails Remediation Program averaged $5.5 million annually since the program began in 2008, translating to ninety-five annual jobs—a federal expenditure of almost $58,000 per job, few of which pay anywhere near that much. But that's short-term thinking. The point, Williams says, is not the immediate jobs-to-investment ratio, but the long-term benefits of a restored and healthy landscape in a state where untouched nothingness—not sloughing roads and poisoned rivers—is the draw. There's a broad economic benefit, he's sure, to clean water and healthy ecosystems, and a corollary political benefit in building coalitions between labor unions and environmentalists.

Montana governor Brian Schweitzer has shown more restorative enthusiasm than any other western-state politician, even as his left hand paves the way to dig up huge chunks of eastern Montana for coal to sell to China. He released a conceptual framework for a five-year restoration plan in 2008, talked the legislature into a $250,000 restoration appropriation, hosted two restoration summit meetings, and issued a report in 2009 employing Missoula's Milltown restoration as a case study. The $113 million spent on that portion of the Clark Fork Superfund restoration accounted for an estimated 3,563 jobs. A third of restoration jobs go to the construction industry (including Envirocon), 15 percent to environmental consultants like Hackathorn, and 10 percent to government offices, with the remainder divided among various support industries. Because restoration so often requires demolition, it often looks on the ground like a construction project. Earthmoving construction projects aren't feasible during the frozen half of the year in Montana, and even when they're underway, big machines do most of the work. The same big trucks that make the Continental Pit a more efficient producer of copper than human miners make restoration, ironically, not labor-intensive enough to pay many human dividends. The dividends that restoration does provide are slim. Unlike Montana's historic mining, the work isn't dangerous enough, or unionized enough, to pay top wages.

Restoration projects also tend to take a while, frequently exceeding any given legislator's political life. "The thing about legislators," Williams tells me, "is that they like to cut ribbons."

In the past, Williams has lobbied Montana's biennial legislature for restoration appropriations. In 2011, the session just past when I talked to him, the statehouse was so overrun with ideological Republican flamethrowers that he didn't even bother to try.

If there's been a singular restoration success story, it's the Clark Fork, an ongoing showcase for the healing powers of deep pockets. Much of that money was squeezed out of ARCO, and there aren't nearly as many ARCOs in the West as there are Clark Forks. Besides, in the current political climate it's considered unseemly for government to create jobs. That's supposed to be the private sector's prerogative.

It hasn't helped, Williams admits, that several case studies commissioned by the Center for the Rocky Mountain West found that even when restoration dollars are appropriated, too many of them end up paying for—there's no nice way to say it—more studies.

Schweitzer, a lame duck in 2011, no longer has staff dedicated to the state's restoration program, and when I ask Williams who today is lobbying for restoration, the answer is "virtually nobody." Organized labor throws its reduced weight around in dribs and drabs, and a few small businesses step up for especially attractive projects.

"I get a feeling that people are turning away from it," Williams tells me. "There's less excitement as the money gets thin. You may be writing about the last major project of this sort"—the Clark Fork—"for fifty years."

# PART VII

# CONFLUENCE

*Who was it said we were invented by water as a
means of its getting itself from one place to the other?*

—BARRY HANNAH, *Ray*

It's not easy to imagine a forested hillside burning if you've never
seen it up close. The temptation is strong to make more of it than
there is. Flames flare here and there, orange lines creep, and charred
spots smolder. The smoke is thick and gray, turning to black when
an individual tree torches in sudden entirety.

That's what I wanted to see. Smoke and flames, thrill and a hint
of fear, weren't enough. I wanted to see a mountain explode.

My dream cabin didn't last. It was never mine. Eight months
after I moved in, I moved out again, this time downstream to Bonner, just across the interstate from where Milltown Reservoir used
to be.

While a 2011 earthquake cracked D.C.'s Washington Monument and New York City huddled in fear of a wayward tropical
storm, the mountains above my house burned.

I was sitting at home, staring at a computer, when my house-
mate pulled into the driveway and came straight to my door. "Oh
my God, have you been outside? It's crazy!" She walked me down
Riverside Drive, peeking over rooftops and yard trees at bruised
plumes of smoke, until we came to an open view and saw the flames.
They'd jumped a ravine and were burning two hillsides now, just
fifteen minutes after she'd first driven past and seen the initial con-

flagration. A gusty wind was blowing east, away from Missoula proper and toward our house at the end of the street.

Bonner is a neighborhood with village pretensions and few amenities. As far as the postal service is concerned, it's Missoula, but its founding was more or less discrete. Bonner grew up around Marcus Daly's and William A. Clark's lumber mills on the banks of the Blackfoot River, a five-minute walk through woods from my door. Across the river is a defunct mill, last owned by a company called Stimson, from which the industrial bedroom communities of Bonner, Milltown, Piltzville, and West Riverside radiate like spokes.

Several stubby peaks line up in a row behind Bonner, and the circumscribed grid of homes, twelve blocks long and three blocks deep, lies along the topographic squiggle where their slopes level into back yards. The fire quickly spread the length of them, and everyone in Bonner came out to watch. We pulled lawn chairs out of trailer parks onto the gravel skirt of the road, or stood on pickup roofs, or walked toward the smoke carrying cameras and vodka lemonades in insulated travel mugs from the giant truck stop across the feeder that serves as Bonner's grocery of first resort.

Between my house and the truck stop is a chain-linked expanse of abandoned flat that used to corral logs awaiting milling. Fire departments from around the state colonized the site as a base of operations. That's where the helicopters landed. They dragged huge rubberized buckets on long tethers, dipped them into the rivers, and flew pendulous patterns, the liquid load swinging out in banking arcs like NASCAR racers. When they got where they were going, to a flaming tongue's closest advance on a house, the pilots triggered the buckets and dumped what looked from the ground like a pitifully ineffective splash of mist on the forest floor.

The next day, driving across the Clark Fork into Missoula, I stopped on a bridge and watched one of the copters dangle its bucket into a wide spot in the river while college kids floating in tubes, towing beer coolers, watched.

The mountain didn't explode. Fallen limbs and pine needles burned off quickly, exposing shale talus, the sort that provides about as much traction as ball bearings on glass. A few full trees did torch, but most just got their bark singed.

The sun, ember-orange behind the smoke-and-cloud understory, was prettier than the inferno proper. The Riverside/Bonner blaze had a pretty good run, encompassing more than 3,000 acres and sucking up more than $5 million in expenses to fight it. A month later they were still mopping up hot spots.

The fire overshadowed most of Missoula's news for a week: the fund-raisers for the new "Max Wave" kayak play wave slated for the Clark Fork downtown; newly released drawings of the state park going in to mark the Milltown confluence; another dead homeless man fished out of the river downtown. On December 10, we watched a total lunar eclipse turn the moon the color of copper.

By August 2010, Milltown Reservoir was gone. A Helena-based contractor had been hired to reshape the Clark Fork's floodplain and carve the river's new channel. Alan Armstrong, an excavator operator, took a break and climbed out of his machine to examine a tackle box his blade had uncovered. Since the contractor was charged with reporting any historic artifacts unearthed in the restoration, he called it in to his supervisor and left it where it was. A dozer operator said he'd found part of a tackle box in the same area several days before, and this one still contained lures and fishing licenses, with phone numbers. The licenses were legible. They belonged to Missoulians Russ Piazza, a financial portfolio manager, and Steve Carey, a media lawyer. An administrator with the state's Natural Resource Damage Program called Piazza's number. Piazza answered.

It had been twenty-five years since Piazza and Carey took a raft fishing on the Clark Fork just upstream of Missoula. They'd run into a snag at a blind bend and flipped the boat, tossing its contents into the river. Neither Piazza nor Carey had changed their phone numbers since.

A few days later Armstrong was back where he'd left the first half of the tackle box when he noticed a mess of fishing line tangled with a bunch of keys chained to a medallion. He rubbed the mud off and tossed the keys on the floor of his cab. Two minutes later his foreman radioed. Piazza had called to ask, on the off chance, whether any keys had been found with the tackle. His mother had given the medallion to his father when he joined the navy to fight in World War II. It was one of the few mementos Piazza had had of his long-deceased parents.

Twenty-five years after it had gone overboard, it came back. On its face was an icon symbolizing the Sacred Heart, Mary, Joseph, and St. Christopher, the patron saint of long journeys. It was the perfect human-interest story dug up from the margins of an abstract river restoration. Things were back where they belonged.

⚘

I'm fascinated by the out of place. Elk antlers in a shallow pit, or a mummified smelterman in a glacier. Things that get lost and then found.

I was married once to a woman whose father had the reputation of being the first man to tumble down Texas's Rio Grande in a johnboat. She had grown up canoeing through the Big Bend. There was a picture of her there, maybe three years old, trailing a rubber ducky with a stick and string from the bow of an old aluminum Grumman canoe while her parents paddled. Her dad had a dozen old Grummans scattered among the various barns dotting his gentleman's farm in Temple. He and his wife let us use one when they took us out on the Lampasas River one summer day. We picnicked on deli meats and cheese and fruit and beer.

On the riverbed under the invisible water that day I found a thin round ruin, a patterned disk carved in sandstone the size of a 45-rpm record and as thick as a thumb. I've kept it with me through half a dozen moves over more than fifteen years now, and only recently did I realize that it's an intact skeet trap that landed in the river and lay there, eroded clay instead of sandstone. It must not have been there long when I found it or it would have turned back entirely to sand already. I loved not knowing what it was, an untranslated treasure. I like it even better now, an almost perfectly transient object, designed to be shattered and, failing that, built to disintegrate. It's remarkable that it's still whole. I can hold it in my hands. I scrunch tissue paper around it every time I pack.

⁜

Less than a year after the Clark Fork flowed freely for the first time since he'd stoppered it, Clark's youngest daughter was located by a journalist, and then died. Huguette Clark was 104 years old when she passed away in a New York hospital on May 24, 2011. She'd come into the world two years before her daddy's dam was built, and she'd outlasted it by three. Her most recent publicly available photograph was more than eighty years old. She had spent the last two decades of her life behind a blanket of privacy, collecting fine French dolls and cared for by nurses in an anonymous hospital room while her multimillion-dollar mansions in California, Connecticut, and New York sat empty. She left a fortune, primed for a squabble, estimated at half a billion dollars.

Huguette's hermitism was breached when Bill Dedman, an investigative reporter at MSNBC, published a series of articles exploring her family history and raising questions about the lawyers who represented her finances and shielded her from family and strangers alike. The article briefly resuscitated the story of William A. Clark, once toe-to-toe with John D. Rockefeller as the richest man in America, but long since forgotten outside Montana.

When Huguette—who never spoke to Dedman—was involuntarily brought to light, Governor Schweitzer wrote her a letter, asking her to steer some of her fortune back to Montana, the source of so much of it. He never got a reply.

The day before Huguette died, it turned out, Butte schoolchildren had started their own letter-writing campaign. They wanted a slice of the family fortune to rebuild Columbia Gardens, the Butte amusement park built by her father at the turn of the century. A newspaper article quoted the kids' teacher saying they wouldn't let Huguette's demise stop them. They'd send their letters to the lawyers.

I wish them luck without holding out much hope. You don't get anything—not a restored river, not a father's respect, not one red cent—for free.

⁜

Since I moved to Montana I've kept an annual log of my river miles: when, what river, which stretch, in what boat, with whom. If I end up dumping, or see a deer swimming the river, or the channel has changed course from the year before, I make a note. It's not impressive by chronic canoeist standards, but like any log it marks a sense of accomplishment. It feels good to record the miles. The most times I've ever put a boat on the water in a season is thirty-three. The most miles I've marked in a year is 350. The latest-season float I've done was in mid-November. This year, 2012, was the earliest I've put in: February 4.

Quinlan and I are having beers to celebrate another Friday when I start talking him into it. I'd been watching the river on my drives up and down Interstate 90 to Opportunity. We'd had several hard freezes already, days when the Clark Fork's banks constricted the flow with shelf ice and the water turned black and filled with a silvery aggregate of floating slush. You could stand on the bridges and hear the sandpapery grind of that slush moving downstream, brushing itself apart against the banks, but each hard freeze had been followed by warmer days and a melt. There were sucker holes between the cold snaps.

Canoeing in the cold is no particular problem, you just dress for it and don't dump, but shore ice is worth avoiding. You need a solid shore for getting safely into and out of a canoe.

I had driven upstream just the day before and seen no shore ice. I tell Quinlan we should go for it. He agrees.

I almost regret it when I wake up the next morning—it's bitter cold before the sun rises over the hills—but a paddling plan engaged is a hard thing to back out of. I drive to Quinlan's house and we strap his big green canoe onto his truck and drive both our vehicles upstream, just beyond Missoula. We pick a nine-mile stretch we haven't paddled before from the guidebook and leave a truck parked in a pullout at its tail end, where a little gravel beach pokes into the river from a bank piled with two feet of snow.

The park that accesses the river is gated closed for the season, so, after post-holing through crusty snow for a quarter-mile to confirm a viable bank, we thread a strap through the seventeen-foot canoe's bow handle and drag it, loaded with waterproof bags stuffed with extra warm clothes, across the snow to the river.

As usual, before putting in Quinlan asks, "You sure you want to do this?"

"Nope."

We step into the canoe, wedging insulated boots under the thwarts to kneel on the foam pads glued to the floor, and snug our thighs tight with nylon straps glued to the hull. The ground is white, the sky is blue, and the black river carries us downstream. For no particular reason, we start laughing at the same time. "Hell yeah," Quinlan says. We're sure now.

Within a few minutes we've passed a real-estate-for-sale sign posted on the left bank—targeting guided out-of-state fly fishers, I imagine—and I launch my daydream script of somehow, someday being able to buy a place like this: on the water, shielded from the interstate, an easy commute to Missoula but far enough away to forget that it's there. The same thing everyone wants. The rarest, most expensive thing.

We're barely out of sight of the little gravel bar put-in when we come to the river's first braid. A thin right channel cuts off from what looks like the river's mainstream and sneaks around a broad island topped with snow like an over-frosted cupcake. As soon as we pass all possibility of hewing right, we see the log dead ahead. It had probably come down the spring before, toppled off its undercut bank, and now reclines at full stretch from bank to bank. We swing the canoe alongside the bank, climb out on the island to portage, and spend half an hour just studying the log.

The upstream curve of it, where the water pillows, has formed a polished convexity of glass-smooth ice, transitioning to craggy drippings that follow the furrows of bark on the trunk's downstream side. The log's limbs, starting midstream and reaching toward us, are hung with heavy, beaker-shaped ice stalactites where water has lapped the limbs' undersides and receded, freezing to icy pearls in the cold air between waves, lapping and layering all night long. Nearer shore, where the limbs thin into branches, dozens of switchy fingers drag in the water, bouncing in and out of the flow, building tiny glass bells where their tips bob.

On shore, the dry limbs sprout fluttery ridgebacks of lattice ice, wings of watery lace melting at the touch of a tongue.

The dead thing blocking our way is an elaborate chandelier of water that will not be here tomorrow, and may never have been here—not like this—before.

Three deer climb the bank ahead of us and stand watching. A baldy follows another baldy upstream over our heads.

There's a lot to like about this stretch of river. There is none of the obvious contamination to be found upstream, no slickened soils, no green cattle bones. The Clark Fork modifies its character below Garrison Junction, near Deer Lodge, where the Little Blackfoot flows in. It gets bigger, for one thing, and relatively steeper. The water moves faster, and since sediment tends to drop out of suspension in slow water, this stretch has seen significantly less deposition of nasties. The gradient also gives the river impetus to cut new channels, and even as hills and then mountains close in on it, adding a flavor of the Blackfoot, the channel migrates across the narrowing valley floor, like the Bitterroot.

Quinlan and I had lived in Missoula more than twenty years between us, and neither of us had ever paddled this stretch of the Clark Fork. Neither of us, well stocked with fishing and boating friends, had even heard mention of anyone paddling it, but it is too good—too close, too silent, too fishy-looking—to be unknown.

We were floating a secret stash. Such stashes are time-honored Missoula traditions, unspoken agreements among like minds aimed at protecting scattered treasures like this piece of river from too much love. This piece of Clark Fork must serve as secret stash to dozens of Missoula river rats who'll never say a word. It's there for the finding, but ask me and I'll tell you there's nothing there.

⁺ϯ₋

There is surely a genuine Montana, but I can't speak to it. I'm a seventh-generation Texan and the culture of that state runs as deep in me as in anyone with a competing claim. Any lack of confidence I may feel in speaking as a Texan, or for Texans, or of Texans, is overwhelmed by sheer pedigree. I judge the world from the vantage of where I'm from. Montanans do too. I'm not from here. My family hasn't been ranching here, or logging, or mining since the nineteenth century, or even the 1970s. I don't hunt. I barely fish.

I can't speak to genuine Montana. I don't particularly care to.

I'm interested in an imaginary Montana. The one that brought William A. Clark from the schoolhouses of Iowa, and me from the pavement preserve of Houston.

There are a few states so overloaded with mythology that they're essentially countries unto themselves. Texas is one. Montana for sure.

In 1941, East Coast literary critic Leslie Fiedler took a job in the English Department at the University of Montana in Missoula. Like visiting professors before and since, he made hay while he was here. "Montana; or The End of Jean-Jacques Rousseau," published in *Partisan Review*, made the case for Montana as a "by-product of European letters, an invention of the Romantic movement in literature." Certainly Fiedler thought so. What he saw was a fatal disconnect between Montana's imported-from-Europe sense of itself as a land of cowboy nobility and the discomfiting fact of that noble self's brutal subjugation of the land's—Rousseau's—noble savages.

Considering the state's identity in terms of psychological self-awareness, Fielder identifies three stages of "Frontier" (stage one being simple survival), and straddles Montana between stages two and three. Stage two, Fiedler wrote, marks a territory "torn between an idolatrous regard for its refurbished past . . . and a vague feeling of guilt at the confrontation of the legend of its past with the real history that keeps breaking through." Fiedler called stage three a "pseudo-Frontier, a past artificially contrived for commercial purposes, the Frontier as bread and butter." The state of Montana, as a function of the American imagination, was becoming a self-parodying anticipatory reflection of what the rest of the country—judging from movies and books—thought it should be.

When Steinbeck drove through in 1960, he stayed one night, maybe two. He bought a hat in Livingston, whose wild Saturday nights Jimmy Buffett later memorialized in song. It was October. Maybe he got cold. Maybe he was duding up; he was soon to meet up with his flown-in wife for an unwritten-about month. He already knew everything he needed to know to write "with Montana it is love, and it's difficult to analyze love when you're in it." That says quite a bit about John Steinbeck, and pretty much nothing about Montana. Steinbeck imagined Montana. He thought it was pretty.

In 2001, *New York Times* columnist David Brooks published *Bobos in Paradise*, his wry, mocking indictment of human attempts to live well. Brooks writes about Missoula with more disdain than might appear seemly from someone whose visits to the state include dude ranch stays. He unfurls Missoula as a blanket for his picnic of pet peeves, which particularly includes well-off liberals. What Brooks found in Montana, oddly, modernly, was a blank slate for his aesthetic distaste. He's not outdoorsy; who would've guessed? He's not spiritually woo-woo; who knew? He resents what he calls Missoula's lack of ambition. He observes that Montana can be cold in winter, and he can't imagine anything to like about being cold.

Brooks's basic charge, which he shares with Leslie Fiedler, is hypocrisy. To Fiedler, Montana was a state wearing mountain-man drag, playing for the coasts. To Brooks, Missoula is shorthand for shallow enviro-spirituality and an overly smug pride in "place."

Norman Maclean, raised by a fly-fishing minister in Missoula, wrote *A River Runs Through It* in 1976. Robert Redford made a movie based on it in 1992. It's frequently noted—though Brooks somehow missed it—that the movie, while largely set on the Blackfoot River, was not filmed there. The Blackfoot was a working river, with a mill, traffic, houses, and drunks on inner tubes. Redford filmed the river scenes on the Gallatin near Bozeman, the Boulder, and the upper Yellowstone, and at Granite Falls in Wyoming. All of them looked more like the Montana river Redford imagined in Maclean.

Even Maclean's novella had neglected to mention the mill that operated at the river's mouth for a century, or the dam that was built when the author was six, past which any Missoulian visiting the Blackfoot had to travel. That's not the Montana America wanted to see.

✢

Missoula is a town where texting teenagers can sprint into the middle of any city street in full and secure knowledge that the pedestrian-loving populace will come to a screeching halt—no matter what risk to traffic—to let them pass. Entire residential sections of town have no stop signs; people are just expected to go slow and keep an eye out, and people generally do. Any artistic performance at all, by child or adult, will be applauded with a standing ovation. Missoula is proud to recount that John Updike once called the one-time Berkeley of the Rockies "the Paris of the '90s," due to the prestige and density of local writers like William Kittredge, Rick DeMarinis, Richard Hugo, James Welch, and James Crumley. The prideful appellation is alleged only. There's no source for it, and when my newspaper contacted Updike for confirmation after yet another sloppy assertion in the daily, he couldn't recall having said any such thing.

It's reputation that counts, and by reputation Missoula is home to more nonprofit organizations per capita than any place in the nation. A quarter of the automobiles purchased in the county are said to be Subarus. Every last waiter in every crummy restaurant, and in the good ones, supposedly has a PhD. Missoula is inordinately proud of all the smart people it has lured away from traditionally productive lives to live in the cocoon. It is a very pleasant cocoon.

While the billboards for traffic headed east advertise skanky Lake Berkeley, those for traffic headed west into Missoula advise visitors to "Stay Cool, Stay Downtown" at the Holiday Inn. The picture is a stock photo of a kayaker playing in whitewater. The Clark Fork is being amenitized. Missoula's economy depends on it.

The river here has been remade every bit as much as restoration is remaking it upstream near Opportunity, and as much as mining remade Silver Bow above that. The Clark Fork was walled out of its natural downtown channel in 1962, scouring the foundations of the historic eight-story Wilma Theatre, and filled in to create Caras Park on the new riverbank. There are bridges running over it, pipelines buried under it, ditches dredged off of it, culverts pouring into it, and busted dams diverting it. On hot summer days, hundreds of floaters emerge from the Clark Fork onto the city's streets, wearing bathing suits, tanned arms threaded through inner tubes, headed back home after an afternoon's drift. Crowded-out fishers call this the "tube hatch." Downtown, a pavilion has been built on the bank from which to view kayakers spinning on the recently installed whitewater, Brennan's Wave, beneath it. Images taken from that view have become ubiquitous in Missoula media.

A shot like that accompanied the blurb when *Outside* magazine named Missoula one of its best places to live—again—in 2011. Trying to distinguish Missoula from a similarly "sports-obsessed burg" like Boulder, Colorado, the writer told one of Missoula's favorite stories about itself: "The former lumber town is in close enough contact with its industrial past to have retained its old grit."

Yes and no. In the case of Milltown's literal grit, certainly not. That grit got outsourced to Opportunity.

Missoula is a beautiful, smart, funny, conflicted town, equal parts outdoorsy playground and industrial HQ, home to hunting hippies and reactionary gearheads. I'm in love with it in the way that one falls in love with people and places and things they can never truly possess, which is all of them. Being in love with Missoula, I'm in debt to Opportunity, but blaming Missoula doesn't make sense. Missoula just wanted the best that it could get, and got it. Opportunity sought the same, and failed. We're all guilty of something. Not everyone can win.

⊹

I'm at home in Bonner, sitting at my desk, papers held flat by a copper ingot the size of my index finger. I bought it off a curio shelf at a bookstore in Butte for $5. The woman behind the counter had snapped that it wasn't for sale, but when I turned it over to expose a price sticker she relented. I wanted copper I could see and hold. Otherwise it's out of sight, in the innards of my digital recorder, my desk radio, my cell phone, my change jar, the rusting strings on an ill-used guitar. It's in the lace guides of my hiking boots and the buckles of my belts and the zipper of the Gore-Tex drysuit I wear when the water's too cold to fall into. It's in the guts of my camera, the memory cards that store my pictures, and the computer on which I edit the photos to look the way I want. The plumbing that carries my water is copper and the wires that power my appliances are copper, and so is the wiring in the wireless router that shoots the e-mail across space to my screen.

The e-mail is from Hong Kong, from the Society of Publishers in Asia. Through a professional relationship in Texas, I've been asked to help judge the society's annual "Awards for Editorial Excellence." I'll be considering a category called "Excellence in Environmental Reporting."

There are five entries to rank. The first one I open is about acute heavy-metal pollution in one of China's biggest, filthiest rivers.

The Xiang River runs generally south to north, like the Clark Fork, on its way to join the mammoth Yangtze, home of Three Gorges Dam. Its watershed supports forty million people in Hunan Province.

The Xiang is lined with tens of thousands of smelters, large and small, legally permitted and otherwise. Since the 1970s it has been known as China's most metal-polluted river. Cancers cluster in riverside villages, and farmland flooded and irrigated with Xiang water has been poisoned.

The award entry reported that China had just named the Xiang a national environmental priority and earmarked $71 billion in Hong Kong dollars for cleaning the river up. A party chief named Zhou Qiang suggested, "The Xiang will turn to the Rhine of the East."

That's just one river in China.

Studies by the Nanjing Agricultural University say as much as 10 percent of the rice grown on China's mainland could be tainted by cadmium—the same zinc-smelting by-product that poisoned five-year-old Bingje Xiaomao to death in 2008 in a village called Xinma, south of Hunan's capital city. A now-defunct electroplate manufacturer called Longteng Industry allegedly poured its smelter waste into open fields while paid-off officials turned a blind eye. Bingje was one of dozens of documented deaths. Her family got a settlement equal to just over $900 in U.S. dollars.

Longteng could afford it. Mining and smelting amount to 70 percent of the watershed's economy.

The country's Institute of Geographic Sciences and Natural Resources estimates that as much as 10 percent of China's farmland is contaminated with heavy metals, including, as on the Clark Fork, cadmium, copper, arsenic, and lead. Up to 90 percent of the vegetables sold in Hong Kong come from the mainland province of Guangdong, one of China's most metal-burdened regions. Lead in Hong Kong market vegetables is almost three times the global standard. Like Anaconda, Hong Kong can only afford to be so safe. As in Anaconda, hard data is hard to come by.

At a certain point, considering China, the stay-at-home Western mind boggles and repetition bleeds the percentages dry, but whether I can comprehend it or not, China is reenacting—at a dwarfing scale—the amped-up industrialization that gripped the United States in the early twentieth century.

There are far more thorough books than this one on the exploding Chinese economy, but a few facts are suggestive. Over the next forty years, 300 million rural Chinese people will move into cities. By 2025, China will have 221 cities of more than a million people. (The United States has nine such cities, three of which are in Texas; the entire state of Montana was projected to welcome its millionth resident in late 2012.) An estimated five million new buildings and 170 new transit systems will be constructed to accommodate China's urban influx. The construction will rely on copper installed by copper-driven equipment made in copper-fed factories. According to a 2007 MIT study, China is taking the equivalent of two 500-megawatt coal-fired electrical power plants online every week, expanding the country's capacity by the size of the entire UK power grid every year. All that power will leave those plants on copper wire. Many of those plants, if Montana governor Brian Schweitzer has his way, will burn coal stripped from the plains of eastern Montana. The state has survived, but not thrived, on a fitful amenity economy, and many residents are eager for a return to the misremembered stabilities of Montana's resource-colony days.

As much as Chinese infrastructure is projected to grow over the next decade, Chinese consumer demand for new copper-based cars, water heaters, refrigerators, and electronics is on track to surpass it. The same modernization—rushed and overdue both—is underway in India as well, where electrical power infrastructure is growing at up to 20 percent a year. Between 1980 and 2010, world copper consumption expanded by an average of 10 percent a year. In 1930, global demand for copper was about 2,000,000 tonnes. In 2007 it was 18,084,000 tonnes. In 2030, estimates suggest, it will more than double to 37,865,000 tonnes, in which case global mining conglomerates will have to unearth as much new copper over the next quarter-century as has yet been produced in all of gilded history.

When copper prices rise, metal theft becomes profitable, and newspapers circulate stories about Detroit gangs stripping copper wire out of telephone company switching boxes and Arizona meth addicts poaching the copper fixtures off farmland irrigation systems and selling them to recyclers for the commodity price.

You can find elaborate "peak copper" hypotheses on the web if you're into that kind of thing, but copper is almost endlessly recyclable, so, unlike oil, copper won't just suddenly be gone when underground supplies run out. Fear of a dwindling copper supply is nothing new. Geologist and copper-mining expert Ira Joralemon warned in 1924 that "the age of electricity and of copper will be short. At the intense rate of production that must come, the copper supply of the world will last hardly a score of years. . . . Our civilization based on electrical power will dwindle and die."

He was obviously wrong. Prophets of end times usually are. Then again, they only have to be right once.

While China, the world's largest copper importer, drives global demand, the metal is increasingly sourced in South America. Chile now produces about 36 percent of world demand, and Peru pitches in 15 percent, making them the top two copper producers in the world.

Chinese mining is expanding, but China is still a relatively small producer of minerals. So China buys mines in Canada, South America, and Asia. Some have smelters associated with their mines, as Butte had Anaconda. Most ship copper concentrate to existing smelters in South Korea and Japan. China puts the finished copper to use in consumer goods and sells them to the United States. Neither country has to look at the smelter cities supplying them. The smelter cities have no view of the mining towns that supply them. Nobody tours either town's dump. Like Opportunity, they disappear from the maps.

Jim Kuipers was flying to Chile to help draft new environmental regulations, ninety years after the Anaconda Company purchased the largest copper mine in the world there. Ecuador, on the other hand, he says, remains a regulatory Wild West. The technology to mine more cleanly, Kuipers knows, exists. Corporate motivation to employ it, at a premium, does not.

It's not hard to imagine the Opportunities.

Every last ounce of the copper currently mined from Dennis Washington's Continental Pit—itself a blip on the contemporary mining radar—is now sold to China. You can hardly buy Butte copper in Butte. The Butte Copper Company gift shop down on the Flats sells hammered copper plates made in India, copper cookware from Indonesia, copper tea kettles from Turkey, and imported braided copper bracelets that are supposed to relieve arthritis. Even the little plastic-boxed ore samples are imported. I may have gotten the last ingot in town.

There is no good day like a good day in Missoula. No one who's ever spent a good day in Missoula will argue the point, and those who haven't just don't know. An early spring day maybe, in mid-March, under a blue sky paled with white wisps. It's sixty-two degrees, a temperature designed for bare skin unsheathed after a winter's swaddling. There's more winter on the way, but it's not here yet.

Maybe you drive a canoe just up the Blackfoot to the Weigh Station put-in and make a short day of it. You'll paddle past the old Bonner mill, through the former holding ponds that log-jammed floating timber and over the half-buried foundation of the old dam that held it back, the Milltown Dam's little brother—the first time anyone's run that in a hundred years. Above you, out of sight but in earshot, earthmovers are digging up a PCB hot spot on the shelf above the river. At the river's edge, your wake breaks against thousands of bare, sawn logs exposed when the reservoir drained and the Blackfoot dropped. You'll pass the old Stimson yard, now leased and temporarily full with a harvest of beetle-killed timber upstream. The logs go on and on. They'll be chopped into fragments and shipped to a paper mill in Washington State.

You'll pass under what Milltowners call the Black Bridge, pedestrian-only, then under the humming Interstate 90 bridges, skirting the nasty hole that's developed downstream of the newly reinforced center piling, and in no more than a dozen paddle strokes you'll lean to your right, flashing your boat's bottom up, and brace the blade of your paddle downstream as the incoming Clark Fork pulls you into its path. The floodplain is expansive and turning green with growth, and the river is swift enough to demand attention, nothing at all like Milltown's torpor just a few years before.

The river narrows again and passes heedlessly through what used to be a dam. On the bluff above, the state has installed an asphalt trail and a half-dozen interpretive signs, not one of which mentions Opportunity. There's a new state park being developed at river right, with a boat ramp. Now the Clark Fork takes a wide sweep around Canyon River, the new golf course subdivision at Bandmann Flats, decorated with fountains and fake waterfalls, then enters the narrows of Hellgate Canyon, the steep constriction that once whirled draining Glacial Lake Missoula into boulder-plucking kolks. Now there are apartments on the riverbanks, and the Kim Williams Trail (named for the Missoula naturalist who was NPR's longest-running guest commentator in the 1970s and '80s), and then UM's Washington-Grizzly Stadium looming on the left as the river splashes over the Jacobs Island weir. I dumped here once, banging a friend's knee on a rock, and even though it's an easy, small, one-drop run, I still get butterflies approaching it.

Three Labs harass a German shepherd on the beach of the Jacobs Island Bark Park, an irrigation culvert cuts back in at river left, then a footbridge, Rattlesnake Creek dribbling in from the right, and the DoubleTree Hotel, with the Finn & Porter restaurant deck hanging out over the rock beach. Sure enough, there's a guy fishing there.

Madison Street Bridge passes overhead, carrying Highway 12, followed by Kiwanis Park, Toole Park, Bess Reed Park, open space and walkways sandwiching the river.

There's nothing like this in Opportunity. There will never be. Nobody from Opportunity will ever kayak in the Clark Fork. Nobody will ever build an artificial whitewater wave. Nobody from Texas, or anywhere else, will ever move to Opportunity for the conveniently located river. Opportunity was born so that Anaconda could live, and now it's dying for Missoula's sake. Every success requires a sacrifice. The slow death of Opportunity is Missoula's cost of living.

Higgins Avenue Bridge is Missoula's centerpiece and pole star, and when you see it from the river, you start getting ready for Brennan's Wave, just downstream. Brennan's Wave is an engineered whitewater feature. Before it was built, the river was marred here with the remains of a busted-up weir dam that had diverted water into the offshoot irrigation channels that still crisscross parts of town. Since it had to be rebuilt anyway, a coalition of kayakers convinced the ditch company and the Army Corps of Engineers and the state to let them build something that would both divert water and entertain boaters. Shaped boulders were cemented into the riverbed in a pattern that creates two recirculating waves midstream in the Clark Fork's two channels. It's named for Brennan Guth, a local kayaker who drowned in a kayaking accident in Chile. I've dumped here twice.

Around another island on the left shore, hugging the Riverfront Trail, and then under Orange Street Bridge with its worldly black lampposts, and finally to the baseball field. The Pioneer League's Missoula Osprey play here in spring. Just under a decommissioned Montana Rail Link bridge is the downtown Clark Fork's third section of mild whitewater. It's a mostly submerged rock garden that kicks up small, confused waves, and it also marks the remains of a decrepit irrigation weir. An organization has formed to build another kayaking play spot here, this one to be called the Max Wave, after another dead kayaker.

I understand and even honor the impulse, but I suspect there may be a limit to the number of dead kayakers one cares to be reminded of every time one paddles a boat through Missoula. I wouldn't fly Lynyrd Skynyrd Airlines, even at a steep discount.

The swaybacked California Street footbridge swings overhead just as you pass the muddy backwater where I used to launch when a business called the Canoe Rack occupied what's now a roofing warehouse up on the right bank.

Now you pass beneath Russell Street, slated for lane expansion, and skirt an almost invisible sand-and-gravel operation along Mullan Road, the thoroughfare a vestige of the first wagon route across the Rockies, completed by army lieutenant John Mullan in

1860. The rendering plant on the high bank is one possible source of the stink that comes over this part of the river on a warm day. It could be the wastewater treatment plant a few hundred yards downstream too. Then under the thrum of Reserve Street, just a few miles from Dennis Washington's world headquarters, and into my favorite stretch of the Clark Fork.

We—the few friends and I who make a habit of paddling it—call it the Stinky Float, for the obvious reason. I've paddled it dozens of times over the course of a decade, sometimes alone, sometimes with company, sometimes, if I'm feeling generous, with newbies I want to let in on the secret. The secret is that after about five minutes of olfactory discomfort, when your brain toggles between the relative merits of sucking that sticky smell through your nose or drawing it into your mouth, it disappears. The river bends, Reserve Street Bridge recedes behind you, and though you're still well inside city limits, and aside from a few unobtrusive power lines camouflaged by the tree line, you might as well be floating through a postcard of predeveloped Missoula.

The stink is the price of admission, and it's the only reason I can fathom that the stretch isn't clotted with floaters—it never is—on summer evenings when the sun stays up till 10:00 p.m. and the Stinky Float amounts to an easily shuttled after-work wind-down. They've been daunted, I imagine, by the river's apparent imperfection. They didn't move to Montana to paddle past the outflow of a municipal sewage treatment plant.

You can't just start over like nothing ever happened. You can't befriend a dead man. You can build a river to modern specs, but you can't rebuild one that's gone. What came before carries over, like water topping a dam. At what point do you decide to write off the imperfect—a blood tie, a landscape—and turn away? What's downstream of disappointment?

Bob would have known why the treatment plant stank on summer days, why it *had* to stink. I hold my nose and my breath.

The Clark Fork slows here—facing the welling of the Bitterroot Range ahead—and braids through a parkland called Kelly Island as it approaches its juncture with the Bitterroot River. Relict channels, buggy backwaters, and quiet sloughs cut off the mainstream, and the mainstream bifurcates to encompass a mini delta decorated with puddles and trickling runs. The Stinky Float is rarely the same river twice. Each spring's high water carves new intricacies into the river's bed and leaves new obstacles in a paddler's path. The first spring rise after the Milltown Dam came out remapped the Stinky Float entirely, silting up channels that had been preferred routes the year before and opening passages that hadn't been paddled in ages. Rivers move sediment. It's what they do.

The best picture I never took is on the Stinky Float, about halfway down, on a panoramic sweep of rock beach at the inside bend of a forested bank. On the beach lay a long bleached log with one rooty arm rising to a small wooden shelf. On that shelf, someone had mounted a classic silver metal mailbox. It was gorgeously incongruous so far from any road, and it wasn't peppered with buckshot, so I was allowed to think of it as some impromptu art piece, or a shore comber's wink to passersby who'd fallen under the spell of the Stinky Float's human-free fantasy.

For a year I paddled past it, late spring, summer, fall, and late December, when a fluffy pile of snow topped the mailbox like a fur hat. Every time I remembered too late and forgot to bring a camera. Every time I reminded myself to bring the camera next time, but the image disappeared from my memory until the next time I saw it. It's like it didn't exist until suddenly I was looking at it, and then, around the next bend, it ceased again.

The following spring it was gone for good. The water had washed it away. It's tempting to follow its path, past the boat ramp takeout, jagging into the Bitterroot, on down the valley into Alberton Gorge, past the Idaho line and through Lake Pend Oreille and on toward the Pacific, with all the mailboxes and golf balls and arsenic and trout. It disappeared while I wasn't looking. The first time I noticed it was gone, I told its absence good-bye.

Upstream, the river I've known is disappearing too, its poisons scooped out and removed to Opportunity, where they join layers of sedimentary disappointment, piled high over the years until they amount to immovable mountains: a father abandoned, a landscape sacrificed, a river redeemed.

It's hard to see from here, floating forward. At this distance, I might not remember Opportunity had ever been there at all. I might even forget it's where I've come from.

# A WORD ABOUT FACTS

*Opportunity, Montana* is a work of nonfiction that combines memoir with reported fact. I have collected and presented the facts of Opportunity, Montana, and the Clark Fork as accurately as I am able. I welcome corrections. For the memoir material I have relied on my memory, which I know to be fallible. I do not welcome corrections regarding my memory. Chronologies, especially personal ones, have been simplified. Quoted material may be considered reliably verbatim, though occasionally condensed for clarity. No locations, persons, objects, or interactions have been invented. For the sake of continuity, people have occasionally been left out of scenes. I trust that their omissions will be taken as what they are— necessary narrative liberties—rather than lack of appreciation for their many contributions.

# ACKNOWLEDGMENTS

The commonplace is that a book bears resemblance to a baby, but this book has grown into less a child than a many-headed debt, for which the following people hold chits.

Jessie McQuillen wrote the article that first drew my attention to the story of Opportunity, and along with colleagues John S. Adams, Matt Gibson, and several generations of Missoula *Independent* staff, helped make the practice of journalism in Montana more fun than is generally allowed with pants on. Austin's *Texas Observer*, especially former editors Nate Blakeslee, Jake Bernstein, and Bob Moser, gave me a professional home and quality steerage at several critical junctures. Editors Ray Ring and Michelle Nijhuis at *High Country News* provided a venue for portions of Opportunity's story and handled my copy with care. Writers Steve Woodruff, Steve Hawley, Timothy J. LeCain, George Ochenski, Steve Hendricks, Ian Frazier, and David James Duncan lent ears, encouragement, and letters of recommendation.

A Knight-Wallace Fellowship at the University of Michigan provided money, time, collegiality, and ideas. Big thanks to Charles Eisendrath, Birgit Rieck, David Uhlmann, and the class of 2010. A residency with Western-writing advocates Fishtrap delivered writing time, money, and the curious chance to brainstorm with high school students. The Fund for Investigative Journalism supplied a generous research grant, and the Society of Environmental Journalists offered much-appreciated support.

*Missoulian* newspaper editor Sherry Devlin and reporter Rob Chaney, among others, have provided ongoing coverage of the Clark Fork cleanup that I have tapped liberally. Missoula's Clark Fork Coalition, especially Brianna Randall and Bryce Andrews, were generous with help and information. Both institutions deserve gobs of thanks for what they've done for the river.

Pat Munday, David Neuman, Pat Saffel, Robin Saha, and Serge Myers provided critical context. Other sources are either named within or preferred not to be. Among them, George Niland, Becky Guay, Connie Ternes-Daniels, Tracy Stone-Manning, Pat Williams, Jerry Hansen, and Jim Kuipers are due special thanks.

Robin Troy, Skylar Browning, and Tom Zoellner read various drafts and offered insights I'm relieved I didn't have to do without. Emily DePrang did the same, even while talking me off a spiral staircase of psychological ledges.

Special commendation of extra-large gratitude to author, bon vivant, and friend Fredric Alan Maxwell, who told me early on that leaving a steady job to write a book was a terrible idea, and then proceeded to cheer me at every turn.

In Montana, I owe boundless personal props to Missoula's Al and Ginger Pils; Nick and Dawn Davis; Matt and Jori Quinlan; and John, Karen, and Chauntel Frakie, and the memory of Peter Sunchild Curley. Joey and Vanessa Parchen were nice enough to put me up in Butte, where Tom Molloy and the late Jackie Corr confirmed and expanded my early interest in this story. David and Katie Madison have been gracious hosts in Bozeman.

John and Marika Suval kindly housed me during layovers in Madison, Wisconsin. Matt Kelly and Marianthe Perce came through with warm and welcome respites on the best deck in Austin.

In Texas, my grandmother Dorothy Tyer and mother, Sharon Lee, are sweetly unwavering in their tolerant encouragement; I hope they know how much it means. In Atlanta, my sister Cameron and nieces Nelson and Bradley are the apples of my eye and motivating joys.

Brandon and Missy Cullum, William Grotewold, Lisa Simon, and my aunt Betty Waters, along with others already named, emerged from the wellspring of affirmation-on-demand that is Facebook to pony up the fees to reprint this book's epigraphs.

Artists Doug Hawes-Davis, Kilian and Tricia Sweeney, and John Harris contributed their substantial skills to the book's betterment. Thanks much to photographers Chris Chapman for the cover and Chad Harder for the flap.

Some people need to be thanked just because. Doug Marx, Andrea Moore, Sheri Guess, Lisa Gray, Randall Patterson, Lorie Rustvold, Susanna Sonnenberg, Chuck Irestone, Ellie Hill, and Steve Bierwag are among them. I would be remiss if I failed to express my gratitude to Missoula's Kettlehouse.

My agent, Deirdre Mullane, and editor, Alexis Rizzuto, at Beacon saw me steadily through unfamiliar territory and saw something in this book before I knew how to describe it properly. Along with copy editor Chris Dodge, they have my thanks.

My gratitude as well to the citizens of Opportunity, whose community I've appropriated for purposes that may or may not align with their own.

Finally, I couldn't and wouldn't have written this book without the panoramic love, support, and editorial savvy of Azita Osanloo. Thank you.

# SOURCES

Proof that Montana's status as a landscape of the imagination is every bit as solid as the mountains it's named for fills a good-sized bookshelf. Among those books not mentioned in the text, the following have been most useful, one way or another, to me.

Native Texan Rick Bass's moving-to-Montana memoir *Winter* (1992) was less a template than an inspiration for my own relocation, and remains as compelling a portrait of a stranger coming home to a strange land as anyone has written. John Steinbeck's *Travels with Charley* (1962) and its drive-by romance with Montana were influential in my daydreams of the early oughts.

Any thoughtful person who spends more than a week in Montana ought to read the collected works of K. Ross Toole—especially *Montana: An Uncommon Land* (1959) and *Twentieth-Century Montana: A State of Extremes* (1972)—if only to understand the bedrock into which later historians have drilled.

Watson Davis's *The Story of Copper* (1924), is the most readable history of the element I could find, and, defying expectations, contains one of the most satisfying sentences I've ever read. Angus Murdoch's *Boom Copper* (1964) is an excellent account of Michigan's copper years.

The best book most people will ever read about Butte is Richard K. O'Malley's memoir *Mile High Mile Deep* (1986). Two more-scholarly works—*The Butte Irish* (1989), by David M. Emmons, and *Tracing the Veins* (1998), by Janet L. Finn—are rightly well regarded. Less so, but more fun, are *It's a Butte Thing . . . The Mules, The Mines, and the Miners* (2004), by Mike Byrnes; *The Truth about Butte through the Eyes of a Radical Unionist* (1917), by George R. Tompkins; *Underground Warfare at Butte* (1964), by Reno Sales;

and *Copper Camp: The Lusty Story of Butte, Montana, the Richest Hill on Earth* (1943), a proud product of the WPA-era Montana Writers Project.

The extent to which the battle of Butte's copper kings excited the national imagination even into the middle of the twentieth century is proved by Marian T. Place's *The Copper Kings of Montana* (1961), of the Random House Landmark Books illustrated series for children. The popular (regional-history-shelf popular) history is C.B. Glasscock's *The War of the Copper Kings* (1935); the rigorous one is Michael P. Malone's *The Battle for Butte* (1981). As for the participants themselves, biographies are remarkably thin. Sarah McNelis's *Copper King at War* (1968), the most involved of the available books, narrowly treats the least remembered of the three kings: Augustus Heinze. Marcus Daly receives only oblique illumination in Ada Powell's *The Dalys of the Bitterroot* (1989) and Miriam Poe Ryan's *Riverside* (1995), a historical novel set at Daly's eponymous Bitterroot mansion, in which much imagination has been applied to the specifics of turn-of-the-century women's clothing. William A. Clark would probably trade for either man's literary legacy—he settles for William Daniel Mangam's *W.A. Clark and His Tarnished Family* (1939), a gloatingly gossipy and weirdly angry ax-grinder of a book denouncing pretty much everything about Clark and his progeny. MSNBC journalist Bill Dedman's coverage of the 2011 discovery of Huguette Clark has been endlessly fascinating, and Dedman's forthcoming book about the Clark family seems sure to set several records straight.

Any community ten times the size would be lucky to have as dedicated a chronicler as Patrick F. Morris, whose companion volumes *Anaconda, Montana: Copper Smelting Boom Town on the Western Frontier* (1997), and *Anaconda, Montana: In Changing Times* (2010), deliver a wealth of street-level detail. Laurie Mercier's *Anaconda: Labor, Community, and Culture in Montana's Smelter City* (2001) layers the town with context. Isaac F. Marcosson's everpresent (in antique shops) corporate history *Anaconda* is indispensable as—and indistinguishable from—corporate propaganda. Publishing in 1957, and fully recruited to the hagiographic cause (his next two books were copper-based industrial histories), Marcosson can be forgiven for not following an environmental storyline. Still, not a word about waste in 370 pages of the densest industrialism you'll ever read strikes me as more than mere oversight.

Vastly more compelling, and dramatically more to the point, Timothy J. LeCain's *Mass Destruction: The Men and Giant Mines That Wired America and Scarred the Planet* (2009) gives a dizzying overview of large-scale strip mining and its consequences, in Montana and elsewhere. Donald MacMillan's *Smoke Wars: Anaconda Copper, Montana Air Pollution, and the Courts, 1890–1920* (2000) makes bountifully clear that the Anaconda Company knew what it was doing well before Isaac Marcosson chose to ignore it.

Regarding the Clark Fork itself, and aside from reports published by the Montana Department of Environmental Quality, Environmental Protection Agency, and a dozen different consulting entities, I kept returning to the spiral-bound *Clark Fork of the Columbia River Basin Cooperative Study* prepared by the USDA's soil conservation, economic research, and forest services (1977). Its maps are beautiful. David Alt's *Glacial Lake Missoula and Its Humongous Floods* (2001) is entertaining and informative in equal measure. When I wanted more literary company, I consulted *The River We Carry with Us: Two Centuries of Writing from the Clark Fork Basin*, published in 2002 by the Clark Fork Coalition and Clark City Press, and *Headwaters: Montana Writers on Water and Wildness*, edited by Annick Smith.

Many of these books, perhaps obviously, are small-print-run, out-of-print rarities. For help tracking them down, my thanks go especially to the staffs of the Missoula Public Library, the Hearst Free Library in Anaconda, and Butte's Second Edition Books.

# CREDITS

Map of Clark Fork River Watershed by John G. Harris with the Cargo Collective, Inc. Copyright © 2012.

**Opening epigraph:**
From "I Come From the Water," words and music by Todd Lewis. Copyright © 1994 Songs of Universal, Inc. All rights reserved. Reprinted by permission of Hal Leonard Corp.

**Part I epigraph:**
From *Travels with Charley*, by John Steinbeck. Copyright © 1961, 1962 by the Curtis Publishing Co. Copyright © 1962 by John Steinbeck. Copyright © 1990 renewed by Elaine Steinbeck, Thom Steinbeck, and John Steinbeck IV. Used by permission of Viking Penguin, a division of Penguin Group (USA), Inc.

**Part IV epigraph:**
From *Standing by Words: Essays by Wendell Berry.* Copyright © 1983 by Wendell Berry. Reprinted by permission of Counterpoint Press, Berkeley, CA.

**Part V epigraph:**
From *The Triggering Town: Lectures and Essays on Poetry and Writing*, by Richard Hugo. Copyright © 1979 by W. W. Norton & Company, Inc. Used by permission of W. W. Norton & Company, Inc.

**Part VI epigraph:**

From lecture by Emmet Gowin, Princeton University, April 1994. Reprinted here with permission.

**Part VII epigraph:**

From *Ray*, by Barry Hannah. Copyright © 1980 by Barry Hannah. Used by permission of Grove/Atlantic, Inc.